The Many Faces of

The Many Faces of Polyamory: Longing and Belonging in Concurrent Relationships provides new perspectives on polyamory and the longing to belong in the relatively uncharted territory of nonnormative relationships.

This volume offers a valuable and compelling account on how to approach polyamorous relationships from the clinical perspective. While there is no uniform answer, Dr. Fosse's compassionate and discerning approach that combines relative neutrality, an open-minded embrace of nontraditional lifestyle choices, and skilful attention to countertransference dynamics is likely to be inspiring. Dr. Fosse exposes the dynamics of love, sex, jealousy, and compersion as they play out in the lives of those interested in polyamory, and more broadly, consensual nonmonogamy. Her focus is on relationships worth having.

With its nuanced clinical focus, *The Many Faces of Polyamory* will be an essential resource for psychotherapists, educators, students, and anyone inside and outside of the mental health field drawn to the intricacies of sexuality, intimacy, and how they are intertwined with relational satisfaction.

Dr. Magdalena J. Fosse is a licensed clinical psychologist and AASECT certified sex therapist in private practice in Cambridge, MA. She works extensively with individuals and couples who identify as polyamorous or consensually nonmonogamous. Dr. Fosse is on the faculty of Psychodynamic Couples and Families Institute of New England (PCFINE), which provides advanced training in couples' therapy to licensed clinicians.

The Many Faces of Polyamory

Longing and Belonging in Concurrent Relationships

Magdalena J. Fosse

Routledge
Taylor & Francis Group

NEW YORK AND LONDON

First published 2021
by Routledge
2 Park Square, Milton Park, Abingdon, Oxon OX14 4RN

and by Routledge
52 Vanderbilt Avenue, New York, NY 10017

Routledge is an imprint of the Taylor & Francis Group, an informa business.

© 2021 **Magdalena J. Fosse.**

British Library Cataloguing-in-Publication Data
A catalogue record for this book is available from the British Library

Library of Congress Cataloging-in-Publication Data
Names: Fosse, Magdalena J., author.
Title: The many faces of polyamory : longing and belonging in concurrent relationships / Magdalena J. Fosse.
Description: Milton Park, Abingdon, Oxon ; New York, NY : Routledge, 2021. | Includes bibliographical references and index.
Identifiers: LCCN 2020052079 (print) | LCCN 2020052080 (ebook) | ISBN 9781138504295 (hardback) | ISBN 9781138504301 (paperback) | ISBN 9781315145969 (ebook)
Subjects: LCSH: Non-monogamous relationships. | Non-monogamous relationships--Psychological aspects.
Classification: LCC HQ980 .F67 2021 (print) | LCC HQ980 (ebook) | DDC 306.84/23--dc23
LC record available at https://lccn.loc.gov/2020052079
LC ebook record available at https://lccn.loc.gov/2020052080

ISBN: 978-1-138-50429-5 (hbk)
ISBN: 978-1-138-50430-1 (pbk)
ISBN: 978-1-315-14596-9 (ebk)

Typeset in Goudy
by MPS Limited, Dehradun

Contents

Preface

When I first came to the States, I was married, and my Norwegian husband was my only family here. Together we faced the challenges of learning the quirks and twists of the new culture. For me, coming to the U.S. was like finding a home, but that was not the case for him. After a heartbreaking divorce, my friendships were my saving grace. A trusted group of friends became my family of choice, and that is who we still are to one another, with ever-deepening bonds of intimate connections and trust. I used the term "family of choice" long before I became aware of its existence in the media and in academic literature. Unconsciously, I must have integrated the term because of its resonance, without yet being aware of the original connotations to the queer and other marginalized communities, historically relegated to the sidelines of culture.

Writing this book made me revisit my personal story of how my friends truly became what I consider the best family I could ever imagine. We are not a commune or cohousing community; like most extended families, we do not live together. In our group, there are those who are single and longing and those who are single and content as well as those who are married, cohabitating, or otherwise committed. There are those who are searching for the right person or people, and those who are ambivalent about monogamy as well as polyamory. We are a multiracial, international mix of open-minded, creative individuals who love to spend time together. There is no one way to define us, with the exception that we are a wildly beautiful family of people who keep the unwritten commitment to one another vividly alive.

Without my friends, my true Family of Choice, this book would not be what it is.

Acknowledgments

"Tell me who admires and loves you, and I will tell you who you are."
—Antoine de Saint-Exupéry

This book starts and ends with a quote by Antoine de Saint-Exupéry, my childhood inspiration to explore the impossible, travel beyond boundaries of what was available to me back then, and explore relationships beyond what I knew but sensed.

This book is my homage to the late Gina Ogden, an inspiring teacher, mentor, and friend, who insisted I embark on this project. Without her wholehearted belief in me, this book would not have come into existence. Thank you, Gina, for your encouragement, wisdom, and shamanic presence. You taught women how to love their sexuality without shame and fear.

My friends are my family of choice, and I am deeply grateful for your presence in my life. You helped me find my place of belonging, and I long to love and dance with you forever. Together we contain multitudes.

Introduction

In the Beginning There was Chaos...

Polyamory means "multiple loves"; it implies the ability to be sexually and romantically involved with more than one person. Unlike monogamy, polyamory comes in a number of permutations, with no fixed number of partners and no set presumption of commitment. As such, it is not one relational format but many, all under the umbrella of consensual, ethical, partnered nonmonogamy. People choose polyamory for a number of reasons. Some are drawn to it; others are thrown into it. Polyamory is simultaneously an idea, a reality, and an aspiration. The reality of it is nothing but complex and complicated; it is less predictable than monogamy and, in spite of its emphasis on boundaries, it may come across as curiously vague.

My aim in this book is to illustrate rather than prescribe how therapists might work with clients in polyamorous relationships. Our understanding of the nature of therapy is still limited in spite of decades of practice and research, with various perspectives of treatment intended and explored. This volume depicts therapy among people with relatively new and different kinds of relationships, and in which the traditional boundaries of coupledom or family are redefined. In his book *Intimacy, Change, and Other Therapeutic Mysteries*, David Treadway observes, "In some respects, the therapeutic role allows many of us to experience a tremendous degree of daily intimacy. From the safety of the therapist's chair, we can risk loving our clients and engaging them at the most vulnerable levels of their lives" (2004, p. xi). In our capacities as therapists, we are more or less directly responsible for holding relationships together or helping them dissolve. Individuals and couples put their trust in our hands, hoping our expertise will guide them to make the best possible decisions. Unfortunately, whether our intuition or even conviction is on the mark is not possible to know until years later, when we may no longer work with a particular couple or formation. Not having crystal balls at our disposal (which are notoriously unreliable), we carry a tremendous amount of responsibility for the relationships entrusted to us. Engaging in polyamorous relationships is risky for many clients. How do we then know if polyamory is right for someone? Can we make sure that the process of opening up will not upend a relationship? How do we know if gains will be greater than losses? We do not. But we know how to listen.

The way I approach people with polyamorous bonds is not very different from the way I approach monogamous couples. At the core, all relationships are about the same issue—a sense of connection and belonging, and hope for a lasting, secure attachment. Needless to say, my anticipation of what is likely to transpire in polyamorous versus monogamous intimacies varies. However, the emotions and relational tensions evoked by attachment and intimacy issues are of the familiar, deeply human sort. From a countertransference perspective, some poly relationships leave me feeling dubious about their commitment, while others instigate my curiosity about the human capacity to sustain the most difficult entanglements. That said, monogamous marriages, too, can be anything from miserable to wonderful. One partner can be enough to make one's life a whirlwind of torment. Likewise, having many partners may not offset the loneliness and despair of a person who feels relationally unseen and unknown. Instead of comparing monogamy to polyamory or the other way around, I am choosing to ascertain relationships for what they are. This is my way of staying focused on what *is* rather than what *should be*. The emphasis is thus on the relational quality and emotional well-being of the people involved and my role as a healer and guide.

A metaphor that helps me to conceptualize relationships is that of tree roots. Relationships are supported by their roots much as trees are. We can understand trees' roots by examining the soil they grow in, their access to water, and the overall conditions in their location. They are the result of biology, ecology, and environment. Some trees have one solid root that reaches deep into the earth; others have widespread root systems. All are meant to ensure the stability and survivability of the trees. They are also expressions of adaptation to circumstances. If we imagine the roots of monogamy, we could perceive a taproot growing vertically, reaching deeper with the passage of time. The roots of polyamory extend horizontally, shallower in appearance, but not necessarily in strength. Each is meant to anchor a person in the relationship of their choice. Roots provide protection and nourishment, and, when the conditions are right, trees and relationships thrive. When the circumstances become too challenging to endure, they topple. Relationships are not guaranteed to succeed, or fail, based purely on the form they take. For relationships to thrive they must be taken care of, not just in the beginning when they are newly formed, but throughout their entire existence.

In the horizontal spread of polyamory, the relational constellations are in flux: New partners are added; marriages fall apart; primary partners become secondary; tertiary become primary; hierarchical arrangements become nonhierarchical; a relationship of three becomes six, then goes down to four. Some partners have sex; some do not. People who would never imagine being in a relationship with one another become *metamours*—those who, willingly or not, become indirectly involved with their partner's other partners.

Polyamory as a lifestyle is meant to be egalitarian; yet, the benefits and privileges are not distributed equally and not always available to all. Dominant partners, those whom others are drawn to, have more of a say than the individuals on the periphery, whose relational and sexual choices are limited. Polyamory is simultaneously abundant and scarce. There are those who have a ball, their dance cards constantly full. Others long to belong, hoping to find the right person with whom to form a primary relationship, or hoping to secure a lover who is content with being a secondary.

Most monogamous relationships go through developmental stages, typically from the passionate beginning through deepening of intimacy to reliable companionship. They involve two people willing to commit to each other, to mature side by side, and to grow old together. All lasting monogamous commitments experience these developmental phases regardless of whether the couple's relationships began at 20, 40, or 60. At each stage, there are separate tasks that need to be mastered for the relationship to evolve and thrive. This developmental succession is closely related but not identical to what people in the polyamorous community dismissively call the *relationship escalator* and which describes a relatively predictable sequence of falling in love, getting engaged and married, having children and grandchildren, and staying together in health and sickness until the final exit.

Finding the escalator restraining and inhibitive, those who choose polyamory embrace less stereotypical alternatives. Developmental stages of polyamory are harder to discern and describe. It might be because polyamory is still early in its own development. It may also be due to its horizontal spreading. Regardless of the explanation, polyamory's practitioners consider this relational format to be more evolved than the calcified monogamy. Are they right? Time will tell.

The practice of polyamory may have the potential of creating something entirely new, a paradigm shift with unforeseen consequences. Yet, like monogamy, polyamorous relationships are not immune to hurt. All relationships come with their own risks. Those who embrace polyamory avoid the familiar source of ache that monogamy has been rehashing for centuries—infidelity. Circumventing old-fashioned cheating, polyamorous people discover other reservoirs of pain. They are willing to immerse themselves in jealousy while attempting to rise above it. Polyamory's practitioners have created a new ideal—the opposite of jealousy—which they call *compersion*. Compersion stands for sublimation of jealous feelings into a joyful celebration of a lover's sexual and romantic pleasure with another person. In setting the stage for this new ideal, the polyamorous lifestyle gives rise to a unique kind of insecurity: the struggle of being a jealous person may be replaced with self-judgments of not being evolved enough to feel compersion.

Writing about polyamory from a therapy perspective begs the question—Is polyamory better suited to contain the complexity of modern relationships than monogamy does? Maybe or maybe not. Robert Sapolsky, a professor of neurology and biological sciences, writes in his tour-de-force treatise on the multilayered correlates of human behavior that humans are neither monogamous nor polygynous or polyandrous (having multiple wives or husbands) but instead profoundly confused (2017). It is in our nature to be bewilderingly inconsistent. Thus, positioning polyamory against monogamy is not only reductionistic, but it is also inaccurate. The best answer might be that our predilection for monogamy versus any of the possible forms of nonmonogamy is simply context dependent. Monogamy is more familiar to most than polyamory, but each is a relational format in its own right.

The Language of Polyamory

If relationships as we know them are undergoing unprecedented transformations, keeping track of polyamorous alterations can be mind-boggling. In a conversation, a colleague shared with a smile that he just learned a new term—*vee*. He expected me to understand his merriment upon learning a new poly term, but for anyone else reading, a quick google search would reveal that vee refers to a formation in which two people are romantically involved with a third, focal, person but not with each other. The person in the focal position is sometimes referred to as a *pivot*.

This anecdote illustrates how complicated it can be to follow the ever-evolving vocabulary of polyamorous relationships. New terms are added, and many clients hope the therapist will be up to speed with the terminology. Yet, it is not necessary for clinicians to know all the words used by poly people; they may not know them themselves. Having a grasp of basic terminology is enough to convey empathy and respect.

Language Convention in this Book

Words have power. Languages have limitations. Gender stereotypes are shaped by language and vice versa. Many of my clients are gender nonconforming, representing the entire spectrum of what nonconformity may entail. In my experience, it is much easier to maintain gender neutrality in relating to an individual in front of me and much harder to do in writing. The English language is stubbornly cumbersome and inelegant when the personal pronouns *he* and *she* are substituted with *they* used as a singular. Until the language evolves enough to solve this problem, I am choosing to stay with the linguistic conventions that make absorption of this material a little easier. There are plenty of complex concepts used in this book, and simplifying what can be simplified, without being insensitive, is helpful.

Writing about relational reality outside of monogamy and heterosexuality is full of other linguistic confrontations. Some terms, such as *mononormativity* and *heteronormativity*, are complex but unambiguous. Other terms hang upon a hyphen, including *non-monogamy* versus *nonmonogamy*; both imply the opposite of monogamy, but with a somewhat different connotation. I decided to follow the convention of the latter and drop the hyphenation to convey that nonmonogamy is a relational choice in its own right, rather than a relational practice defined by negation.

Another convention used in this book allows certain terms to be used interchangeably; among these are *polyamory, open relationships,* and *consensual nonmonogamy.* Polyamory is a form of an open relationship, and many people who decide to "open up" find polyamory more appealing than other forms of nonmonogamy. It might be because of the positive representation of polyamory in the media, but also because poly (more) and amory (love) seem to promise a more mature and complete form of relating than other, predominantly sexual, forms of openness.

Other terms that I use interchangeably are *client* and *patient.* Neither one is perfect; both have pros and cons. The term *client* implies that a person seeking therapy is ready to negotiate the terms of interaction. It has a double connotation; on the one hand, it points to the collaboration and co-construction of treatment, which is highly desirable. On the other hand, it creates an association with the therapist as a contractor who is there to perform a predetermined service. To that point, I had an inquiry from a prospective client asking not about my fees, but about "my quote." Therapy is not a mechanical construction built from standard materials that can be arranged in a predictable way. People do not always know what they need from therapy, but they do know that they are struggling and want help. The term *patient* comes from the Greek word that means "suffering," and therapy aims to alleviate suffering. This is very different from the more common association that being a patient means being passive. Rather than asserting that client is better than patient, or vice versa, I embrace both.

Organization of the Book

The book consists of six parts, each organized around a central theme relevant for understanding the reality of polyamory from a clinical perspective. The parts are conceptualized as concentric circles, from a general grasp of the phenomenon of multiple loves through a more specific delineation of love, sex, and jealousy as innate and unavoidable relational factors, to the relevant psychological theories and perspectives, culminating in therapy narratives representing common polyamorous challenges and reenactments.

Part I, the broadest in scope, provides an overview of polyamory's relational position on the biological and cultural map. Part II focuses on love and different ways to conceptualize what love is. Part III is centered on the theme of sexuality in polyamory. Part IV discusses jealousy as a topic of particular relevance in poly ways of relating. In Part V, selected psychological perspectives germane to understanding of polyamory are detailed. Finally, in Part VI, narratives reflecting the many faces of polyamory are presented. While shorter clinical vignettes illustrating relevant points are included in the preceding parts of the book, the stories presented in Part VI portray in greater depth the kind of therapy dilemmas a clinician working with a poly population is likely to encounter.

References

Sapolsky, R. M. (2017). *Behave: The biology of humans and our best and worst.* Penguin Books.

Treadway, D. (2004). *Intimacy, change, and other therapeutic mysteries: Stories of clinicians and clients.* The Guilford Press.

Part I

Charting the Map of Polyamory

1 Polyamory: Bewildering and Evolving

The Polish language has a wondrous, slightly surreal expression *Jak to się je?*, which roughly translates to *How do you eat it?* Contrary to how it sounds, it is not used with reference to novelty food, but instead serves to exclaim curiosity and bewilderment when encountering something unfamiliar and confusing. When I first conceived this book, there was but one definition of polyamory. *Poly* conveys multiple, and *amory* denotes love. Polyamory implies the possibility of being involved, sexually and romantically, with more than one person. As straightforward as this definition was by yesteryear's standards, it nonetheless perplexed the lay public and the majority of clinicians. At the time of this book's publication, it is no longer necessary to spell out the term, but the bewilderment regarding this lifestyle is far from diminished. There are so many extensions of the original definition and notion of polyamory that it can be hard to know what is talked about. By some characterizations, love in polyamory could be for almost anything—partners, lovers, nonromantic involvements with dear friends, lifestyle, families of choice, communities, even the planet (Anderlini-D'Onofrio, 2009; Barker & Langdridge, 2010). How do we eat *that?*

We are dealing with an ever-expanding universe with ambiguous boundaries. From being a relatively specific phenomenon, polyamory is undergoing diffusion rather than consolidation. Polyamory is a lifestyle; it might be a sexual orientation, and it is also a social and cultural movement. In the widest understanding, almost any kind of openness and embrace of nonnormative relational expression and life strategy could be considered poly.

What is polyamory then? The prevailing understanding is that there is no one definition of polyamory. Poly structures can be complex and immensely varied. A few years ago, the dominant polyamorous constellation was hierarchical in nature. At its core there was a couple, oftentimes a married one. The spouses adopted the name of primary partners. When a primary partner got involved with somebody else, this new person became a secondary partner. If more people were involved, they were considered tertiary or, alternatively, they got assigned the designation of orbits, implying casual, consensual lovers. Since then, the discourse has shifted toward nonhierarchical polyamory, in which all partners involved are considered to be equal in status. Hierarchical or not, polyamorous constellations fluctuate; examples of common arrangements include *triads, quads,* and *polyfidelious families,* to name a handful of the more familiar ones (for definitions, consult the glossary at the end of the book). For clinicians working with poly clients, keeping track of who is involved with whom can be baffling. Similar to genograms depicting family ties, poly relationships are often presented visually. The common strategy is to represent each person as a sphere and then draw the lines connecting the globes. No graphic distinction is given to males, females, or gender-nonconforming individuals. Portrayed this way, poly configurations look like chemical molecules, which earned them the name of *polycules.*

Sexual orientations, relational preferences, and lifestyle realities can be intertwined in highly intricate ways. A person identifying as poly may or may not be in a polyamorous relationship. An individual whose preference is for monogamy may be intimately involved with someone who is poly. Relational status provides a lot of information about lifestyle orientation, but they are not one and the same. Many individuals navigating this complex relationship landscape are choosing, or staying with, partners based on availability and commitment rather than personal preference, sometimes alternating between monogamy and nonmonogamy. The cases of mismatched relational preferences and actual relational status are characterized by considerable vulnerability, oftentimes sending these individuals and couples to therapy. It is not uncommon for these clients to face judgments on all sides, from their monogamous families and friends, from their poly peers, and from mental health practitioners whose help they seek.

My introduction to the complexities of polyamory from the therapy perspective was full of qualms and surprises. One spring afternoon, a man I will call Nick left me a vaguely hesitant message wondering if I would be fine working with someone who has an interest in polyamory. His voice trailed off: "Anyway, I hope to hear back from you …" I then listened to the next message. It was from Sophie. She inquired about my availability, adding that she was in a somewhat unusual relational situation. "I've read that you work with consensual non-monogamy," she said, "and it seems like you'll be a good match." I scheduled Nick for a Wednesday the following week and Sophie for the day after.

Nick's open face and mild manner made him instantly likeable. He explained that polyamory intrigued him and he wanted to explore his feelings about this lifestyle. Nick was married and concerned about his marriage not surviving if he were to suggest opening up. He loved his wife and had no intention of ending the marriage, but he was struggling with his conflicting desires. As we were nearing the end of the session, Nick looked at me and asked, "Would you have any problems working with me if you're going to work with Sophie as well?" I was mystified. Was it the same Sophie who I was supposed to meet the next day? If so, how did he know? Seeing my bewilderment, Nick elaborated that he and Sophie knew each other, but had not known until a few hours earlier that each had scheduled a session with me.

I learned that they were postdocs in the same lab on the brink of developing a relationship. Collaborating on a project, their work relationship had morphed into friendship, and, soon enough, they discovered their mutual interest in polyamory. Both were married and, upon realizing their attraction toward each other, they decided to seek therapy "to do things right." Armed with this decision, each set off to search for a suitable therapist. Unbeknownst to each other, they happened to find my qualifications and approach appealing, leading to their respective inquiries. The revelation of this parallel experience felt like a confirmation of their spiritual connection. Hurriedly exploring their feelings about this coincidence, they concluded that, as long as I agreed, it might be helpful if they both worked with me.

If the sequence of events was less unexpected, I might have hesitated more. If it happened now, rather than several years ago, I might have suggested they inquire with other therapists before making a decision. But back then, polyamory was *terra incognita* to the absolute majority of clinicians. Nearly every client told me about their difficulty finding a therapist who knew what polyamory was, and how relieved they were to work with someone who would not be judgmental about their lifestyle. As it stood, I scheduled a follow-up session with Nick, giving both myself and him time to process this unusual situation.

In my meeting with Sophie on the following day, I received similar re-assurance that she was eager to work with me. Bright and engaging, Sophie described her marriage as committed and, overall, highly satisfying. She had friends who were polyamorous, so she knew about potential pitfalls if she and her husband were to open up. She also knew that it was possible to transition to nonmonogamy without upending the marriage. Coming from a blended family, she saw the value of being intimately involved with more than one person. Just as with Nick, I scheduled a follow-up session, giving Sophie and myself more time to reflect.

Given the relatively small size of the poly community, I anticipated that, sooner or later, I might be facing the dilemma of needing to disclose a po-tential conflict of interest. What I could not imagine is that this conflict would present the way it did. It made me wonder—how can a therapist maintain clear boundaries and avoid breaches of confidentiality when working with polyamorous clients? How can she handle countertransference? Countertransference issues may arise even before an individual or a couple walks through the door. In traditional therapy, there is virtually no need to clarify the boundaries of coupledom; transgressions and betrayals are easy to locate within the system. Furthermore, the therapist's boundaries regarding ethics are clearly delineated; the limits of confidentiality are routinely espoused, and dual relationships are carefully avoided. As I was learning, therapy with people in polyamorous relationships was going to test this fa-miliar known on multiple fronts.

Working with Nick and Sophie on parallel tracks helped me refine my rules. They did not seek my services as a couple, but their goals and motivations were tightly intertwined. Because of their connection and shared focus, I found it helpful to think of their burgeoning relationship from an individual as well as a couple's therapy perspective. From the beginning, I told Nick and Sophie about my rules of privacy and confidentiality—I was not going to share any information, privileged or mundane, about the other person, unless something was common knowledge or I had explicit permission from both to talk about it. They could talk about their therapy experience as much as they wished, or not at all—that was their line to establish. If something came up in a session that I had a sense would be important for them to discuss, I would encourage them to bring it up with the other person for further exploration, but I would not mention any of it unless they did. Periodically, I checked in with each to see how they felt about working in this fashion and was reassured that the parallel format felt enriching rather than limiting.

Nick and Sophie's therapeutic journeys overlapped a lot. Both were in what might be called *mono-poly marriages*, struggling with similar issues in their respective relationships. Early on it became apparent that their spouses, without being physically present, played significant roles in the treatment process. Meghan, Nick's wife, and Damien, Sophie's husband, had no interest in polyamory but felt powerless to stop this already-moving train. Although I came to know that Meghan and Damien never talked in person and only knew about each other's preferences from what their spouses conveyed to them, they felt more confident knowing that they were not alone in their desire to prevent, or at the very least delay, the process of opening up.

With time, both Nick and Sophie agreed that it would be helpful if their individual therapy courses shifted to couple's counseling. Meghan joined Nick in his treatment, and Sophie came in together with Damien. With this shift in emphasis, each couple was able to focus more directly on what opening up would mean to them. The couples talked with greater honesty about the pain and doubts they were experiencing. It was not an easy process. There were tears, anger, guilt, shame, fear, and despair—the whole gamut of emotions one could expect in a situation like this. But there was also hope. As Meghan and Damien came to realize, their spouses meant what they said—they had no intention of ending their marriages. Nick and Sophie just hoped that their respective relationships could tolerate and eventually embrace an expansion of love.

Finding themselves on the opposite side of the spectrum—valuing monogamy more than polyamory—Meghan and Damien found their strange alliance reassuring. They had no interest in getting to know each other as it felt like too much to add to their already-conflicted emotions, but they felt comforted by what they knew was going on for the other person. There were, of course, other times, too, when one or the other felt uneasy, assuming that his or her "ally" was more on board with the process of opening up.

Transitioning to polyamory for mono-poly couples is particularly arduous, and the risks of the relationship ending are high. The way these different relationships in my office happened to be balanced was fortuitous; it was not easy for anyone, but no one felt left out. Still, a lot was at stake. In spite of their earnest attempts at slowing down, Nick and Sophie were experiencing *new relationship energy*, or *NRE*, and, with their spouses' permission, hoped to become physically intimate. For Meghan and Damien, this movement toward increased intimacy was still advancing too fast. Much of the work at this stage of therapy involved giving voice to each person's respective insecurities and desires and managing the progression of opening up. To prevent their relationships from imploding, the married couples had to prioritize taking care of their marriages. As hard as it was for them, Nick and Sophie kept their agreement to hold back on their budding relationship.

Transitions of any sort represent opportunity and loss, and each person and couple in this poly-centered constellation was dealing with a mixture of hope and grief. After a few months of careful negotiations, Nick and Sophie were finally due to spend their first night together. We discussed in detail what they were "allowed" to do. They could kiss and cuddle but without progressing to any form of sex. To Meghan and Damien's relief, the night went as planned, but there was a lot to digest. Nick and Sophie were disappointed with the slowdown but agreed that, to avoid unrepairable ruptures, the speed of their burgeoning intimacy had to be negotiated all over again.

The process of therapy is rarely smooth, and this was definitely true in the case of these four people. There were as many discoveries of what is relationally possible as there were setbacks. Over time, Meghan and Damien officially consented to partially open their marriages. The partial opening meant that Nick and Sophie could take further steps in their relational exploration, but they were not to add any more partners. Meghan and Damien still did not find polyamory appealing, but came to appreciate that the conflict was not theirs alone. Likewise, Nick and Sophie came to learn how hard their spouses were willing to work to ensure the well-being of their marriages.

There were inevitable breaches of trust, most of them unintentional. One day Nick's car broke down and Sophie had to give him a ride. It meant that she was late coming home to dinner with Damien. It was a blow of betrayal. It took several weeks of therapy to repair this rupture but, overall, the focus on honesty, openness, and transparency—the binding agents of polyamorous relationships—was paying off. Each person and couple was learning that it was possible to reach new levels of relational integration as long as everyone's concerns were respected and heard. "Doing things right" involved a copious amount of processing, not only during our sessions but also outside of therapy.

Eventually, the weekly couples' sessions became biweekly, and the moment came when both therapy tracks came to an end. We parted ways with an understanding that we could resume therapy should the need arise. Nick and Meghan came back several months later to work through some difficulties related to his family of origin. I learned then that Nick and Sophie were still seeing each other, maintaining the kind of balance that appeared to work for everyone involved. They were all tired of the endless processing needed to sustain this delicate balance, but affirmed their interest in making each of their relationships evolve and grow.

Working with Nick and Meghan, and Sophie and Damien, provided me with a valuable meta-perspective that I would not otherwise have. Their parallel tracks forced me to be in a constant dialog with my counter-transference, and I gained great insights from this process. This is not to say that I recommend other therapists follow suit. It is a personal judgment call how to approach situations of this level of complexity. What I have learned is that therapy boundaries do not have to be rigid to be safe, but they do need to be transparent, predictable, and negotiable. Whenever I am willing to alter the course of treatment, or be somewhat flexible about whom I accept as a new client, I emphasize that it is something we can try out as long as we are open about the process and are willing to change course if needed.

References

Anderlini-D'Onofrio, S. (2009). *Gaia and the new politics of love: Notes for a poly planet*. North Atlantic Books.

Barker, M. J., & Langdridge, D. (Eds.). (2010). *Understanding non-monogamies*. Routledge.

2 Paving the Road to Polyamory: From Free Love to Multiple Loves

"How come you therapists always use food metaphors?" a patient once asked. Until that moment, I was not aware of this particular predilection clinicians apparently have. Food as a clinical metaphor makes intuitive sense; we all need to eat in order to survive; thus, everyone can relate. But food is so much more than the calories needed; food is about love and oppression, nutrition and depletion, cultural influences, and elaborate perceptions of right and wrong. In other words, there is nothing simple about food and eating. So, returning to the question that frames this book—if polyamory is a new kind of cuisine that is here to stay, how do we eat it?

Human behavior is governed by biopsychosocial factors—a powerful combination of biology, ecology, environment, and culture in a specific moment of time. Biopsychosocial factors form and inform who we are; therefore, humans of the 21st century are both similar and different from our ancestors. Not having direct access to the past, we can only make educated guesses, but from what researchers can conjecture, it is highly unlikely that our forebears were monogamous. Present-day hunter-gatherer cultures, the living examples of our ancestral existence, are not monogamous. They tend to practice *polygyny*, in which one man has multiple female partners, or, less frequently, *polyandry*, in which one woman has multiple male partners (Sapolsky, 2017). Hunter-gatherer cultures are rich expressions of what kind of coupling is possible and acceptable. From this perspective, the argument in the poly community that monogamy is not natural is accurate. But it also misses the point. The argument of the unnaturalness of monogamy is predominantly biological in nature and, to a large degree, it excludes environment, ecology, and culture as other formative factors relevant for situating the particulars of human behavior in a specific moment in time.

As a parallel example, some of our ancient lineages were patrilineal; others were matrilineal. Neither kind was natural or unnatural; each was an expression of a complex context. All of this is true in modern times as well. Our perception of the basis and expression of human sexuality is going through rapid revisions. Advances in knowledge, assisted by evolving technology, create new narratives. The standard of polarized sexuality, the male versus the female, has been rightfully discarded as too narrow. Some babies are born as biologically male, some are biologically female, some are in between, and others are both. Biological sex and gender expression might be concordant or not. The biggest sexual organ in all genders and sexes, the part of us that is responsible for our varied desires, is not between our legs. It is our brain.

Until relatively recently, our knowledge of the brain implied an understanding of the male but not the female brain. Female brains were not studied with differences in mind; if discrepancies were noted, they were discarded as confounding noise. The expanding field of brain science, which looks at the interplay of genetics and epigenetics, the role of hormones and neurotransmitters, and so on, is changing our understanding of human sexuality. Adding to it, advances in technology play a surprisingly large role in modifying our perception of what is normal and what is not from a sexual point of view.

As much as anything else in the past, pornography is shaping human sexual expression and expectations. Pornography with its three As, Availability, Accessibility, and Affordability, is everywhere, obtainable at all times, and at no cost. It is the teacher that youngsters and adults consult free of charge. Pornography might be free, but due to the distortions embedded in its presentation of human sexuality, its "teachings" can be painfully costly to an individual and a couple. Many consumers become desensitized to normal sexual stimuli, finding themselves seeking images of more and more extreme versions of sexual acts. Is that natural? Or merely contextual?

The history of marriage is full of examples of contextual adaptations, too. A marriage in medieval times can hardly be compared to marriage in the Victorian era; both are vastly different from the modern invention of marriage for love. One may also ask, would we have polyamory if not for the Internet and social media? It is hard to say. Wide-sweeping social movements have emerged without the aid of the World Wide Web; it just took longer for them to get established. We humans are constant shapeshifters.

It is hardly a surprise that monogamy is under scrutiny. That the challenge takes the form of polyamory (among other forms of open relationships) is but an example of our shape-shifting tendencies. Various social forces and cultural waves contributed to the emergence of polyamory and consensual nonmonogamy in the second part of the 20th century. The socioeconomic and cultural transformation in Western countries since the 1960s gave rise to so-called *reflexive modernization* (Beck & Beck-Gernsheim, 1995; Beck, Giddens, & Lash, 1994; Giddens, 1991). One aspect of this new modernity is of particular relevance. It regards the changed assumption about life trajectories. Until the end of the 1950s, an individual's life trajectory was fairly predictable. This track involved heterosexual courtship followed by marriage and raising children. This was the *standard biography* of the nuclear family.

Reflexive modernity is immersed in a very different relational philosophy, referred to as *do-it-yourself biography*. Familial roles and assumptions are no longer defined by gender; the old expectations of courtship, marriage, and family apply with reservations. The do-it-yourself process of individuation and individualization makes space for a previously rare sense of personal autonomy within the standard narrative of heterosexual relationships. It is a transformation of relational life; the range of what is acceptable is far wider than in the past.

The women's movement and gay-rights activism paved the road to previously unimagined social changes. Taking a closer look at the achievements of gays and lesbians over the past three decades provides an intriguing backdrop for polyamory and, more broadly, consensual nonmonogamy. In *Same Sex Intimacies: Families of Choice and Other Life Experiments* (Weeks, Heaphy, & Donovan, 2001), the authors observe that this social transformation was a dual process. As the non-heterosexual community expanded, becoming more confident about its right to exist and thrive, a greater sense of agency started to emerge. A mere affirmation of gay identity was no longer enough; the bigger and more important task involved championing of the new relational ethos. This recognition coincided with the broader context of change in traditional family structures, paving the way to new gender and family boundaries. The steadily expanding alphabet of the LGBTQ+ community makes it evident that this is an ongoing (r)evolution.

Questioning the standard narrative is no longer renegade. In his seminal treatise on the history of sexuality, Michel Foucault (1978/1990) argued that to truly evolve, old models of dominance and subordination, of which heterosexual assumption is the prime example, need to be rejected and revised. A new practice of life, which he called the *aesthetic of existence*, focuses on friendship, autonomy, and the exploration of pleasure. The aesthetic of existence transcends and expands the familiar and, for the most part, socially accepted forms of sexual expression, including heterosexual, gay, lesbian, bisexual, and pansexual assertions. In this new realm of relating, monogamy and traditional coupledom may still exist but no longer dominate in their conventional format.

The open narrative is not a futuristic fantasy either; among gay men in committed relationships, the practice of nonmonogamy is widely accepted, as is the custom of consensual sex with multiple partners. Similarly, coupled bisexual individuals who by mutual agreement are free to engage sexually with people of both genders are by definition nonmonogamous. Perhaps it is not a surprise that heterosexuality as the remaining bastion of monogamy is under such scrutiny. Compared to non-heterosexual orientations, which more readily embrace wider ranges of sexual expressions, monogamous exclusivity may feel like an animal on the brink of extinction, ill-fated as a result of its lack of adaptive skills.

A question I often get is: How is polyamory different from the free love of the 1960s? This is a question of particular interest to therapists who, more or less directly, happened to experience the impact of the unfolding sexual revolution. To those who encountered the first wave of relational openness and are now witnessing the second, it is an understandable query. Comparing these two can make the unfamiliar more approachable, considering how the past hinted at the possible future. What I hear implied in this question is that the free love movement, with its implication of multiple partners, eventually evolved into "one love" after all—the majority of hippies settled down and with time came to espouse more traditional values. The communes in which free love was professed failed to survive. Could that be the fate of polyamory? If so, how should clinicians assist their clients? Encourage or discourage them? What kind of container, from Wilfred Bion's perspective, can therapists provide?

Not many mental health professionals are aware that one of the most influential and admired therapists of all times, Carl Rogers, explored the alternatives to traditional marriage by examining the life of intentional communes in the early 1970s. He shared his observations in a deeply personal book entitled *Becoming Partners* (1973/1978). Rogers spent hours conversing with the members of a commune that welcomed his inquiry. He earned their trust with his signature warmth and unconditional regard. Rogers described how at that time an estimated 2,000–3,000 wildly different communes and intentional communities were in existence, "growing, changing, closing, and starting, with a rapidity which outdates at once anything which can be written" (p. 132). His words resonate. Polyamory and nonmonogamy today are growing and changing with a rapidity that resembles the climate Rogers experienced. What especially interested Rogers was how the members of these communal groups were coping with marital, sexual, and interpersonal relationships. It was not easy, he observed, but the effort put into making it work was hard not to admire.

References

Beck, U., & Beck-Gernsheim, E. (1995). *The normal chaos of love*. Polity Press.

Beck, U., Giddens, A., & Lash, S. (1994). *Reflexive modernization: Politics, tradition and aesthetics in the modern social order*. Stanford University Press.

Foucault, M. (1978/1990). *The history of sexuality, Vol. 1: An introduction*. Vintage Books.

Giddens, A. (1991). *Modernity and self-identity: Self and society in the late modern age*. IntiNet Resource Center.

Rogers, C. R. (1973/1978). *Becoming partners. Marriage and its alternatives*. Constable & Company.

Sapolsky, R. M. (2017). *Behave: The biology of humans and our best and worst*. Penguin Books.

Weeks, J., Heaphy, B., & Donovan, C. (2001). *Same sex intimacies: Families of choice and other life experiments*. Routledge.

3 Relational Dreams and Fantasy Bonds: Commitment, Belonging, and Fitting in Poly Relationships

The Paradox of Monogamy: Social Versus Sexual

The raison d'être of the practice of polyamory is rooted in the paradox of monogamy. Biologically, we are not programmed to be monogamous. Socially, monogamy is challenging to maintain. Helen Fisher, an anthropologist who studies relationships and mating behavior noted that "Only 16 percent of the 853 cultures on record actually prescribe monogyny, in which a man is permitted one wife at the time" (2016, p. 50). The vision of sexual exclusivity over the entire lifespan makes even the most monogamous at heart smile with sad disbelief. Furthermore, there is no specific expiration date on one's sex life. Long life expectancy in the West combined with steady innovations in sexual medicine increase cultural expectations to remain sexually active until an advanced age. The combination of the longer life span and monogamous lifestyle is counterintuitive, yet seldom questioned. Against powerful odds, humans somehow manage to promote monogamy.

In their illuminating text *The Myth of Monogamy: Fidelity and Infidelity in Animals and People*, David Barash, a zoologist and professor of psychology, and Judith Eve Lipton, a psychiatrist, examined sexual behavior in a wide variety of species, including humans. They concluded that multiple mating is the norm rather than the exception in the animal world, and humans are not any different. Even pair-bonding birds, traditionally referred to as paragons of monogamy, are not very likely to mate with just one partner if other options are available. They do not broadcast their extra-pair copulations but instead employ ingenious strategies to avoid being caught. Thus, from the biological perspective, there is no convincing evidence for sexual exclusivity in the animal world, and more specifically, "there is powerful evidence that human beings are not 'naturally' monogamous" (2001, p. 1). However, under certain circumstances, monogamy might be a sensible choice, even if it goes against the grain of our species' biological inclinations.

Distinguishing social monogamy from sexual exclusivity paints a more accurate picture of pair-bonding reality. For animals whose progeny depends on extensive parental care, social monogamy is adaptive; it ensures greater survival rates for the offspring. This kind of pair-bonding applies to humans and birds and a handful of other species. Sexual exclusivity often accompanies social monogamy, at least overtly. Polygyny, which is a far more common form of sexual partnering in the animal and human world, refers to one male mating with multiple females. There is ample anthropological evidence of polygyny being dominant in humans when the conditions permit. However, throughout the different stages of humanity's development, only a handful of men were ever able to afford polygyny. To have multiple wives or multiple liaisons requires wealth and power. Polygyny was the privilege of rulers and their men. In contrast, the beta-male, a commoner with limited resources, was better off ensuring access to one woman than none. Monogamy affirmed such access. In Barash and Lipton's words, "Polygyny … is a condition of elitism, in which a relatively small number of fortunate, ruthless, or uniquely qualified men get to monopolize more than their share of the available mates. With monogamy, by contrast, even the most successful individual cannot have more than one legal mate; as a result, even the least successful is likely to obtain a spouse as well" (2001, p. 136).

Many patients I have talked to think of polyamory as an equalizer and monogamy as a monopolizer. They forget, or are not aware of, the equalizing power of monogamy, as described above. However, monogamy does not prevent infidelity, and in a long-term relationship, the chances of one or both partners straying at some point is high. Divorce and breakups lift the burden of monogamy, at least temporarily. But discarding a well-established relationship for the sake of sexual variety is a drastic measure. As a sex therapist, I have worked with numerous couples who describe their relationships as highly fulfilling and rewarding overall. Their primary complaint is about their sex life. It may seem like a small measure compared to their overall relational satisfaction; yet, many people seriously consider divorce when their sex life disappoints.

When, under the pressure of mononormativity, divorce feels like the only ethical solution to the dilemma of human biology, it creates a ripe condition for serial monogamy. However, an honorable breakup in the spirit of avoiding infidelity is not pain free, either. The conflicted spouse's integrity may be preserved when cheating is avoided, but this same integrity becomes the source of her partner's pain. Enter polyamory, the seemingly perfect answer to the puzzle of our biological-relational contradictions.

Firestone and Catlett, in their book *Fear of Intimacy* (2006), make an important observation that not many long-term relationships consist of what the authors call *high-level partner choices*. The majority of people have access to a limited pool of candidates regardless of when and where they live. At any given time, only a select few are fortunate to have access to a great number of high-end partner prospects. To be able to psychologically cope with this limitation, people find ways to justify their lower-level choices by making them appear more flattering than they are. Anyone who has tried online dating is aware of the limited supply of high-end options among seemingly endless possibilities.

In my experience, contrary to what people may hope for, the polyamory world does not offer any better selection of partners than the monogamy world. High-level prospects are as coveted in poly circles as they are among those who prefer monogamy. It is possible that on some unconscious level, the appeal of nonmonogamy might be due to this reality of limited options. While not being able to grant access to high-level partner choices, the polyamorous lifestyle at the very least provides access to variety. The perspective of being stuck for life with a default, presumably lower-level, partner might thus be amended.

Making one relationship work is demanding; maintaining multiple relationships is a considerable task. It requires much skill and effort and, above all, time. Choosing polyamory may yield access to variety, but it does not expand time. Nor does it ensure ease of effort. By necessity, to support multiple relationships, a person's attention has to be divided. This division of focus often comes at the cost of deepening intimacy. A concept that helps to explain this phenomenon is that of *fantasy bonds*. Developed by Robert Firestone (1987), this concept illuminates how people attempt to deal with these kinds of relational limitations.

A fantasy bond is a defense mechanism that lets people see love and conjure a loving connection where authentic love and genuine affection are missing. The imagined bond substitutes weariness and disappointment of the existing ties with an illusion of greater connection and closeness. The fantasy bond allows people to assuage loneliness by pushing aside the reality of emotional distance. The formation of a fantasy bond affects the flow of both giving and receiving love. Such bonds are characterized by a routinized, mechanical, going-through-the-motions action in an intimate relationship: goodbye and hello pecks on the cheek with no affection, mandatory "I love you's" in a voice empty of emotion, perfunctory lovemaking if it still exists, and so on.

Stale exchanges between partners, void of real interest in each other, are different from numbed interactions that are stilled by insecurity and fear. In the latter, when the anxiety lifts, the warmth returns. In the first, little sparks of interest quickly die, only to be replaced by indifference. Fantasy bonds can be discerned in long-term couples whose platitudinous interactions propel them to open up. They may reside in poly relationships maintained by a nutrient-poor formula. Polyamorous long-distance dating might be an example of the latter. A considerable number of poly individuals maintain relationships with people they see no more than once or twice a year, but whom they still consider to be intimate partners. In poly terminology, they are aptly known as *satellites*. Like satellites, fantasy bonds transmit but do not connect.

As a species, humans are immensely flexible, capable of adapting to most circumstances and demands. Fantasy bonds assist this adaptation. Yet, this process does not occur without a struggle. Adaptation in polyamorous relationships involves the capacity at least to tolerate, and at best to embrace, the other romantic pursuits of one's partner. As I have time after time observed, it often results in a confrontation with what can be called the case of not being chosen. A client described her grief when the attention of the man she deeply loved turned elsewhere, leaving her confused and hurt. With his other partner, the man experienced not only a new relationship energy (NRE), but also a shared, passionate political interest. No longer feeling chosen, my client tried to reassure herself that their connection was too strong to be broken by a third party. This belief made her dismiss his lack of attention as temporary and overlook the reality not matching her fantasy bond.

Regardless of how much the advocates of polyamory try to neutralize the experience of rejection associated with NRE, the sense of loss is not gone when alliances shift. It is not any different in cultures in which polygyny has been sanctioned for centuries. Women in polygynous societies rarely want their husbands to take on junior wives, nor do women prefer to be a junior spouse. The subordinate position comes with few privileges, offering pseudo-independence rather than genuine interdependence. The difference between polyamory and polygyny is that in polyamory, the case of not being chosen is not limited to women. Men are as likely to find themselves in this position. Fantasy bonds may help to sustain relatively weak liaisons but without offering the deep sense of connection. It is not a surprise, then, that fantasy bonds so often become the focus of therapy.

Commitment, Belonging, and Fitting In

At the core of any romantic experience is the question of love and belonging. They are inseparable entities; love belongs with belonging. As critical as they are to life, our ability to measure and properly describe these relational concepts is limited. "Everyone who risks explaining love and belonging is hopefully doing the best they can to answer an unanswerable question," cautions Brene Brown (2010, p. 25). Brown has devoted her research to understanding vulnerability, authenticity, and what it means to belong. She makes a key distinction between belonging and fitting in. To me, this distinction is crucial for understanding the struggle with polyamory that so many people experience. Fitting in is motivated by a desire to be approved of. As adaptive as this process might be, it requires adjustment in order to be accepted. In contrast, belonging does not require adjustments; it springs from being who one is.

According to the belongingness theory, people form social bonds under most conditions, even adverse ones (Baumeister & Leary, 1995). However, to be experienced as genuine, the sense of belonging needs to be mutual, with equal measures of giving and receiving shared between two people. Without mutuality, there is no romantic bliss. When the balance of belonging is consistently thrown off, the relationship is not likely to last. The experience of receiving love without wanting it is not rewarding; the experience of giving love without receiving much in return can be agonizing. Unrequited love, the prime example of one-sidedness, is associated with angst and torment. Being a rejector is distressing, too; refusing another person's offer of love induces guilt.

When clients open the first session with the carefully worded phrase "I'm poly?"—the question mark hovering in the air—it is a statement laden with meanings. Sometimes it underlies worry about not being accepted should one stray from mononormativity. At other times, it is akin to what many LGBTQ+ people first say when finally daring to admit their sexual orientation to themselves or others. Early on in my practice, when polyamory was unfamiliar to most, this opening statement represented a test of the therapeutic waters; clients were looking for signs to determine whether they belonged with me. Later on, for some people it represented what I came to call a reverse doubt; they believed in polyamory on principle but were no longer sure if they fit in with it. Another meaning of this phrase emerged as I started pondering the nature of love and belonging in polyamory. To what degree could this phrase be capturing some unconscious unease regarding the sense of belonging in multiple loves? Exploring poly travails with a wide range of patients made me aware of how frequently the talk about belonging actually reflects anxiety about fitting in.

The sense of belonging in polyamory is convoluted. On the one hand, having multiple partners may increase one's sense of belonging. Rather than solely relying on one's only partner to fulfill diverse relational needs, there are more people to turn to for love, connection, and support. On the other hand, the presence of multiple partners can diminish the sense of belonging, especially when there is a discrepancy between relational preferences and desires. The extensive poly vocabulary attempts to classify different kinds of romantic ties. From loosely connected metamours to primary partners, a language filled with code has developed in polyamory circles. Knowing the terms is another way of asserting one's belonging to the community. Creative labels denote relational constellations and positions; to a degree, they classify the levels of commitment. What these labels fail to convey is the emotions associated with those designations. It is understandable—sobriquets and feelings are two different things. Making adjustments to fit in is not the same as having a sense of belonging.

Some years ago, the predominant format of polyamory was hierarchical, with primary, secondary, and tertiary partners. Nowadays, clients are as likely to describe their relationships as nonhierarchical. As informative as these terms are, the labels do not remove relational ambivalence and may even mask emotional ambiguity. As an example, a hierarchical structure involving three partners may become nonhierarchical, giving the impression of equal commitment among everyone involved. However, the emotional reality of nonhierarchy might be egalitarian only in theory. It is rare for three (or more) partners to be equally invested with one another.

Shifts in poly arrangements are typically due to the dominant partner's desires. A person in the central position may propose a move from hierarchical to nonhierarchical polyamory. His partners more or less contentedly agree, but what feels like a promotion to one person may feel like a demotion to the other. Ryan's relationship with Rose and Katarina speaks to this complexity. Ryan's original involvement was with Rose, with whom he transitioned from monogamy to polyamory. The hierarchical structure they formed became nonhierarchical on Ryan's insistence after his relationship with Katarina became serious. Both women conceded, each considering her relationship with Ryan too important to give up on. Presenting as a poly family, they claimed that this was their ideal arrangement. It was only in their respective individual sessions that I learned each woman was longing to be the primary one. Katarina felt good about her step up in the relationship hierarchy but secretly wished for greater exclusivity. Rose felt demoted, unsure whether she wanted to stay or leave. The women were respectful of each other, doing their best to curb jealousy, but their connection was forced. They were not choosing each other; what they had in common were their feelings for Ryan. They maintained a semblance of a relationship for his sake, and the arrangement suited him well. Ryan, who was particularly adept at compartmentalizing, was aware of the women's lack of connection, but since there was no open conflict, he was disinclined to make any changes.

Another example of convoluted feelings associated with labels is represented by the term *anchor* or *nesting partner*. The phrase is ambiguous. In technical terms, it is a contranym; that is, its meaning changes depending on where the person stands. A former primary partner might be relegated to a new position of an anchor. He represents a live-in partner who anchors the connection, perhaps because of marriage or finances. At the same time, this assignation may reflect a sexual demotion. An anchor provides security but is no longer the person one desires to have sex with. The experience of mutuality in this anchor's sense of belonging has shifted. If his romantic attachment is still strong, being demoted can be very painful.

On the opposite end of the anchor spectrum, an individual might be longing for a deep sense of connection and security with one special person. It is exemplified by this poly blog: "… A poly friendly, OKC [the dating site OK Cupid] date asked what I wanted. And I answer as I always do, 'Truly what I want is one person in this world who gets me. An anchor. Two or three people would be great, but really, everything after one gravy' [sic]" (Cunning Minx, 2010). Even in a poly context, the note of longing for that *one special person* is hard to overlook. This longing is romantic and dyadic at heart. It is a longing for genuine bond.

Commitments to Partners Versus Commitment to Lifestyle

To meet in mutuality is powerful; two people wanting the same thing at the same time with the sense that it will last is magical. Envisioning three or more people wanting the same thing at the same time in equal measures, hoping that it will stay that way, is magical thinking. Describing existing commitment patterns in a poly relationship is easy. Predicting their stability over time is far more complicated, not the least because the approach to commitment in poly relationships is cautionary. People who practice polyamory revel in consensual agreements to be together for as long as it lasts without the risk of false promises. In the words of Franklin Veaux and Eve Rickert, the authors of *More Than Two*: "This means not just being realistic about your other commitments now, but about the flexibility you may require in the future when a new partner enters your life" (2014, p. 263). To translate, in polyamory, it is advisable not to commit too strongly because, when the relational energy becomes old, it might be time to look for a new source of romantic flare. This openness to new energy is based on an assumption that once a person becomes poly, they will always prefer this way of life.

"Once poly, always poly," a sentiment often expressed by polyamorous clients, implies that polyamory is too compelling to be abandoned for the restrictions of monogamy. In my experience, what is often overlooked is that commitment in polyamory is more often to the *lifestyle* than to a particular person or people. However, a large portion of polyamorous explorations start with a couple who hopes to maintain their partnership as it is, with minimal shifts in priorities. They hope to form additional relationships but without sacrificing the well-being of their own. That is what most patients assume will happen. Their confrontation with the reality of nonmonogamy can be daunting. Poly relationships fluctuate; they require the flexibility that many people do not have. When new partners are added, priorities change following the ebbs and flows of new relationship energies. Experiencing these shifts can be painfully shocking; they are sometimes followed by a confusing sense of being misled. Feeling deceived can be an unusually lonely experience—what feels like a betrayal was embedded in the very agreement to open up.

Belonging to a Community

If individual poly commitments tend to be fluid, committing to this lifestyle provides people with a sense of belonging to a unique community that by and large is open-minded and supportive. But, like any strong-minded community, this one too has its prejudices. Relational choices indicative of monogamous inclinations may be treated with distrust in poly circles. People who decide to abandon the polyamorous lifestyle for personal reasons, but remain poly-friendly in spirit, may lose connection with the community. They may no longer be invited to poly gatherings even if they are still friends with other poly people. Similarly, those who decide to marry while remaining polyamorous may no longer feel supported by others. Their reasons to marry are likely to be similar to those of monogamous couples, sans the promise of sexual exclusivity. But the very decision to marry may be met with criticism rather than approval in the poly community. It is typically expressed as "Why bother being poly if you are going to marry?"

Transitioning from Monogamy to Polyamory

The term *opening up* refers to the process of untying the boundaries of monogamy. The degree of openness varies, from the permission to engage in occasional sexual trysts outside of marriage to the full embrace of concurrent romantic relationships. People who are drawn to polyamory find its premise and promise persuasive. This is not surprising, given the captivating portrait of polyamory presented by its advocates. Combined with the grim picture of modern marriage and the difficulty of maintaining monogamy for life, the quest for more compelling alternatives is understandable.

Many of my monogamous clients admit that they are curious about non-monogamy, or that deep inside they feel polyamorous even though they would be reluctant to open up. I hear similar confessions from acquaintances and strangers who happen to know about my expertise in this area. Polyamory might be challenging to practice, but its ethos reflects a widespread unease with the current relational picture. Therapists face questions they cannot easily answer: Do the virtues of polyamory outnumber the consequences of opening up? What can be said about the longevity of relationships within polyamory? How can therapists best guide their clients through the process of discerning what is right for them?

The process of transitioning to nonmonogamy can be made easier by paying attention to the three Ps of Preparation, Prediction, and Prevention. A metaphor I often use is that deciding to open up is like watching an approaching weather front and doing one's best to be prepared. Going through this process is like being hit by a line of storms; their impact is not always easy to predict, but the consequences are usually significant. Some rifts resulting from this stormy process can be addressed relatively well; other damages might be irreparable. Individuals and couples presenting in therapy at the early stages of polyamorous exploration are usually highly aware of the potential risks, but far less equipped to deal with the consequences. Like with the powerful storms of nature, preparation helps but it cannot predict nor prevent all damage.

Polyamorous guidelines on how to open up are plentiful; they are rich in procedural details and abundant in advice (e.g., Taormino, 2008; Veaux & Rickert, 2014). Most of them include the caveat that polyamory is not for everyone, urging the interested to do a thorough self-examination using the questions provided. The questions range from an assessment of one's beliefs regarding monogamy to a calculation of how much time and energy one will be able to devote to multiple lovers. However, the guides' focus is predominantly on what can be won (plenty) and less so on what might be lost (presumably not much compared with the gains). The overall tone may give the impression that as long as everyone follows the instructions, polyamory is relatively easy to manage and that the rewards are worth the challenge. It is less readily acknowledged that the relationship one hopes to keep while transitioning to polyamory is likely to be changed beyond recognition or may cease to exist altogether. Some guides go as far as to say that perhaps the relationship that got lost was not worth having. Indeed, for some couples, opening up becomes an opportunity for what can be described as *soft divorce*, a slow separation of relational ties. However, not all relationships are ready to be discarded. Many clients are not prepared for the challenges of open relationships and may desperately hope to reverse the process. Slowing down the process tends to be beneficial, but it is not always possible to salvage a relationship riddled with the multiple rifts caused by opening up.

Guidebooks offer fair warning that polyamory is not the solution for a broken relationship. But concluding that something must have been wrong with marriage because it ended up in divorce oversimplifies the picture. The clinical reality is that many marriages that end up dissolving due to opening up are not necessarily bad. On the contrary, they are often well functioning after years of relational fine-tuning and are generally highly satisfying. The most common ground for considering polyamory is a relative lack of sexual satisfaction or a desire for greater sexual variety. Sexual novelty running its course is a dilemma facing all long-term couples, but surprisingly, many people are not ready to accept this reality of life and assume it must be their partner's fault. From an object relations perspective, it is a struggle with the *depressive position*, which will be elaborated upon in Part V. The term *depressive position*, introduced by Melanie Klein, has somewhat unfortunate associations, but so far nobody has managed to suggest a better one.

The depressive position implies an ability to perceive the world realistically and to accept the inevitable limitations and sense of incompleteness of any relationship. It involves acceptance of responsibility and the capability to grieve a loss. There is no easy way around the loss of sexual novelty unless we somehow manage to alter human biological responses. It is hard to admit to sexual restlessness, especially when everything else appears to be working fine in a relationship. Because regardless of how refined it sounds, *it is not a desire for more love that prompts opening up*. I have not yet met a couple who would say, "We love each other very much, are best friends, have great families, work well together, and have great sex, but miss having more love in our lives, so we decided to open up." Sex and love are intertwined, but it is rare for love without sexual desire to instigate the exploration of polyamory. People who want more love invest in children, family, friendships, or pets, without feeling the need to change their monogamous status. Experiencing a strong emotional connection with someone new may lead to conversations about nonmonogamy, but not because these feelings are platonic. Emotional affairs are considered affairs because they are highly preoccupying; they are usually accompanied by some degree of sexual tension. The emotionally transgressing partner who brings up the possibility of opening the relationship does so because she hopes to become physically involved with the object of her affection.

References

Barash, D. P., & Lipton, J. E. (2001). *The myth of monogamy: Fidelity and infidelity in animals and people*. W. H. Freeman & Company.

Baumeister, R. F., & Leary, M. R. (1995). The need to belong: Desire for interpersonal attachments as a fundamental human motivation. *Psychological Bulletin, 117*(3), 497–529. doi:10.1037/0033-2909.117.3.497

Brown, B. (2010). *The gifts of imperfection: Let go of who you think you're supposed to be and embrace who you are*. Hazelden Publishing.

Cunning Minx, (2010, November 15). A replacement for "primary/secondary. *Polyamory Weekly*. http://polyweekly.com/a-replacement-for-primarysecondary/

Firestone, R. W. (1987). *The fantasy bond: Structure of psychological defenses*. The Glendon Association.

Firestone, R. W., & Catlett, J. (2006). *Fear of intimacy*. American Psychological Association.

Fisher, H. (2016). *Anatomy of love: A natural history of mating, marriage and why we stray*. W. W. Norton.

Taormino, T. (2008). *Opening up: A guide to creating and sustaining open relationships*. Cleis Press.

Veaux, F., & Rickert, E. (2014). *More than two: A practical guide to ethical polyamory*. Thorntree Press.

Part II
Poly Dynamics of Love

4   In Love Versus in Life: Has Marriage for Love Failed?

What are the determinants of love? Can love last or is it doomed to fail? Is it better to invest in multiple loves than to hold on to one that may not last? The dominant form of marriage throughout human history has been what is called "marriage for reason"; this concept safeguarded a bond but sacrificed the feelings of those involved. The reasons to marry varied: to secure a bloodline, to protect assets, to enforce racial or religious integrity, to institute political powers, or to maintain monarchies. Love was the least important factor in those equations. It was an appreciated side effect, but not the main goal. When marriage for love replaced marriage for reason, it came with a beautiful promise; it suggested that following one's heart is more in alignment with who we are relationally. Yet, marriage for love, as revolutionary as it was, has not delivered on its promise. Love has a limited lifetime if the divorce rates are taken into consideration, but the longing for love endures.

Passionate and companionate forms of love appear to be universal; however, their value is culture specific. Even within one and the same culture, the importance of love may change over a relatively short time span. In the 1960s, only 24 percent of college-aged women in the U.S. considered marrying for love to be essential while 65 percent of their male counterparts considered it important. Marrying well meant something different to men and women of that era. Two decades later, more than 80 percent of both men and women considered love a prerequisite to marriage (Coontz, 2005).

Nearly 30 years ago, in his book *The Transformation of Intimacy: Sexuality, Love, & Eroticism in Modern Societies* (1992), a prominent sociologist, Anthony Giddens, predicted changes in sexual and gender dynamics, anticipating a shift in what it means to be in a romantic relationship. Giddens saw romantic love as harbinger of a so-called *pure relationship*, a relationship rooted in sexual and emotional equality in which traditional gender dynamics no longer applied. A pure relationship was made possible by *plastic sexuality*, characterized by the emancipation of sexuality from the burdens of reproduction. Plastic sexuality liberated women's pleasure; desire became autonomous and free from fear of pregnancy. It also became free from the rule of the phallus, which implied the domination of male sexual experience. Women's pleasure became equally important to that of a man. The phallus got demoted to the role of a mere penis, no longer an omnipotent, but rather a fallible organ.

"Romantic love presumes that a durable emotional tie can be established with the other on the basis of qualities intrinsic to that tie itself" (1992, p. 2), wrote Giddens. The echo of this sentiment can be discerned in polyamory; the intrinsic qualities of polyamory supposedly attest to the superiority of this lifestyle. Giddens asserted that romantic love depends on projective identification, a process in which prospective partners are attracted and then bound to one another. The process of mutual projective identification creates a sense of wholeness.

On the opposite end of the spectrum of the projective identification of romantic love, Giddens saw *confluent love*. He described confluent love as active and conditional, incongruent with the "for-ever" and "one-and-only" qualities of classic romantic entanglement. Being conditional, confluent love does not presuppose sexual exclusiveness and monogamy. Pure relationship and confluent love are valid "until further notice," that is, until the existing relational terms are ready to be renegotiated. According to Giddens, confluent love emerged as a result, not the cause, of the separating and divorcing society.

Giddens's observations foreshadowed the rise of polyamory. Like polyamory, confluent love is negotiable; it presumes equality in emotional and sexual give and take. To some, intimacy seen as a demand for constant emotional closeness, is oppressive. To others, it is synonymous with a mutable relationship between equals. "The more confluent love becomes consolidated as a real possibility, the more the finding of a 'special person' recedes and the more it is the 'special relationship' that counts" (p. 62). In my clinical observations, in polyamory, that special relationship so often is...*polyamory*. This is an important notion. In the spirit of confluent love, partners are ultimately replaceable. The relationship they form is expected to last until the terms have changed; for example, another partner has risen in prominence. What remains unchanged is the oath of allegiance to polyamory as a lifestyle. Herein lies a certain paradox; while the practice of polyamory is considered more evolved than monogamy, a similar commitment to the lifestyle, as in monogamy, is expected.

In my work with polyamorous and polycurious clients, I cannot help wondering sometimes if expectations toward love have been replaced with the expectation to be constantly in love. People marry for love, but they equate love with being *in love*. They take the fireworks of passion and effortless energy of the early stages of romance for signs of true love. When the fireworks die down, to be replaced by a deeper sense of connection and intimacy, as is the case in any long-term commitment, it is only mildly comforting. For many, the lack of sparks gives rise to marital anxiety. The adjustment from being in love to being in life is difficult; I have heard the same complaint from countless couples, often expressed in almost identical words: "We love each other very much but are no longer in love." These couples' distress is very real, and they are not easily reassured. The expectation to be in love prevails, combined with an assumption that love should be effortless and organic. Any effort required to maintain a passionate connection is dismissed as "not spontaneous." When the neglected spark of passion refuses to ignite, it is taken to mean that the marriage is failing. Spouses blame each other for depleting the tank, spending copious amounts of energy listing their grievances. Refusing to reengage feels safer than reassessing the situation and trying to engage in an authentic manner. It is a perfectly vicious cycle; recounting the blows justifies the lack of effort. The majority of individuals and couples who seek therapy in the context of polyamory find themselves being in life rather than in love and are unsure how to deal with the absence of in-love feelings. They do what they are familiar with—they blame the other for the failure of love.

Relationships are living, breathing organisms. They need nourishment to survive and thrive. Without due attention, marriages for love inevitably fail at staying in love. In his book *Becoming Partners: Marriage and Its Alternatives*, Carl Rogers (1973/1978) shared reflections on his own marriage. He humbly admitted how little he knew about his wife's pleasure when they had sex. Rogers assumed she had orgasms because she seemed to enjoy their relationship. Only when they began "[t]he frightening process of talking—really *talking*" (p. 33), did he learn that she did not find their sex life satisfying. This was the beginning of their process of being truly open with each other, a process that involved expressing their satisfactions and dissatisfactions, and that required weathering of criticisms and rejections. This process lasted throughout their life, in a never-ending commitment to being *vulnerable together*. It led Rogers to conclude that "the dream of marriage 'made in heaven' is totally unrealistic, and that every continuing man-woman relationship must be worked at, built, rebuilt, and continually refreshed by mutual personal growth" (p. 39). As I mentioned earlier, *Becoming Partners* is more than an introspection of Rogers's marriage. It is also an exploration of marital alternatives as they started to proliferate in the late 1960s and early 1970s. Rogers's conclusion regarding his own marriage has resounding poignancy regarding the alternatives. A continuous effort is required to become true partners, and replacing monogamy with non-monogamy only moves the target without addressing the cause. Monogamous marriages and polyamorous relationships can both flourish as long as "the frightening process" of genuine engagement is maintained. To turn a catchphrase into a relational mantra, ask not what love can do for you—ask what you can do for love.

References

Coontz, S. (2005). *Marriage, a history: From obedience to intimacy or how love conquered marriage*. Viking.

Giddens A. (1992). *The transformation of intimacy: Sexuality, love, & eroticism in modern societies*. Stanford University Press.

Rogers, C. R. (1973/1978). *Becoming partners: Marriage and its alternatives*. Constable & Company.

5 Maps of the Heart: Capacity for Love

By combining the words *multiple* and *love*, the word polyamory thus implies *knowing* love. But what is love? How can it be defined? The sheer fact that countless numbers of philosophers, poets, scientists, and therapists have attempted to penetrate the nature of love says a lot about its ambiguity. Love is a physiological phenomenon and a social convention. The biology of love is manifested by the feeling of butterflies in the stomach, the racing heart, and the spinning head. Love is also a social construct that defines who we may or may not love, sometimes in accordance with our biology and sometimes against it. This social aspect of love explains why the laws of attraction are rather elusive. It illuminates why we find some people appealing and others not, regardless of their physical attractiveness. Queer love, interracial love, and polyamorous love are all examples of socially permitted love bonds that were inconceivable in the not-so-distant past. In many parts of the U.S. and in the world, they still are.

I have always loved maps. To this day, when I travel to new places, I look for paper maps that I can unfold. As much as I rely on smart devices for directions, examining a physical map helps me to locate myself in a new terrain. A concept of a map is applicable to the study of the intertwined dynamics of love, romance, commitment, and sex. Early love experiences shape a child's capacity for love later in life. The sum of these experiences forms an inner map that adults may use to navigate the complex relational world (Goldbart & Wallin, 2001).

I envision this inner map as drawn in visible and invisible inks. The visible lines represent childhood memories of being loved and cared for by one's parents or caregivers. The invisible lines are not consciously accessible but are as deeply etched into the love map as the visible lines. To be able to perceive these contours, a special activating agent, a trigger, is needed. Triggers are reactions to real or perceived relational threats that reveal unhealed wounds underneath faded scars. A person may not be aware, or capable, of describing the original wound and might even be dismissive of the scar. The triggered responses, usually discordant to situations, indicate the presence of old injuries.

The child's love map continues developing as she matures. The cross-lines of new relational experiences fill the map, sometimes healing and sometimes concealing early developmental rifts. The invisible lines are not erased; the right kind of trigger may bring them out, usually to the partner's startled dismay. It is like falling through a concealed crevasse when hiking through a seemingly safe and even terrain. The surprise and hurt get mixed with confusion and fear. The triggered individual, unaware of the old relational fractures, reacts to the partner, blaming him for bringing on the pain.

The visible and invisible layers of the inner love map shape our relational expectations. They may reinforce a person's deepest fears or assist the process of healing from earlier relational ruptures. Goldbart and Wallin note, "The key (without which we are lost) is to recognize that we have all been mapmakers—and that, for better or worse, we are also made by our map" (p. xiv). Every person who yearns and dares to love is likely to encounter some amount of pain caused by unhealed attachment wounds. With patience and support, the invisible outlines of a love map may become more discernible. This is the terrain of relationship-oriented therapy, whether the couple in focus is monogamous or polyamorous, or somewhere in between. Intuited by Freud and his followers, object relations and other psychodynamic perspectives have gained new recognition in light of rapid advances in the interdisciplinary fields of psychobiology and neuropsychology. Specifically, the vast role played by the unconscious in the brain's processing of emotions is no longer disputed. This is the same unconscious that was, until recently, dismissed as belonging to the obscure psychoanalytic past. The unconscious not only applies to our emotions; it also shapes our perceptions, our behavior, and our ability to love and be loved.

Winnicott offered a beautiful metaphor of turning ghosts into ancestors when dealing with the intricacies of love, and the image resonates. In therapy, I frequently refer to the ghosts from the past, and each time the response is similar. A person or couple in front of me nod in thought, regardless of how pragmatically they approach life. There is a visceral recognition of the impact of ghostly shadows written in invisible ink on their inner map. Relational ghosts evoke emotional reactions, and any attempts at treating them as irrational only intensify the affect. In a sense, emotions need to "hear from" other emotions before they can "listen to" rational explanations. A father impassively telling his young son that there are no monsters under the bed, so he should go to sleep now, is not reassuring to the child. The son knows the monsters are there; he *feels* them and is now even more frightened because the monsters in their viciousness managed to scare away the father from the room. The son is alone and terrified. His fear was not soothed by his father's dismissive comment; it has intensified. The same father patiently sitting down on the edge of his son's bed to hear about the monsters underneath renders the beasts less scary. The child believes they cannot possibly be so bad if the father is not afraid of staying in the room. The father's soothing voice and playful games invented to chase the monsters away comfort the child. He sees that only dust bunnies are hiding under the bed. The father's emotional joining creates a sense of safety, and it is now reasonably safe to go to sleep.

A woman reacting with a ferocious outburst to something innocuous her partner says is responding to him *and* to a scary ghost from the past. The partner, taken aback by the intensity of her emotions, dismissively asks her to take it down a notch and stop being ridiculous. He wants her to calm down and have a logical conversation, like all "rational adults." What he does not realize is that his reply just added more fuel to the fire. Her outburst was irrational and he can see it as clear as day, but she stubbornly refuses to listen to his amends. She cannot hear him, not until her affect is validated rather than dismissed. It is not a matter of being stubborn. That in his eyes makes her even more unreasonable, so he wants to stop her from behaving so foolishly and start listening to logic. Neither one understands the other; both feel hurt and wounded, powerless to break their impasse. They have reached a familiar standstill with no hope of resolution in sight. The emotions eventually cool down, but the wound remains unhealed.

To reiterate the metaphor, emotions want to talk to other emotions first before listening to the rational. In fact, they *need* to be heard first; otherwise, the vicious cycle is going to be repeated. At the same time, the rational craves rational responses and considers emotional explanations as an unhelpful diversion. The couple's attempt at recovery, as they explain what was going on for each one of them, brings them back to the familiar impasse, with more hurt feelings in tow. The woman says, "You did this," hoping her partner will understand what it was about "this" that was hurtful to her; the man fires back with a logical explanation of his behavior, not understanding why she, once again, is getting more upset. The dance goes on until both partners collapse in exhaustion. What both are missing is how much they yearn to be at ease and understood by the other; they hope the other person will understand their inner map. They are unaware of how their respective solutions to the problem have this same goal in mind. Both partners desperately want to recover from the rupture and, in order to get there, they need to *feel seen*. Feeling seen and known by the other is the most powerful relational experience there is; it is a building block of trust, admiration, and respect. The opposite, not feeling seen in spite of genuine attempts to connect, is desperately painful. True love cannot exist without the person feeling known; enduring love cannot survive without respect and appreciation of the other person's inner love map.

Reference

Goldbart, S., & Wallin, D. (2001). *Mapping the terrain of the heart: Passion, tenderness, and the capacity to love.* Aronson.

6 From Passion to Compassion: Different Shades of Love

Each individual has their own love map. Each couple creates their unique atlas of love. With so many love maps in existence, it is hard, if not impossible, to come up with a unifying theory of love. Love is a feeling, a state; it is an aspiration, preoccupation, confusion, frustration; the list goes on. Love can be as fleeting as fireflies, frenziedly alive for a few summer weeks, and love can last a lifetime. Writing about polyamory from a clinical perspective pleads for some way of conceptualizing love. Are concurrent loves, as practiced in polyamory, different from a singular love?

A handful of psychological theories have been proposed to capture the elusive nature of love.

Ellen Berscheid and Elaine Hatfield's (1974) theory identifies two elemental components of love—passion and compassion. Passionate love is characterized by strong sexual attraction combined with intense affection and anxiety. Passion is transitory by nature, usually lasting from about 6–30 months. When unrequited, passionate love can cause immense distress; when reciprocated, it makes a person feel profoundly alive. It is commonly anticipated that with time, passion will morph into compassion. Compassionate love is based on a deep sense of mutual respect, commitment, affection, and trust. The early passion does not need to die out, but it is unlikely to remain as intense as it was in the beginning. However, the popular cultural expectation has it that, rooted in the stability of a secure attachment, deep passion should co-exist with compassion. When compassion detaches from passion, it generates disappointment and, for many, a sense that the relationship has failed.

Robert Sternberg (1986, 1988) proposed a triangular theory of love. According to him, love consists of intimacy, passion, and commitment. An interplay of these three components accounts for the varying degree of depth and longevity of loving feelings. When characterized by only one component, love is not going to be fulfilling in the long run. A *crush* is fueled by one element only—passion; when an element of intimacy is added, it becomes a *romance*. Long-term relationships based on commitment, but lacking in passion or intimacy, are stable but seldom satisfying. A *companionate* love that has its base in a deep sense of intimacy and commitment is likely to be gratifying, even without the fireworks of passion. A *consummate* love combines all three components; it is the strongest and most enduring kind, but also the rarest.

The main implications of Berscheid and Hatfield's, and Sternberg's theories are that love changes over time. In contrast, John Lee's (1973) "six elements" proposal depicts love more as categories, rather than as transitions. Lee's analogy is of a color wheel, with its primary and complementary colors. The three dominant styles of love are Eros, Storge, and Ludus. *Eros* is a passionate, highly erotic, and preoccupying kind of love. It is a love for another, often idealized, person. *Storge* stems from the Greek and implies a familial or friendship-based type of love that is characterized by natural affection. It exists between parents and children, between siblings, and among extended family members. It develops in friendships built upon shared interests and mutual affection. *Ludus* is a game-playing kind of love, fun and noncommittal. It is appealing to those who are wary of deep intimacy and lasting attachments. When the primary colors of love are combined, they form secondary love styles. Eros and Ludus create *Mania*, an obsessive kind of love. *Pragma*, a practical and realistic type of love, combines Storge and Ludus. Finally, *Agape*, or selfless love, stems from a combination of Eros and Storge.

What these different theories have in common is the tension between transient passion and enduring compassion, between lustful intimacy and steady commitment. In my clinical observations, the majority of polyamorous explorations start with a search for passion or play. A number of individuals hope to experience deep emotional intimacy characteristic of new relationship energy. For many people, their initial expectations will change over time, and they will form a desire for a deeper commitment. For others, Ludus, a play-based kind of love, will remain the major attraction of poly possibilities.

Theories of love, however accurate, provide little comfort regarding the shifting nature of love. Talking about love can be painful—the very fact that it is brought up in therapy conveys doubt about its permanence. In English, the language of love is limited. The same word is used to communicate incomparable feelings: we love our partners, children, parents, friends, pets, coworkers, lattes, cars, vacation trips, and so on. Gary Chapman (1992, 2015) aimed to expand this limited terminology by suggesting that people tend to use and respond to a handful of distinct expressions of love. He called these expressions the *five love languages*. The languages include words of affirmation, quality time, receiving gifts, acts of service, and physical touch. Chapman's theory may lack empirical support, but it has proved to be immensely popular; the book *The Five Love Languages* has been on the *New York Times* bestseller list since 2009. Clearly, having a more nuanced vocabulary is helpful; love's meanings and motivations can be refined and reassessed.

Love conceptualized as distinct languages makes intuitive sense. People show love differently. Presented with a language they do not recognize as love, they feel unloved. Inviting patients to reflect on what love languages they respond to, perhaps identifying their own variants, diminishes the sense of hurt. Examining fused relational dynamics from the perspective of different love languages brings love back to the therapy room.

Conceptualizing Different Love Styles in Polyamory

Eros in Polyamory

Those who have ever experienced passionate, romantic love are not likely to forget its vibrant vitality. Monogamous couples wistfully remember the delights of early passion before the intimacy of companionship set in. Sometimes their longing makes them stray from monogamy, either covertly or more directly, which leads to the suggestion that they open their relationship. Polyamorous individuals who have experienced the power of passion may seek it with the extra ardor available to those who do not have to hide their longings.

A subset of polyamorous individuals presenting in therapy is driven by the endless quest for passionate love. These people may move from one romantic pursuit to the next, never satisfied with what they have. When a new relationship energy dissolves into companionate feelings, they may search for a new person who will again evoke the sense of exhilaration they desire. This is parallel to the quest for confluent love, understood as a search for the near-perfect passionate romance of equals, noted by Giddens (1992). A relationship that is not delivering constant, renewable passion is somehow at fault. Evoking Giddens's observation, confluent love becomes an ideal in a society where almost everyone has a chance to become sexually accomplished. We live in such a society. Mutually satisfying sex has the power to sustain a relationship; the lack thereof may lead to its dissolution.

Returning to a crucial point, none of the people who have ever contacted me for therapy say they are thinking about polyamory because they are *in love*. On the contrary, they make an appointment because something appears to be amiss. Loving one's partner, but no longer being in love, is often considered a problem that warrants counseling. Obviously, there is more to it; a transition from being in love to a relationship characterized by companionate love is typically not enough for people to consider polyamory. It almost always happens because whatever was left of passion has dangerously dwindled down or disappeared. The impetus to seek more is not because of the hope for companionate, measured love; it starts with a desire to be in love or to have more sex: more of it, more variety, more spontaneity. In other words, the longing for the promise of starting anew takes over.

Countless studies indicate declining sex to be a strong predictor of diminished relational satisfaction. Thus, deteriorating sex is not merely correlated with lower levels of relational fulfillment; it is actually causing it. However, I will dare to proclaim that many people have learned to expect more while doing less, oftentimes oblivious to the fact that considerable effort is required to make passion last. As Peggy Kleinplatz's (2006, 2010) research on optimal sexual experiences indicates, contrary to popular belief, great lovers are made not born. The key finding in Kleinplatz's research is that extraordinary lovers, as defined by those who are middle-aged and older and who have been in the same relationship for 25-plus years (monogamous or consensually nonmonogamous), had to unlearn everything they learned about sex when they were young. Everything! One of the prevailing myths about sex is that it is spontaneous and requires no labor. Nothing could be further from the truth. Magnificent sex in the context of a lasting relationship involves time, preparation, outstanding communication, and a number of other factors pointing to *sustained* effort. Extraordinary sexual experiences are not limited to those who are young, able-bodied, and conventionally beautiful. They belong to those who are willing to invest in the relationship and capitalize on the power of preparation to make something spectacular happen.

Storge and Pragma in Polyamory

There are moments in therapy that stand out, not because of some brilliant intervention or empathic attunement, but because they offer unexpected insights. One such moment occurred when a couple I worked with casually remarked that people who succeed at polyamory are "low on drama." When I asked about their observation, they told me about a discussion with a group of poly friends in which they reached this conclusion. Their comment was aligned with what I have been observing in my practice for a while, which is that couples who are able to transition from monogamy to polyamory without falling apart are those who are deeply attuned to one another's processes. They are those whose reflective functioning abilities are well developed.

The love styles of Storge and Pragma are characterized by low emotional reactivity. Individuals with these love styles respond in a relatively unperturbed way to emotional storms. Because of their seemingly collected demeanor, they may appear to be unruffled by opening up. Still, the process of transitioning from monogamy to nonmonogamy can be dramatic; from the moment polyamory is suggested and throughout its progression, nothing stays the way it used to be. The love styles of Storge and Pragma may give the appearance of secure attachment, as the following example illustrates, but other attachment styles may be in play as well.

Zach and Becca, like many of the couples I have worked with, decided to open up when their sex life had ceased to exist. Now in their mid 30s, they were high school sweethearts, married, with four young children. Their values were in alignment since they had started dating in their teens; both dreamed of getting married after college and having many children. However, their shared dream did not spring from a similar source; their respective backgrounds were very different. Zach came from a large family with countless aunts and uncles and their offspring. Family gatherings were festive opportunities to be merry together, and the cousins still spend time in one another's houses. When reflecting on his desire to open up, Zach thought back on his family experiences, concluding that with so many people to love and share his life with, in his heart he had always been poly. In spite of its large size, Zach's extended family was cohesive and stable. Hetero- and mononormativity prevailed; there were no divorces to speak of, nor were there any gay people among his relatives. His upbringing was secure, and he reached his developmental milestones without much conflict. As he said, with smiling eyes, he *belonged* in a large family.

Becca, by contrast, came from a family of four—her parents and an older brother. The family had very little contact with other relatives. Becca appeared to be companionate in a quiet, self-assured way; however, it became apparent in our work together that her upbringing was far from stable. Her family of origin avoided open conflict, but there was simmering tension between her parents. Until therapy, Becca did not question her decision to have several children, even if it meant that she was in constant demand. She assumed it was just what she and Zach had agreed upon. Exploring how her upbringing came to influence her life decisions, she realized that, paradoxically, having four kids allowed her to keep a distance from the hassles of too much closeness. Switching attention from Zach to one child and to the next created enough space to not feel overburdened by the individual interactions. When Zach proposed polyamory, she reacted the way most people do at first, wondering if he was no longer invested in their relationship. When he explained that his desire was to expand and not to replace, she found it reasonable, given his close-knit family experience and her growing understanding of how she regulated distance and closeness in her intimate relationships.

Zach and Becca's pragmatic styles and overall agreeable personalities made it possible to transition to polyamory without overt drama. Over time, Becca found reassurance in Zach's continuous commitment to her and their children, and Zach was grateful for her support of his needs. Since their children were used to interacting with lots of relatives from the day they were born, Zach and Becca did not have to worry about explaining the presence of more people in their lives.

The Power of Ludus

The realm of Ludus may explain the appeal of polyamory to males. After all, consensual nonmonogamy provides access to a wider range of sexual possibilities without the weight of commitment. Indeed, the research on love and sex attitudes reveals consistent gender differences between men and women, with men endorsing a self-focused, game-playing kind of love the most, and women embracing it the least (Hendrick & Hendrick, 1987, 2004, 2006). However, men are not the only ones who cherish sexual novelty. Women too value access to greater sexual variety. According to some studies, sexual novelty may actually be more important to women than to men (Martin, 2019). At the same time, the appeal of polyamory to females cannot be solely explained by the allure of Ludus. Women tend to be more practical and commitment oriented in their endorsements. They are also more likely to admit to possessiveness; however, in the context of polyamory, they tend to manage this tendency more effectively. Overall, polyamory reduces the risks associated with sexual betrayal and the possible loss of a partner as a result. It is possible that women's greater focus on friendship combined with their pragmatic approach is what makes polyamory attractive to them. Interestingly, the early endorsers and most vocal promoters of polyamory, Dossie Easton, Janet Hardy, and Deborah Anapol, were all females. Indeed, many of the strongest voices advocating for polyamory continue to be female.

Sexual expansion aside, couples in committed relationships struggling with their sex life are deprived of more than sex; they are frequently deprived of touch. Our *need to belong* (Baumeister & Leary, 1995) is based on intimate connections with others, where "intimate" implies physical contact. Of all the forms of physical contact, the sexual one has the largest implications because of its meaning. However, when sex disappears, it not only leaves a vacuum; it often takes away touch. Polyamorous communities recognize the power of touch as a part of play. For some poly individuals, the access to play—from nonsexual touch in cuddle parties to consensually sexual exchanges in kink events—is very appealing. A patient, Marissa, described what she finds so special about these gatherings: "You know, I just love touching and being touched. It doesn't have to be sexual, but if it turns that way, with the right person or people, it's just great. Sometimes my partner is present and sometimes he isn't. Before attending, we discuss what we're comfortable with, and what our boundaries are, and that feels very authentic and respectful."

The Meaning of Love in Polyamory

Intimate connections within polyamory are far from equal. Different kinds of love, including Eros, Ludus, Pragma, Storge, and Agape, are all mixed together. Mania, with its possessiveness, is the only love style not sustainable for poly relations. From a clinical perspective, the greatest appeal of polyamory, at least initially, lies in its connection to Eros and Ludus; however, loving more does not give automatic access to more romantic love. On the contrary, loving more is likely to imply surrender to other kinds of love, while perhaps still longing for Eros. The attitude of Pragma makes the acceptance of new relationship energy easier, but without necessarily reaching the levels of Agape. With Eros being as elusive as ever, only a few are likely to be hit by his arrows. A desire for the passionate merging of two people in a romantic union might be substituted by similar, although usually less fulfilling, highs of a crush or infatuation. Ludus may become the distracting alternative, sheltering a person from not being able to secure a deeper kind of "more."

As the theories reviewed above illustrate, trying to capture the nature of love in any meaningful way is tremendously difficult. For many, the main challenge lies in the expectation that love should be synonymous with being in love. However, since there is not one kind of love but many and love is not a static state but a fluid continuum, it should be reasonable to expect that loving feelings would morph and transform over time. Conceptually, it makes sense; emotionally, it is a struggle for many patients in therapy. Social context, sociodemographic factors, the type of relationship that one is in, and their stage of life, all have influence on how people experience love. Given this complexity, perhaps the dictum inherent in polyamory—that in a contemporary society it is necessary to further expand the boundaries of love—is not far off. As long as one is capable of adapting to the changing nature of love, loving feelings may not evaporate and, instead, mature into something uniquely new and unexpected. Yet, the power of new love tends to be overwhelming, and when it strikes, it does not differentiate between monogamy and nonmonogamy. As the following chapter illustrates, people in polyamorous relationships do fall in love, although they may theorize about it differently.

References

Baumeister, R. F., & Leary, M. R. (1995). The need to belong: Desire for interpersonal attachments as a fundamental human motivation. *Psychological Bulletin*, 117(3), 497–529. 10.1037/0033-2909.117.3.497

Berscheid, E. S., & Hatfield, E. (1974). A little bit about love. In T. L. Huston (Ed.), *Foundations of interpersonal attraction* (pp. 355–381). Academic Press.

Chapman, G. (1992). *The five love languages: How to express heartfelt commitment to your mate*. Northfield Publishing.

Chapman, G. (2015). *The five love languages: The secret to love that lasts*. Northfield.

Giddens A. (1992). *The transformation of intimacy. Sexuality, love, & eroticism in modern societies*. Stanford University Press.

Hendrick, S., & Hendrick, C. (1987). Multidimensionality of sexual attitudes. *Journal of Sex Research*, 23(4), 502–526. 10.1080/00224498709551387

Hendrick, S., & Hendrick, C. (2004). Sex and romantic love: Connects and disconnects. In J. H. Harvey, A. Wenzel, & S. Sprecher (Eds.), *The handbook of sexuality in close relationships* (pp. 159–182). Lawrence Erlbaum Associates.

Hendrick, S., & Hendrick, C. (2006). Styles of romantic love. In R. J. Sternberg & K. Weis (Eds.), *The new psychology of love* (pp. 149–170). Yale University Press.

Kleinplatz, P. J. (2006). Learning from extraordinary lovers: Lessons from the edge. *Journal of Homosexuality*, 50(3/4), 325–348.

Kleinplatz, P. J. (2010). Lessons from great lovers. In S. Levine, S. Althof, & C. Risen (Eds.), *Handbook of adult sexuality for mental health professionals* (2nd ed.). Brunner-Routledge.

Lee, J. A. (1973). *The colours of love: An exploration of the ways of loving.* New Press.

Martin, W. (2019). *Untrue: How nearly everything we believe about women, lust, and infidelity is wrong and how the new science can set us free.* Little, Brown Spark.

Sternberg, R. J. (1986). A triangular theory of love. *Psychological Review, 93,* 119–135.

Sternberg, R. J. (1988). *The triangle of love: Intimacy, passion, commitment.* Basic Books.

7 Falling in Love in Polyamory: New Relationship Energy

There is a Roman proverb that states, *Omnis amans amens*, meaning "every lover is crazy." Requited love generates an intense sense of fulfillment; it is a source of seemingly endless vitality. People in love have trouble thinking about anyone and anything else but the beloved. Identifying as poly does not change this basic equation of love's preoccupations. In polyamory, the overwhelming power of new love is not denied; instead, it gets renamed.

The act of renaming is always significant, but what accounts for this need to re-present the familiar madness of love under a name that omits any mention of love, even while embracing self-identification, as *polyamorous*? Perhaps because admitting to being under the spell of NRE sounds less ominous than confessing to being in love? NRE conveys the sense of temporality and, conceptualized in this way, it attempts to defuse the threat associated with new love. By suggesting a name that implies temporary distraction, polyamorous ideology aims to provide a sense of safety from the threat of a new love toppling the balance of existing attachments. It is possible that, on some unconscious level, polyamorous individuals recognize that in order to make space for multiple loves, the power of new love needs to be contained.

In her blog, Zhahai Stewart describes how she coined the term *new relationship energy* in the 1980s. When she first used it in an online discussion group in 1993, the term took off almost immediately, revealing the need to name a familiar experience. Stewart acknowledges that there are certain relational challenges associated with the state of NRE, while simultaneously asserting that they are relatively minor compared to the gains: "NRE may well be the ultimate aphrodisiac. People are often surprised at the erotic artesian wells that burst forth from within to meet and match the overflowing energies of their partners. This is indeed one of life's sweetnesses, a blessing from the Gods to sustain us on a sometimes difficult path. From my viewpoint, it's one of the sacred pleasures of incarnating in this species!" (2001).

It is worth highlighting that when people fall for someone, the desire to merge with the other person takes over. Whether one chooses monogamy or polyamory, the experience of being in love transcends any boundaries; the relational format in which this new love occurs is secondary. If there are more than two people involved, the desire to merge occurs as well but may not be equally shared by all partners.

The polyamory community offers a wealth of pragmatic advice on how to cope with NRE, which in itself speaks to the disruptive power of this experience. Most of these suggestions take the form of behavioral modification. Negotiating boundaries and managing expectations are certainly important, but they may not be sufficient to assuage the relational threat brought on by NRE. Relationship-centered therapy makes space for understanding clients' motivations and responses and for processing their meaning, something that poly guides are not equipped or meant to provide.

"The deepest principle in human nature is the craving to be appreciated"—these words by William James expound why polyamory can be a struggle for some of its proponents. Being one of many partners dilutes the feeling of being that special person who stands out among others. As one client, Adrian, whose wife became involved with another man, poignantly described, the desire to be the chosen one does not vanish with the embrace of the poly lifestyle. The intrusion of NRE directed at someone else makes it painfully obvious how the craving to be the center of attention of one's beloved is intrinsic to human nature. NRE is a sexual and emotional vortex. Being at the center of it is exhilarating; trying to embrace it as a witnessing partner can be immensely difficult. The vortex of NRE creates an inevitable split, leaving behind an emotional wake for one's partner to deal with. For Adrian, the split triggered new relationship agony, which he was not prepared to deal with. His heartache was as intense as that of anyone who experiences relational breakup. In some ways it was worse, as it was expected of him, and he expected of himself, to get swiftly over his heartache.

NRE might be about something more fundamental to human nature than the mere dopaminergic craving to be cherished. The yearning to merge, which is the hallmark of belonging, makes some people jump from relationship to relationship in a quest to satisfy an unrecognized emotional thirst. Referred to as NRE addiction in poly circles, this urge speaks to the desire to feel intensely connected, if only for a moment. The consequences of NRE compulsion are significant; recognizing it as an individual need that begs to be honored does not eliminate the harm associated with this behavior. Individuals displaying the signs of NRE addiction are likely to be ousted from the poly community once their pattern becomes apparent. The impact on those who were involved with such a person varies—some feel used; others become disillusioned about polyamory; and a handful may become disheartened about relationships in general.

To recapitulate, the presence of NRE represents a near-universal challenge to the existing relationship. The difference between relationships that are solid and those that appear solid is not always apparent until the bonds are tested by NRE. Helping couples to strengthen their relational ties so that they can withstand these challenges is one of the most common tasks in therapy with nonmonogamous partners. It is also one of the more challenging therapeutic endeavors.

Experiencing NRE, just like being in love, is characterized by an irresistible desire to merge with the new partner. Energy is directed toward the new relationship rather than toward the old one(s). There is no need to create a boundary between the freshly formed dyad and the intruding world; it already exists, fueled by the yearning to be together.

Reference

Stewart Z. (2001). *What's all this NRE stuff anyway?* http://aphroweb.net/articles/nre.htm

8 Polyromanticism: Polyamory's Love with Itself

The polyamorous community frequently references "the polyamory bible," a 1997 book by Dossie Easton and Janet Hardy, *The Ethical Slut: A Guide to Infinite Sexual Possibilities*.

People interested in exploring polyamory are invariably directed to this book, which shapes their perceptions and expectations. Many new guidebooks on polyamory have been published since then, with the market almost exploding (that is, exploding for what is still a niche market). *The Ethical Slut* has gone through transitions manifested by the evolution of its subtitle in the subsequent editions: *A Guide to Infinite Sexual Possibilities* became *A Practical Guide to Polyamory, Open Relationships & Other Adventures* (2009), followed by the most recent edition, *A Practical Guide to Polyamory, Open Relationships, and Other Freedoms in Sex and Love* (2017). The arc of sex and love is expanding, with a decreased focus on sexual adventures and an increased emphasis on freedom of love.

When I first read *The Ethical Slut* and other guidebooks on polyamory, I was struck by the idealizing tone. These pioneering publications are still the dominant source of information for clients and therapists alike. Many of my clients tell me how inspired they are by these books; they make them feel prepared to embrace the world of ethical nonmonogamy. Later, the realization that polyamory is not so straightforward can be confusing and disappointing—even the best guidance on how to open up does not throw the gates open to easy, wonderful loving.

At their core, most polyamorous writings consist of vivid personal accounts around which the authors endorse the premise and promise of polyamory. These publications promise a deep transformation in which people not only become more evolved, but they also contribute to the creation of a better world. Eleanor Wilkinson calls this phenomenon "polyromanticism." She observes how "polyamorists are portrayed as some wondrous beings who have an amazing capacity to have many lovers" (2010, p. 244). Easton and Hardy talk about "advanced sexuality" in *The Ethical Slut*, and in her book *Polyamory: The New Love Without Limits* (1997), Deborah Anapol argues that "polyamory benefits us all": it accelerates personal development, has the power to stabilize families and promote an ecological lifestyle, makes people better prepared for the future as it ends the war between the sexes, and it helps to build a new culture. Serena Anderlini-D'Onofrio (2009) takes it a step further and claims that polyamory is good for the environment, nature conservancy, and human rights, and is, in short, beneficial for the entire planet. In other words, polyamory is good for the individual, for families, for communities, and for the earth—it is a romantic promise.

A specific aspect of polyromanticism involves the perception of superiority regarding sexual ethics. Because polyamory implies love and not just sex, the advocates of polyamory often consider themselves to be ethically superior to proponents of other forms of consensual nonmonogamy, such as swingers. Thus, the polyamorous lifestyle is not only positioned against monogamy, but it is also declared to be more mature and responsible than any other format of sexual and romantic involvement.

A throwback of polyromanticism is present in what might be called "poly-pressure." On the one hand, advocates of polyamory more readily embrace differences and nonconformity than monogamous people. This includes greater acceptance of bodies of all shapes and sizes, nonnormative sexuality, and gender nonconformity. On the other hand, polyamorous communities are less tolerant of monogamy and other aspects of the heteronormative lifestyle. This is perhaps best illustrated by the experience of some people who, for various reasons, decide to go back to monogamy. As Taormino (2008) notes, "If you've spent a lot of thought and energy rejecting traditional monogamy, it may seem as if you're stepping backward to decide your decision should be monogamous" (p. 216).

The community as a whole may subtly, or not so subtly, reject those individuals and couples who return to monogamy by no longer including them in polyamorous events. By the same token, previously polyamorous people who decide to sidestep the lifestyle may struggle with self-judgments about their choice. Both ways, the freedom to choose may become a prison of choice. Owning one's choice is a therapeutic issue. I vividly remember a moment when a client remarked with exasperation, "I just so badly want to make it work because ideologically it makes perfect sense." She had struggled with polyamory from the beginning, but once she decided to embrace non-monogamy, she did it with full sincerity. After a few years of trying her best, even when it was abundantly clear that polyamory did not suit her sensibilities, she was reluctant to give it up—giving up on polyamory felt like a betrayal of ideals that she held dear. The real freedom she sought, however, was being able to accept herself.

When advocates of polyamory reject monogamy as hopelessly romantic and unsustainable, they simultaneously embrace a relational viewpoint that is not any less romanticized. Realizing this paradox often comes as a surprise; polyromanticism makes it hard for some people to give up on the idea of polyamory, even if the reality of this relational approach does not work well for them. Being critical of other relational formats is easy; genuinely examining one's own choices requires a different kind of honesty.

The tone of polyromanticism makes it hard to imagine monogamy as anything but limiting; however, dealing with loss is inevitable in *any* kind of relationship. A marriage that presumes monogamy comes with a loss of sexual freedom; a polyamorous bond that presupposes openness diminishes the sense of security associated with one-to-one commitment. The loss is inescapable; the question is what kind of loss is easier to endure?

References

Anapol, D. M. (1997). *Polyamory: The new love without limits: Secrets of sustainable intimate relationships*. IntiNet Resource Center.

Anderlini-D'Onofrio, S. (2009). *Gaia and the new politics of love: Notes for a poly planet*. North Atlantic Books.

Easton, D., & Hardy, J. (1997). *The ethical slut: A guide to infinite sexual possibilities*. Celestial Arts.

Easton, D., & Hardy, J. (2009). *A practical guide to polyamory: Open relationships and other adventures*. Celestial Arts.

Easton, D., & Hardy, J. (2017). *The ethical slut: A practical guide to polyamory, open relationships and other freedoms in sex and love*. Celestial Arts.

Taormino, T. (2008). *Opening up: A guide to creating and sustaining open relationships*. Cleis Press.

Wilkinson, E. (2010). What's queer about non-monogamy now? In M. Barker & D. Langdridge (Eds.), *Understanding non-monogamies* (pp. 243–254). Routledge.

Part III
Sexuality in Polyamory

9 Love and Sex: Separate and Intertwined

As a sex therapist, I engage in extensive conversations with individuals and couples about their sexuality. Inevitably, the nature of these exchanges varies depending on the presenting problem. Contrary to what one may assume, it is the monogamous clients who are eager to explore this subject. Polyamorous patients, both those who just opened up and those who are immersed in this relational lifestyle, are more likely to talk about emotions than sex. Yet, it would be an error to assume that monogamy leads to sexual difficulties while polyamory ensures a healthy sex life. It would also be wrong to assume that poly people are highly sexual and always ready to engage physically and experiment with beyond-vanilla sex.

With very few exceptions, it is not possible to talk about relational satisfaction without looking at the interlocking dynamics of love and sex. Anthropologist Helen Fisher's studies on the correlates of love (2004, 2010, 2016) differentiate among three interdependent behavioral systems: lust (sex), attraction (passionate love), and attachment. These distinct neural networks evolved separately to serve the purposes of reproduction, mate bonding, and parenting, but over time, these systems became intertwined. Each system is governed by a different set of neurotransmitters, which accounts for their somewhat conflicting nature.

Although these systems are relatively autonomous, the mounting evolutionary evidence indicates that they are also highly intertwined. This interconnectedness explains the innate human need to connect on a deep level, have sex, and, when relevant, to have children with the same person one hopes to be with for a long time, perhaps until death does them part. This same interplay of lust, love, and the search for relational security shapes the dynamics of monogamy as well as polyamory.

The Unbearable Lightness of Sex?

If human sexuality and the ability to love and connect were shaped by eons of evolution, our sexuality over the past several decades has been shaped by revolution. The sexual revolution released humankind from the liabilities of reproduction, but it also resulted in an unexpected casualty—sex got liberated, but its seductive power got depleted (Bauman, 2003). "It was emotion, ecstasy, and metaphysics from which the seductive power of sex used to flow—as it would do now, but the mystery is gone and so the yearnings cannot but stay unfulfilled..." (p. 47). Sex without mystery became sex focused on performance, and performance is about physical prowess and not transcendence. But it is metaphysics, not physics, that opens the door to ecstasy. Liberated sex is "overflowing with expectations beyond its capacity to deliver" (p. 47).

Bauman's words point to the frailty of our liquid modernity. With no fixed or durable bonds characteristic of the past, feelings of insecurity are rampant; loneliness and disappointments lurk around the corner. "When the quality lets you down, you seek salvation in quantity. When duration is not on, it is the rapidity of change that may redeem you" (p. 58). This sentiment, which describes our consumer-based economy and its focus on pleasure and satisfaction, combined with the constant search for greener pastures, may as well depict certain aspects of polyamory. When monogamy does not deliver the quality of love and sex people expect, the solution is that people invite multiple lovers into their lives. Ideally, this should occur without falling in love, because that would interfere with the romantic ideal of polyamory—loving many without a threat to any. NRE is presumed to be different—it is perceived as more contained than the risk-laden madness of being in love. NRE is less likely, at least in theory, to threaten the existing, fragile bonds. Also, when a lover disappoints, she can be replaced. And replaced again. Shallower connections are meant to offer protection against the vulnerability of love.

The sexual revolution opened the doors to free love and the open marriages of the 1960s and, after the panic of the HIV epidemic in the 1990s had subsided, to the increasingly liquid relationships characteristic of our current time. The nature of sex is changing faster than the nature of love, but in spite of the opportunity that liberated sex provides, only some are opting for polyamory. Many people continue looking for depth and commitment. What approach works for whom can be, at least partially, explained from the perspective of sexual scripts that shape and inform our intimate interactions.

References

Bauman, Z. (2003). *Liquid love: On the frailty of human bonds.* Polity Press.
Fisher, H. (2004). *Why we love? The nature and chemistry of romantic love.* Henry Holt.
Fisher, H. (2010). *Why him? Why her? How to find and keep lasting love.* Henry Holt.
Fisher, H. (2016). *Anatomy of love: A natural history of mating, marriage and why we stray.* W. W. Norton.

10 Sexual Scripts: Who, What, Where, and How

Flexible and Inflexible Sexual Scripts

The concept of sexual scripts helps us to examine an individual's assumptions about sex as well as their expectations of the relationship to accommodate for it (Gagnon & Simon, 1973/2011, 2004). These assumptions are rooted in the recognition that sex is not merely biologically driven but also socially scripted. A person *becomes* sexual through interactions with others and the world. These interactions form the basis of a sexual script that is later recognized as located within, rather than outside, the individual. In other words, consciously and unconsciously, we develop sexual scripts, and these narratives come to define who we are. Implicit and explicit messages about sex, combined with subjective personal experiences, help us to interpret situations that we come to understand as sexual. We then make sense of the body's responses to these situations. Taken together, these reactions and interpretations shape our sexual expectations toward ourselves and others.

Sexual scripts can be flexible or inflexible. Flexible scripts allow for greater adaptation to changed life circumstances. As an example, people confronted with a life-threatening disease, such as cancer, may develop sexual difficulties. The most common effect of prostate cancer treatment is the inability to engage in penetrative sex. People with flexible scripts are able to accept that sexual pleasure may no longer be derived from intercourse but is still available through other forms of stimulation. In contrast, a person with inflexible scripts will not be able to make suitable adjustments and may avoid sex altogether. In the flexible case, the access to pleasure is altered, but not gone; in the inflexible one, the possibility of pleasure is rejected.

There are three layers of sexual scripts—cultural, interpersonal, and intrapsychic:

- *Cultural scripts* reflect the dominant views of one's culture. They define what sex is and how it is to be done based on ideas provided by religion, science, education, and common-sense knowledge. These direct and indirect messages are conveyed in a variety of ways: through media, including books, films, porn, blogs, lectures, and teachings; as well as through gossip and sharing of personal stories.

- *Interpersonal scripts* are formulated by actual sexual interactions with others. They are subjective equivalents of "how-to" manuals, providing clues to behaviors and their interpretations (e.g., how to flirt, how to negotiate sexual boundaries, how to engage sexually). Gender roles and behaviors related to sexual orientation also play a role in the shaping of interpersonal scripts.
- *Intrapsychic scripts* are represented by sexual fantasies, replays of real-life scenarios, and other reflexive processes regarding sex. The intrapsychic scripts are in dialog with interpersonal and cultural scripts, helping to outline and refine one's sexuality.

These three levels of sexual scripts are intertwined and always located within the social context. Their interplay accounts for the complexity and fluidity of human sexual behavior. Flexible and inflexible scripts play a role in determining who may consider polyamory and who may succeed at it and who may not. Magazine articles, books, blogs, podcasts, and social media sites geared toward consensual nonmonogamy are proliferating. Rich in advice, they outline strategies to handle interpersonal scenarios. These writings reflect *polyamorous cultural scripts*. Armed with such advice, individuals and couples entering the world of polyamory tend to feel prepared and ready to begin. This response is in line with polyamorous cultural scripts that convey ease of use, as long as the recipe is followed. However, as I so often witness, many therapy clients conflate intellectual preparedness with emotional readiness. The idea of manageable concurrent romantic relationships may be very appealing, but the picture one envisions is an alluring fantasy, not necessarily a reality. The actual experience can be anything from rewarding to disappointing to painful, just as a recipe that is terrific on paper may yield mediocre results, depending on one's cooking skills and the ingredients available.

For many people, embracing polyamory involves reassessing one's intrapsychic sexual scripts. For some, it is relatively easy; their ideological beliefs and actual relational experiences are in alignment. For others, contemplating polyamory requires a deep reexamination of their personal ethics and attitudes. There are many things to consider, among them concerns regarding the family of origin, work situation, and children and their schools. Loving more is an enticing promise with a limited guarantee. Loving more may even come with the surprise of having less love than one expected. In order to flourish, relationships require a deep commitment and investment over time. The amount of love may not be finite, but the amount of time is. Maintaining multiple relationships necessitates the spreading of resources, the most indispensable of which is time. Time as a resource is not evenly distributed, either. Individuals with limited commitments whose partners are busy elsewhere may have more time to fill than they wish.

The subjective experience of time varies as well. Relational time is measured subjectively rather than objectively. A night full of NRE is always too short; a night spent in conflict lasts forever. Some relationships are simply more rewarding than others, even without going to these emotional extremes. Poly relationships are not created equal, and they are not free of deceit in spite of the ethos of transparency and honesty. The level of such deceit may depend on the degree of connection. Some relationships may last for years, held together by a thin thread of expectation that they should continue, because they are already formed. Reflecting back on her experience, a former member of one of the longest-lasting nonmonogamous communes of the past century, called Kerista, conceded that "What was really bad about it [was] that there could be situations that went on for years where one or both people in a given dyad [an intimate pair within the family] would know, in their hearts and minds, that they weren't really in love. Yet because of all the other things and relationships going on, they could sort of pretend that all was well" (Even, 1993). I will return to the example of Kerista in the chapter discussing jealousy.

The proliferation of communes in the second half of the 20th century were examples of large-scale social experimentation involving consensual nonmonogamy. While contemporary polyamory rarely involves communal living, many of the same principles still apply. Both reflect cultural, interpersonal, and intrapsychic trends, and both are examples of flexible sexual scripts. Carl Rogers, in his observations on the communes of his time, noted, "All I can say is that this open, sharing of *all* of one's self nearly always, in my experience, leads to personal growth. I can also add that I believe it is very rare that a person who knows this way of living prefers to go back to living with the façade, the armour, the self-deceiving 'front' which characterizes the great majority of people" (1973/1978, p. 157). By this, Rogers did not imply that people who have experienced nonmonogamy would be unwilling to return to monogamy. His focus was on self-deception as a defense against the reality of one's relational circumstance. Rogers was clearly impressed with many of the people he had interviewed. He observed, "As I have known people who have left communes, or have rejoined in the 'straight' community, or have joined a new commune, it is my strong impression that they have moved *on*, not backward" (p. 161).

Moving on sometimes involves making choices that, to an undiscerning witness, may look like going back. Exploring different relational lifestyles, and examining one's motivations, allows people to learn something important about themselves. Choosing monogamy over nonmonogamy, or vice versa, and *knowing* which is right for an individual or couple, is another example of a flexible sexual script. People with high psychological maturity are able to stand by their choices, even if these choices are in disagreement with the dominant norms of the group they belong to.

Gender-Role Behaviors in Poly Relationships

Gender roles represent another form of scripts, and adhering to these norms can be rigid or flexible. Somewhat surprisingly, gender roles in poly relationships are sometimes more stratified than in monogamy. Polyamory has many advantages for women, among them providing more freedom to choose whom to live with and whom to sleep with. It may, then, come as a surprise that in some respects, women's roles appear to be more traditionally female in polyamory than in monogamy. Emotional processing is traditionally a female domain, and that pattern continues in poly relationships. Men become more used to it as a result of following the poly ethos; however, the burden of carrying through the processing usually falls on women. Other traditionally female tasks, such as taking care of the house, continue unchanged and may even increase. While men are busy with their other partners, the challenges of running a household and taking care of the children fall to the women. Even in cases of nonhierarchical polyamory, where a woman lives with two male partners, these burdens may not be eased. A client, Ginny, an accomplished woman in her late 40s, describes how, in spite of living together with two men she loves, she cannot count on them to be available when she needs them—not only emotionally but instrumentally as well. Each of her partners appears to cede responsibility to the other man, each assuming the other will provide what is needed. Ginny's lifelong struggles with anxiety are not ameliorated by her access to "more love"; on the contrary, her sense of loneliness is greater than when she was monogamous. It is not something she wants to admit, because it gives credence to the ethos of nonpolyamory, and that is often perceived as a betrayal in poly circles. Ginny, like many others who embrace polyamory, remains deeply loyal to her lifestyle of choice. Unable to resolve this inner impasse, she blames herself for not being generous enough toward her partners' desires to pursue other relationships.

Ginny's example illustrates how being a part of a poly family involves handling of more intra- and interpersonal conflicts than might be the case in a dyad. In a triad, quad, or other multi-partner format, cross-purposes are inevitable. Managing these cross-motivations well is an ongoing challenge. Flexible scripts make concurrent relationships possible but, as noted earlier, they do not guarantee relational ease or fulfilment. In addition, in polyamory, people tend to focus more on individual needs than relationship needs. Flexibility sans the dedication to nourish and protect the existing commitments may not be enough to maintain a relationship worth having.

References

Even, E. (1993, Spring/Summer). Afterword: What happened to Kerista? *Kerista Commune.* https://www.kerista.com/what.html

Gagnon, J. H., & Simon, W. (1973/2011). *Sexual conduct: The social sources of human sexuality.* AldineTransaction.

Gagnon, J. H., & Simon, W. (2004). *An interpretation of desire: Essays in the study of sexuality.* University of Chicago Press.

Rogers, C. R. (1973/1978). *Becoming partners. Marriage and its alternatives.* Constable & Company.

11 The New Place of Belonging: Polyamory and Bisexuality

Not surprisingly, by virtue of nonconformity, the polyamory community attracts diversity and vice versa. Although reliable data is still limited, about half of one survey's respondents who identified as bisexual or pansexual were also likely to describe themselves as polyamorous (Balzarini et al., 2019). Pansexuality implies attraction toward others that is independent of sexual or gender identity. Transgender or gender-nonconforming individuals, too, tend to find a place of belonging in polyamory circles.

Historically, sexual orientation has been polarized and dichotomous. Heterosexuality implied normalcy, and homosexuality indicated abnormality; this was the basis of the mental illness model of sexuality. Between these two polar opposites, there was seemingly nothing, or even less coherently, there was adult bisexuality. From the psychoanalytic point of view, being bisexual was an indicator of inhibited psychosexual development, variably explained as repression or denial of homosexuality. It was not until 1973 that the American Psychological Association (APA) made the decision to remove homosexuality as a clinical diagnostic category. It took several more years for the APA to embrace bisexuality from an affirmative perspective, as a legitimate sexual orientation rather than a merely transitional phenomenon in gay and lesbian identity development (Fox, 2003).

While acceptance of same-sex sexual preference is no longer new, bisexual identity defies easy conceptualizations. However, discerning between different kinds of bisexuality in therapy with polyamorous clients is often relevant. Klein (1978/1993) identified four types of bisexual orientation: historical, transitional, concurrent, and sequential. *Historical* affinity indicates a past attraction to the same or another gender among predominantly hetero- or homosexual individuals. Bisexuality as a *transitional* phenomenon implies a phase in the coming-out process as a lesbian or gay. In *concurrent* bisexuality, an individual may have simultaneous relationships with both males and females. *Sequential* orientation indicates shifting sexual preferences toward either men or women, but without overlap. Other forms of exploration relevant for the understanding of polyamory include *experimental* bisexuality, in which transient sexual engagement with individuals of the same gender takes place (Ross, 1991).

With the increasing interest in polyamory, both platonic and nonplatonic, bisexuality is becoming more accepted, to the point of being taken for granted in poly circles. As such, "bisexual orientation" is frequently used as a catch-all phrase, with little or no discerning of a person's actual affinity or preferences. The implications of this are often substantial; there is a significant difference between sexual experimentation with partners of the same or other gender and sequential or concurrent bisexuality.

Many therapy clients come to polyamory with limited past sexual experiences and assumed sexual orientation, without much or any exploration of their identity. With the dominance of hetero- and mononormativity, it is not a surprise that the majority of people take their identity and orientation for granted. Exploring polyamory may solidify their existing preferences, but it may also lead to confusion. Being suddenly thrown into a world of possibilities that, depending on the circumstances, can be exciting or overwhelming is often bewildering. Long-forgotten questions of identity formation, or "Who am I?," are likely to resurface.

The terms *nonmonogamous, polyamorous, pansexual, demisexual, bisexual, asexual,* and *kinky* are all examples of how confusing it can be for someone new to polyamory to orient themselves. For adults who do not have any reason to question their identity, or who thought they had figured it out a long time ago, the renewed question of who they are involves more than a definition. It is like being an adolescent again, but this time with an expectation that at this point in life, they should *know.* I described earlier how common it has become to mistake an infatuation for polyamorous longing. Similarly, people who have sex for the first time with a person of the same gender may start wondering what it means in terms of their sexual orientation.

Women's sexual fluidity is more widely accepted that male sexual fluidity (Diamond, 2009). However, there are many examples of men who have sex with other men while still considering themselves straight (Savin-Williams, 2017). Over time, I have worked with a handful of men who, in late middle age, found themselves having clandestine sex with other men. None of these males identified as gay or even bisexual. They all had been married, oftentimes for decades, had children, and denied ever having any gay longings. The question of identity arose when their transgressions were discovered by their wives. The level of pain and confusion these men and their spouses experience can be profound. On the one hand, they wonder if their marriages were based on a false premise. On the other hand, their out-of-nowhere fluidity does not fit any recognizable category that would explain their behavior. While, strictly speaking, this is not an example of identity confusion in polyamory, it nonetheless speaks to the complexity of sex being mixed with longing for connection, intimacy, and love. Many of my clients experiment with sexual options that do not align with their orientation because of an underlying yearning for intimacy and closeness. If the person you are with is distant for some reason, the caring attention of somebody else, regardless of their gender and sexual orientation, may be very welcome.

Not all relational threats are equal; for predominantly heterosexual polyamorous couples, a realization that one of the partners is interested in sex with same-gender individuals tends to be less ominous than if they express interest in someone of the opposite gender. In my experience, a heterosexual man in an open marriage whose wife connects with a new man is likely to react more adversely than if she expresses an interest in another woman. The reverse is less common; heterosexual poly men are more likely to look for female rather than male partners. They may engage in occasional sexual exchanges with other men but typically express no desire to *date* men.

Relational threats are directly connected to the experience of jealousy and its close cousins, envy and rivalry. Conversely, compersion, which can be conceived as a sublimation of jealous feeling into the opposite, is associated with the lack of relational threats. It is not possible to explore polyamory without encountering jealousy; the following section deals with jealousy as a nearly universal and inescapable part of polyamorous life.

References

Balzarini, R. N., Dharma, C., Kohut, T., Holmes, B. M., Campbell, L., Lehmiller, J. J., & Harman, J. J. (2019). Demographic comparison of American individuals in polyamorous and monogamous relationships. *The Journal of Sex Research*, 56(6), 681–694. 10.1080/00224499.2018.1474333

Diamond, L. M. (2009). *Sexual fluidity: Understanding women's love and desire*. Harvard University Press.

Fox, R. C. (2003). Bisexual identities. In L. D. Garnets & D. C. Kimmel (Eds.), *Psychological perspectives on lesbian, gay and bisexual experiences* (pp. 86–129). Columbia University Press.

Klein, F. (1978/1993). *The bisexual option* (2nd ed.). American Institute of Bisexuality.

Ross, M. W. (1991). A taxonomy of global behavior. In R. A. P. Tielman, M. Carballo, & A. C. Hendriks (Eds.), *Bisexuality and HIV/AIDS: A global perspective* (pp. 21–26). Prometheus.

Savin-Williams, R. C. (2017). *Mostly straight: Sexual fluidity among men*. Harvard University Press.

Part IV
Jealousy in Transparent Love

12 No Size Fits All: Jealousy Is a Complex Relational Experience

With jealousy, it is not always easy to know what is real and what is distorted, what belongs to the here and now, and what is exacerbated by painful experiences from another time and another context. "Born in love but propelled by rage, jealousy is a complex relational experience," write Scheinkman and Werneck (2010, p. 486). "It is a visceral fear of loss, a set of paradoxical feelings and thoughts, an action and reaction," the authors continues, and observes further how, puzzlingly, the word "jealousy" is more or less absent in literature on couples' therapy.

Polyamorous communities pride themselves on their management of jealousy. In polyamory, jealousy is considered a complex phenomenon too, consisting of many underlying emotions and affective states, including sadness, anger, anxiety, insecurity, low self-esteem, possessiveness, territoriality, envy, and fear of abandonment. The actual presentation of jealousy varies from person to person, and how it manifests depends on the context. In *More Than Two*, Veaux and Rickert (2014) invoke Shakespeare by calling jealousy "the chameleon emotion"; sometimes it is straightforward and easy to recognize, and at other times it is concealed and denied. Regardless of the manifestation, in the authors' view, jealousy is an opportunity to do some soul-searching. The goal is to identify the underlying feelings and to test their legitimacy. *More Than Two* provides point-by-point steps for dealing with jealousy: (1) accepting one's feelings, (2) separating triggers from causes, (3) understanding the feelings, (4) talking about them, and (5) practicing.

Like other authors of books on polyamory, Veaux and Rickert assure the reader that it is fine to experience jealousy, but that the responsibility for confronting the feeling falls on the person who is dealing with this emotional state. In this, polyamorous ideology reverses the traditional understanding of jealousy, which implies that one's partner must be doing something wrong, because why would someone feel so terrible otherwise? By placing responsibility on the person who is experiencing jealousy, this approach takes the blame away from the partner who is the source of these potent feelings. Holding oneself accountable is relevant, but, just like with the conventional view, perceiving jealousy as an intra- rather than interpersonal problem is oversimplified.

The polyamorous community's discomfort with jealousy is covert. On the surface, there is swift acknowledgment of the pain of this reaction; underneath, there is a veiled wish to abolish the feeling. Many a conversation in my office is about the secondary sting of jealousy; it is bad enough to experience it in the first place, but it is even worse to admit to this emotion. The resistance to call the affect by its name usually comes in the form of self-judgments: "Something must be wrong with me for feeling this way; I must not be evolved enough." If I inquire what "feeling this way" means, the answer is often an anguished, "You know, I don't like that he is spending so much time with her, but I should be able to deal with it, shouldn't I?"

What is amiss is that jealousy is a complex *relational* experience, not a one-person emotion. Jealousy does not discriminate between monogamy and polyamory; neither relational form prevents the feeling from invading a person and the system. However, by their very nature, polyamorous explorations provide more opportunities for jealousy to arise. Managing many loves requires many rules and strict procedures, including not just jealousy but the *display* of jealousy. Indeed, the display of jealousy appears to be milder in nonmonogamous communities; however, the rules to keep the emotion under control are highly rigid and time-consuming (Pines, 1998).

If jealousy is a relational experience, what does it say about a partnership in which this feeling resides? Are polyamorous partnerships different from monogamous ones? In some ways, yes; in other ways, not really. The definition of a couple will vary, and in nonhierarchical polyamory, it may no longer apply. However, even a triad (or quad and so on) consists of dyads; albeit, some triads are better balanced than others. Making relationships work requires dedication and determination. It involves managing the tasks of being a couple—a challenge that is easy to dismiss and to mishandle (Scheinkman & Werneck, 2010).

To establish relational security and to manage jealousy well, three relational tasks need to be addressed. These tasks include: (1) the co-creation of mutually acceptable boundaries, (2) the maintenance of balance between security and freedom, and (3) the development of effective strategies to manage personal insecurities and the uncertainties of love (Scheinkman & Werneck, 2010). Although the authors address normative relationships, their observations apply equally well to polyamorous commitments. There is nothing inherently easier about polyamory compared to monogamy. When any of these tasks is mismanaged, the relational balance gets tipped, and jealous feelings may get incited. If two or all three of the tasks are mishandled, jealousy is bound to erupt.

Mutually Acceptable Boundaries

The co-creation of mutually acceptable boundaries involves keeping a particular couple's bond separate from all the other bonds. In a nonhierarchical triad consisting of two women and one man, the tie between, say, Christina and Peter, is inevitably different from the bond between Peter and Anna. Christina and Anna's connection is unique as well. In addition, each dyad has to shield their bond from other demands, including work, family of origin, technology, ex-partners, and so on.

Balance Between Security and Freedom

In order to thrive, most couples need to find a balance between security and the freedom to explore. Too much focus on risk avoidance stifles most relationships, but the opposite is true, too. A couple that practices unbounded autonomy may be a couple in name only, that barely operates as one. Finding this balance can be tricky, especially when attachment bonds are insecure. Some individuals may crave as much closeness as possible and react intensely to threats of distance. Others may be happy with a "commuter" relationship characterized by sporadic encounters. In both instances, the partners try to find an equilibrium, but when the individual needs are too disparate, maintaining the balance becomes difficult.

Personal Insecurities and the Uncertainties of Love

As much as some may wish otherwise, in love we have little control over the mind and heart of one's beloved. Daring to love means exposing oneself to the uncertainties of love. The loved one can betray us, experience NRE with someone else, move on, get ill, or die. The vulnerabilities that stem from love are countless. At the same time, for love to flourish, we have to develop trust that our loved one(s) will be available when we need them. Couples who have developed effective strategies for managing personal insecurities and the uncertainties of love tend to view jealousy as part of love. For them, jealousy is a sign alerting partners of a need to reaffirm their importance to each other.

In what I am tempted to call "serial polyamory," having multiple partners can be a welcome strategy for avoiding feelings of insecurity and inadequacy. Just like in serial monogamy, some people move from one relationship to the next, discarding the one that requires effort in favor of a new one that holds a promise of ease. The excuses to move on and not attach come in many flavors, but what all of them have in common is a search for an ever-elusive perfection. Serial polyamory may be a sign of an avoidant approach that prevents people from facing the vulnerabilities brought about by love and relationships.

There is no doubt that jealousy can be disruptive, and even destructive, to a relationship. One component of jealousy, loneliness, warrants a closer look. From a relational perspective, jealousy is a form of separation distress, a real or imagined threat resulting from the failure to have one's basic attachment needs met. Typically associated with interpersonal conflicts and dissatisfaction, loneliness arises in response to poorly addressed relational rifts. Weiss (1973) defined loneliness as an emotion that signals unsatisfied needs for proximity, security, and love. When the significant figures in one's life fail to meet these needs, in a circular fashion putting the burden back on the already distressed individual, the person is left to deal with powerful feelings of separation and disconnect. In the words of a patient, Joshua, "I get that it matters that she is transparent and honest, but it still sucks. I miss her, and she is too busy taking care of her other relationships to really understand. She says she gets it, but she really doesn't. She cannot erase my loneliness by her honesty."

There is no other remedy for loneliness but a healing connection. The perception in polyamory of jealousy as an intra- rather than interpersonal dynamic is to a degree dismissive of this basic need for closeness, which requires accessibility and willingness to work *together* rather than separately at diminishing the distance. Simultaneous maintenance of several relationships requires a vast amount of effort, effectively limiting access to that special person who happens to be evoking the strongest feelings. It is a price that comes with polyamory, and one that most people new to that lifestyle are seldom aware of.

Jealousy, Envy, and Rivalry

Jealousy, envy, and rivalry are emotional close cousins that reflect distinctive relational challenges. The presence of a romantic triangle is what makes jealousy unique and different from envy or internal rivalry in the relationship. Jealousy is always triangular, and "This triangle includes a primary relationship (between the jealous person and the beloved), a secondary relationship (between the beloved and the rival), and a rival relationship (between the jealous person and the rival)" (Guerrero et al., 2004, p. 313). It is not any different in polyamory; there are just potentially more triangles in play at any given time.

Another distinct feature of jealousy is possessiveness. A woman may become possessive when *fearing the loss of something she has* (i.e., her romantic partner). In contrast, envy evokes feelings of *wanting something somebody else has* and one wishes to have. Envy can be intense and hostile, but it does not make a person possessive of the specific item, or the perceived quality in the other person. People are often envious of somebody else's material assets, attractiveness, success, ease of being, extroverted personality, and so on, but without feeling possessive of these attributes.

The distinction between jealousy and envy is relevant. Many polyamorous clients approach jealousy as envy, doing their best to identify their needs and asking for these needs to be met. They might be dismayed when the negative feelings do not go away after they have done their part to speak up. Not surprisingly, the needs represented by envy may have been met but the fear of loss has not been addressed.

Rivalry is associated with jealousy and envy. It is helpful to distinguish between internal and external rivalry, as they often induce different emotions and reactions. *Internal rivalry* is different from both jealousy and envy in that both partners compete for what neither has but both desire. In poly reality, this can be described as two partners competing for the love and attention of the third partner. *External rivalry* occurs in response to competition, for example, when a new, relatively nonthreatening, person is added to the polycule. For the sake of distinction, I will call such a suitor an "Intruder." The Intruder's presence may provoke feelings approaching jealousy but without the aspect of possessiveness. The Intruder increases competition for time, if not for affection or love. To summarize:

Jealousy:	Occurs in a romantic triangle
	Involves fear of losing one's partner to somebody else
	Evokes a degree of possessiveness
	May induce a sense of loneliness
Envy:	Involves desiring something that someone else has
	Is commonly a hostile reaction
	Does not need to be triangular
Internal rivalry:	Occurs within the triangle
	Involves competing for what neither partner has
External rivalry:	Occurs with a competitive suitor—an Intruder
	Perceives the Intruder as relatively nonthreatening
	Evokes mild to moderate emotional reactions

Jealousy, envy, and rivalry are more than semantic distinctions; discerning among these emotional states allows for more nuanced processing in therapy. In addition, each of these affects is likely to evoke old feelings of judgment, shame, or guilt.

My patient, Jeremy, referred to his feelings as a "tight knot." He was in a primary relationship with Amanda, and Amanda was married. Admitting to his, as he put it, "uncharitable" reactions, Jeremy alternated between pangs of jealousy and envy. In spite of Amanda's reassurances that Jeremy was her primary, he could not stop thinking of her marriage as a threat to their bond. He often imagined a "burning house" scenario, wondering whom she would rescue first, fearing that it would be her husband—if not for his sake as a romantic partner, then for his sake as the father of their children. When I wondered what made him feel so threatened, Jeremy confessed that he wished to be like Amanda's husband, who was a successful entrepreneur. Jeremy felt that he could not win; when he did not fear the loss of Amanda, he was envious of her husband's accomplishments.

At first, Jeremy struggled with conceptualizing jealousy as a complex relational experience. As he complained, jealous feelings were supposed to go away once you identified what they consisted of and asked for what you needed. Amanda was responsive to his needs, so what was wrong with him?

"How is she meeting your needs?" I asked.

"She gives me permission to be kinky with other women ..."

"It satisfies your external need," I pointed out, "but what about the internal ones?"

"That's the knot," he replied. "She says she is doing what she can, but between her kids, her job, her other lover, and her husband, there is a limit to how much she can offer."
"And you're still her primary?"
"That's what she tells me. But I wonder if, as a primary, I should be able to expect more, no?"

Differentiating between jealousy and envy helped Jeremy realize that he needed to address his jealous feelings *with* Amanda rather than dealing with this affect on his own. Exploring his envy was a different matter; the wish to be more like Amanda's husband did not belong with her. It was not her doing that, in spite of his education and potential, Jeremy felt less than accomplished in his career.

It is easy to pathologize jealousy and overlook the fact that jealousy is a protective reaction against a threat to a valued relationship. The key words are *protective* and *valued*. It is easy to grasp the connection between a highly valued relationship and jealousy. What is harder to understand is how jealousy serves as protection. The psychological tendency is to see jealousy as damaging. However, it is envy, the darker cousin of jealousy, that is often more destructive. Envy is a hostile reaction toward somebody else who has something one wishes to have. Envy explains why triggered individuals may feel resentful toward the intruder, this new object of interest bestowed with the attention that one wishes was theirs. The intruder is projected upon, and if she happens to be in a position of power due to status or physical attraction, the feelings of jealousy and then envy are born. We are jealous because we wish to protect, and we are envious because we desire what the other has. The greater the imbalance of power dynamics in a couple, the greater the chance that these feelings will arise. Jealousy as a protective reaction aims to bring back the sense of security and balance.

Internal and External Components of Jealousy

Jealousy is complex and multidimensional; its manifestation can be cognitive, affective, and behavioral. Jealous reactions arise in response to the threat by a third party to the existence, or quality, of one's primary relationship (White & Mullen, 1989). The threats can be real or perceived and, as clinicians often experience when dealing with jealousy in therapy, it is often irrelevant which is which. Perceived risks can evoke as intense a response as actual relational jeopardies.

Jealousy consists of internal and external components (Pines, 1998). The internal ones occur in response to a relational risk and are represented by emotions, thoughts, and visceral sensations experienced *within*. Frequently, these reactions are relatively invisible to others, as a lot of effort goes into concealing them. Sadness, insecurity, quiet rage, fear, grief, and pain are examples of specific feelings that jealousy may evoke. On the cognitive level, negative thoughts about oneself (self-blame, self-pity), about one's romantic partner (resentment toward him), toward the third party (comparisons with the rival), and regarding the public image (fear of judgment, wounded ego) are often mixed together. The physical symptoms are similar to those present in anxiety—shallow breathing, sweaty palms, shakiness and dizziness, rapid heartbeat, and difficulty sleeping.

External components are the internal reactions made visible—emotions loudly expressed, crying, fiery anger, hostile and resentful comments, disbelief and fear, acting out, sarcastic humor, elaborate fantasies of retaliation, and so on. Polyamorous strategies for coping with jealousy are effective when it comes to external components. Learning to express one's thoughts and feelings in a constructive way is highly valuable relationally; it promotes intra- and interpersonal growth. Suppressing certain wounded reactions and learning instead to self-soothe are other important relational tools. There is a clear connection between the external expressions of thoughts and feelings and the internal reality; cognitive-behavioral therapy is a prime example of the effectiveness of this approach.

It is easier to control the external expressions than to abolish the internal experiences. As Pines points out, "No known culture, including those in which jealousy is considered shameful and undesirable, is completely free from jealousy." She adds, "A culture can socialize people against expressing jealousy, but it cannot keep them from feeling jealous when they perceive a threat to a valued relationship" (1998, p. 127). When the underlying feelings do not go away in spite of the efforts put into the management of jealousy, it sometimes creates a different, much deeper, sense of conflict. Outwardly, people may no longer appear jealous, while remaining keenly aware of their pained internal state. They may seek further help and support from their poly friends, but when it still does not make much of a difference, they may feel inadequate and broken.

References

Guerrero, L. K., Spitzberg, B. H., & Yoshimura, S. M. (2004). Sexual and emotional jealousy. In J. H. Harvey, A. Wenzel, & S. Sprecher (Eds.), *The handbook of sexuality in close relationships* (pp. 311–346). Lawrence Erlbaum Associates.

Pines, A. M. (1998). *Romantic jealousy: Causes, symptoms, cures*. Routledge.

Scheinkman, M. D., & Werneck, D. (2010). Disarming jealousy in couples relationships: A multidimensional approach. *Family Process, 49*(4), 486–502.

Veaux, F., & Rickert, E. (2014). *More than two: A practical guide to ethical polyamory*. Thorntree Press.

Weiss, R. S. (1973). *Loneliness: The Experience of emotional and social isolation*. MIT Press.

White, G. L., & Mullen, P. E. (1989). *Jealousy: Theory, research, and clinical strategies*. The Guilford Press.

13 Jealousy: Learned Pathology or Universal Affliction?

With the prevailing view in polyamory that jealousy is an unavoidable but ultimately learned response, it becomes more or less optional to be jealous. Presented with such a choice, many poly clients feel ashamed of their jealous feelings. However, there is abundant research involving highly diverse cultures and societies around the world which points to jealousy being a universal experience. Perhaps the widest substantiation for the universality of jealousy comes from evolutionary theory (Buss, 2000, 2018). Darwin considered jealousy to be intimately connected to pair-bonding processes and, as such, a part of natural selection. Pair bonding is an adaptive strategy with numerous benefits, including social, emotional, and financial. It allows for a more effective sharing of resources, and historically, it ensured the confidence of paternity.

According to evolutionary theorists, the greatest risk to the pair bond comes from infidelity. Dealing with infidelity is costly and extremely disruptive; thus, preventing it from occurring in the first place is generally more adaptive. Jealousy can be fairly effective as a preventive mechanism against infidelity (Buss, 2013). There is ample clinical and research evidence of the intentional induction of jealousy. Between 60 and 85 percent of college students admit to deliberately provoking jealousy in their partners. They do it for a number of reasons: to assert commitment, to seek revenge, to gain control, and so on. None of these conscious maneuvers are random. On the contrary, all are calculated and strategic (Goodboy et al., 2012).

Assessing jealousy in the lab reveals that it is a cascade of heightened neurochemical reactions that appears to be hard-wired as a response to relational threats. Numerous studies have identified the connection between jealousy and lowered levels of relational satisfaction (Guerrero et al., 2004). Couple's therapists know this all too well. Nonetheless, positive aspects of jealousy do exist. After all, human emotions are essentially evolutionarily adaptive, even though some may become maladaptive (Sapolsky, 2017). Emotions have evolved in response to the world around us, helping people navigate the maze of complex human bonds, including romantic relationships. Emotions are signals—identifying what one feels and what seems to be causing that feeling—and they allow us to react adequately to internal and external stimuli. Without emotions, we would not be humans; without feelings, we could never be lovers. With love, powerful affects come to life, and we experience our greatest feasts as well as our greatest fears.

When not destructive, a certain amount of possessiveness might be welcome; it reassures one's partner of her desirability and value. With increased relational comfort, one may feel taken for granted. Jealousy can be an emotional wake-up call, reminding partners of their importance to each other. With the sudden rise of jealous feelings, one perceives one's partner more clearly, and the fear of losing him awakens the relationship. Jealousy is a response to a threat; threats represent a danger that needs to be warded off. The adaptive value of this complex relational response is clear: jealous feelings may avert transgressions. They signal to intruders to stay away or to adjust their intentions. Furthermore, increased relational alertness may renew feelings of passion in the relationship.

Unlearning Jealousy

If jealousy is universal, yet possible to unlearn, what does it take to pacify this "green-eyed monster"? Ayala Malach Pines has been researching romantic jealousy since the early 1980s. What is unique about her research is that she has focused on both monogamous and open relationships, thus providing insight into the experience of jealousy in monogamy and consensual non-monogamy. Significantly, the members of one of the longest-lasting communes, Kerista, mentioned earlier, became curious about Pines's investigation and volunteered to participate in her studies. In addition, she studied other urban communes and, more generally, open marriages. The results of her research offer valuable clinical observations that parallel Rogers's inquiry into the internal reality of communal love.

Kerista was established in 1956 in New York City and, by self-description, was an "egalitarian, nonmonogamous, utopian community." It existed in its most cohesive form for 20 years, from 1971 to 1991. The Keristans coined the term *compersion*, defining it as "the positive warm feeling you experience when you see two of your partners having fun with each other. It's the antonym of jealousy" (quoted in Pines, 1998, p. 140). The Keristans practiced polyfidelity, which implied a totally faithful sexual commitment to all the partners involved. Sexual contact with anyone outside of the commune was prohibited. At the time of Pines's interviews, Kerista consisted of 15 members. Life in the Kerista commune was highly structured, with a codified social contract called The Standards, to which all members were expected to adhere. A considerable amount of effort was devoted to the elimination of jealousy. The members claimed that it was their commitment to polyfidelity, resulting in complete trust in one another, that helped them to eradicate jealous feelings. Indeed, their interview reports indicated a surprising lack of jealousy.

Interpreting this finding is complex. How reliable were the Kerista reports? Were all 15 of them truly free from jealousy, or were at least some of them in self-denial? It is a known fact in social psychology that people often report what they want to believe in, not necessarily what is actually true. There is no way of testing this theory, so, taking the results at face value, it is relevant to ask what made it possible for the Keristans to live a life free from jealousy? It is conceivable that a highly structured, closely monitored living arrangement among multiple people can offer freedom from this complex emotion. Kerista's practice of polyfidelity, which is sexually closed rather than open, appeared to be an essential regulating factor. Polyfidelity helped to eliminate possible relational threats from the outside, and the internal threats were handled through an exhaustive group process, inspired by Fritz Perls's Gestalt therapy, called Gestalt-O-Rama.

If living in a highly sheltered environment where a vast amount of effort goes into handling the relational threats is what it takes to overcome jealous feelings, then it speaks to the immense power of jealousy. We are wired to protect what we value. Perhaps, with the exception of the few lucky individuals who claim not to experience jealousy, the majority of people need to spend a lot of time and energy to free themselves from this feeling. Conquering jealousy so it does not damage a relationship is an effort that polyamorous people voluntarily take upon themselves. However, as Pines's experiences with other utopian but less tightly structured communities and group marriages indicate, conflicts related to jealousy are the norm rather than the exception. Many people in these groups discovered that the energy needed to keep a marriage strong while remaining open was too much effort. Failure to abolish jealousy was not the only factor leading to the demise of these communes, but it played a significant role.

Jealousy might be a blessing when it inspires partners to identify their needs and teaches them to communicate clearly about existing relational difficulties. Because it is such a far-reaching, complex experience, it may appear that successfully dealing with jealousy would not only strengthen the relationship, but it would also make it more immune to ruptures. Clinically, this is not always the case. Jealous feelings can be distressing and unsettling; minimizing their destructive power usually benefits the relationship. Having said that, handling jealousy well does not necessarily lead to an increase in relational satisfaction. I have worked with couples where both partners became adept at recognizing component elements of their jealous experiences and learned to express their feelings in constructive ways. Their efforts were productive, leading to the de-escalation of conflicts and increased ease in approaching relational dilemmas. In spite of this obvious progress, many of these couples remained dysthymic, trying to find reassurance in their advancement, but without being able to reignite a spark. Being in the room with them could feel heavy and sad, and it was easy to empathize with their confusion. There was a striking contrast to the energy felt during the earlier days in therapy, when they were actively exploring triggers of jealousy. In the case of these couples, jealousy was the effervescence masking the underlying relational burnout.

Behavioral, Psychodynamic, and Systemic Approaches to Jealousy

The very statement that jealousy is learned suggests that behavioral solutions will be sufficient to eliminate the feeling. Indeed, behavioral techniques can be effective in the management of jealousy. Many patients benefit from learning how to communicate better and from examining their habitual responses; however, as the example of the dysthymic couples indicates, managing jealousy well is only a part of the answer. Looking only at behavioral attitude does not take into account past relational disturbances and developmental traumas that, left unaddressed, are likely to cast a shadow over the relationship.

To make the connection between adult expression of jealousy and childhood experiences, I make use of the exercise called "Jealousy as the Shadow of Love" (Pines & Bowes, 1992/2016).

This examination is psychodynamic rather than behavioral in nature and involves thinking back to the earliest times one can remember. The exercise includes questions such as: Who took care of you? Who taught you the meaning of love? What were the most important characteristics of these people? What was their relationship like? What did they give you? Was there something you wanted, but did not get? Were they faithful or unfaithful to each other? Were they jealous?

Examining one's past can provide insights into unconscious motivations underlying love and jealousy. There are couples who rely on jealousy to experience passion or to make sure their feelings for one another remain intense. They may not find reassurance in loving calmness, taking it as a sign that something is amiss. For those couples, learning to eliminate jealousy without attempting to understand what role it plays in their relationship may be a relational killer rather than healer.

Behavioral and psychodynamic approaches are predominantly individual-oriented. From a systems perspective, however, it is not enough to unlearn behavior or to deal with unconscious motivations or childhood traumas in order to address jealous feelings. As I have come to see over and over again, jealousy is not solely an individual issue but a couple's problem, and it profits from being treated as such. In addition, a couple as an entity is affected by the biopsychosocial context in which it exists. Social trends and cultural norms influence relationships as much as biology and learning does and, for the treatment to be effective, all of these factors need to be taken into consideration.

Relationships affected by jealousy are likely to benefit more from couple's therapy than from individual treatment. Yet, the perception that jealousy is an individual rather than relational problem persists. The majority of my clients seeking therapy due to jealousy come as individuals. When I encourage them to invite their partner(s), they often resist, feeling embarrassed by their jealous reactions. Considering jealousy as a sign of personal failure, they assume they have to deal with this emotion on their own. Pointing out to clients that learning more about jealousy *together* can benefit them as a couple sometimes comes as a revelation. As my patient Katie exclaimed, "You mean that I'm not solely responsible for what we're going through? That we're both contributing to our messed-up dynamic?" She fell silent. "I'm trying to take in what you're saying, but cannot help but think that it's still my fault. I'm the emotional one, with all the outbursts. Michael is the calm one. And even if it isn't all my fault, I don't think I'll be able to convince him to do couple's therapy. He says he doesn't need therapy." Katie folded her arms around her shoulders and started to cry. A few weeks later, Michael agreed to join us for "a session or two, to give it a try."

Sexual Versus Emotional Jealousy

Sexual and emotional jealousy are often mixed together, even if they can also be experienced independently. Those who embrace the approval of sex with multiple partners in polyamory tend to become adept at mitigating sexual jealousy. Sex with others may no longer be perceived as a threat; however, who one has sex with and what actually happens can still be deeply unsettling. As a result, jealous reactions in polyamory tend to be a unique mixture of sexual and emotional.

People in poly relationships spend a lot of time discussing, oftentimes in extraordinary detail, the boundaries of sexual involvement with others. It is done in the spirit of avoiding hurt and averting betrayal, but this level of detail can also represent a defensive reaction against sexual openness. Sexual boundary discussions are also a health measure intended to prevent sexually transmitted infections, or STIs. One of the typical negotiations involves "fluid bonding." Fluid bonding refers to the exchange of bodily fluids during kissing, oral and anal sex, and intercourse. The exploration of what, when, and where such exchange is allowed can be very elaborate. Many primary couples draw a line between fluid bonding and other sexual practices; thus, fluid bonding becomes a way to distinguish the primacy of their relationship over the others.

In spite of all of these preventive measures and seemingly endless processing, it is not possible to avoid transgressions altogether. Some lapses are accidental; others, more ambiguous. A particular kind of transgression frequently explored in therapy involves conflict avoidance. As an example, a man may agree to set safe-sex practices and boundaries with respect to fluid bonding with his primary partner, but fail to use a condom with his secondary partner if she expresses a dislike of it. His fear of alienating the partner he is with at the moment overrides his intention to honor his agreement with his primary partner. The conflict in front of him is acute; the other one is temporarily removed, and the present discomfort takes precedence over the future clash. In another example, a woman may agree not to use a particular sex toy with her secondary partner/lover, reserving the use of it for her primary relationship. When her lover surprises her with a similar kind of toy, she may agree to include it in their sex play in order to avoid hurting his feelings.

The potential for boundary violations is high when it comes to creating rules around kissing; oral sex, anal sex, and intercourse (with or without male and female condoms); the use of vibrators and other sex toys; kinky exchanges; submission/dominance play; and so on. The reality tends to be more ambiguous than the principles one agrees on. When boundaries are defied, it *feels* like a betrayal. What constitutes betrayal in polyamory might be considerably different from betrayal in monogamy, but the emotional reaction is the same. It hurts. It undermines trust and triggers fear of loss. It evokes the same response: "How could you?"

Emotional jealousy can be provoked by seemingly random events or innocuous words. A partner coming home later than he promised might be greeted with angry words because he failed to honor the agreement. His explanation that he had to take care of his other partner who was not feeling well may assuage some of the anger but fail to address the hurt and sadness of the one who is waiting. In that moment, she, the waiting one, feels secondary because her metamour's needs came first. It does not stop there; she also feels guilty for feeling wounded. The cascade of primary emotions is unleashed, but it often ends at an impasse when the secondary reactions of guilt and embarrassment are released.

Whether jealousy is sexual or emotional in nature, it shakes the couple's sense of comfort and trust. Being able to recognize this disruption as a beneficial alarm bell is likely to support the healing process. When partners actively engage in making the relational repair, they are bound to feel better about the relationship than they did before. Nevertheless, acknowledging this positive aspect of jealousy does not imply that jealousy should be accepted as inevitable and left unexamined.

References

Buss, D. M. (2000). *The dangerous passion: Why jealousy is as necessary as love and sex.* The Free Press.

Buss, D. M. (2013). Sexual jealousy. *Psychological Topics,20*(2), 155–182. https://www.researchgate.net/publication/285913868_Sexual_Jealousy

Buss, D. M. (2018). Sexual and emotional infidelity: Evolved gender differences in jealousy prove robust and replicable. *Association for Psychological Science, 13*(2), 155–160. https://labs.la.utexas.edu/buss/files/2018/03/Sexual-and-Emotional-Infidelity-PPS-2018.pdf

Goodboy, A. K., Horan, S. M., & Booth-Butterfield, M. (2012). Intentional jealousy-evoking behavior in romantic relationships as a function of received partner affection and love styles. *Communication Quarterly*, 60(3), 370–385. 10.1080/01463373.2012.688792

Guerrero, L. K., Spitzberg, B. H., & Yoshimura, S. M. (2004). Sexual and emotional jealousy. In J. H. Harvey, A. Wenzel, & S. Sprecher (Eds.), *The handbook of sexuality in close relationships* (pp. 311–346). Lawrence Erlbaum Associates.

Pines, A. M. (1998). *Romantic jealousy: Causes, symptoms, cures.* Routledge.
Pines, A. M., & Bowes, C. F. (1992/2016). Romantic jealousy. *Psychology Today.*
https://www.psychologytoday.com/us/articles/199203/romantic-jealousy
Sapolsky, R. M. (2017). *Behave: The biology of humans and our best and worst.* Penguin
Books.

14 Attempts to Sublimate: Compersion

Compersion

Perhaps the most bewildering aspect of polyamory is represented by the idea of compersion. Compersion denotes a possibility of not only overcoming jealousy, but also of finding joy in the involvement of one's partner with somebody else. Polyamorous people are quick to add that compersion is not limited to embracing the sexual ecstasy of one's partner with another lover. Having nonsexual fun with one's other partners is also referred to as compersion. However, these forms of sympathetic joy, or *mudita*, as it is known in Buddhism, seldom cause distress. After all, anyone who has ever been in a rewarding relationship has experienced joyful feelings upon witnessing one's partner happily engaged with others. It is not simply about the presence or absence of the feeling of joy; it is about who these other people are and what activities they engage in.

The way I approach it in therapy is to understand that compersion lies not in what it *is*, but in what it *does*. As with many poly-related things, ideas swiftly become ideals, and these ideals sometimes become impossible aspirations, having a very real impact on how a person perceives herself. As one patient remarked when feeling blue about her limited capacity to be more accepting: "You know, it's because of that compersion thing. I don't have it in me, and I don't think I ever will. I'm not doing polyamory right. I feel like a fraud." There was profound sadness in her voice, a real questioning of whether she is cut out for polyamory, not because of its other challenges, which she felt she was managing, but because of her inability to feel compersion.

The polyamorous lifestyle, with its embrace of honesty, transparency, and openness, may not be as emotionally liberating as it may appear on paper. If betrayal is touted as a failure of monogamy, the difficulty with experiencing compersion is the unspoken equivalent of a letdown in polyamory. To complicate the matter further, there is a tacit pressure to learn to feel it. While some guidebooks assure the readers that "[n]ot experiencing it [compersion] doesn't mean you're broken, or that you can't still benefit from having metamours in your life" (Veaux & Rickert, 2014, p. 399), other texts are less forgiving, considering compersion an acquired skill akin to acceptance that, with patience and practice, can be learned (Anderlini-D'Onofrio, 2009; Taormino, 2008). "The first step to achieving compersion is to work on unlearning jealousy—letting go of feelings of insecurity, possessiveness, and fear. You're striving for a *shift in consciousness*," writes Taormino (2008, p. 176, emphasis mine). Benson (2008) is even more direct: One should aspire to achieve compersion because "your love for your partner means that you genuinely want your partner to have a joyous, rich life. *Compersion is thus a form of empathy*" (p. 171, emphasis mine).

From the perspective set forth in the guidebooks, polyamory as a lifestyle can be predesigned. Suggested arrangements appear simple enough to put into practice. Strategies involving designing one's preferred relationships include: drawing the outline, filling in the details (who, what, when, where), making space for negotiation, diagramming rules and agreements, and drafting the relationship contract (Taormino, 2008). Individuals interested in polyamory learn about its axioms of ethics, such as "Axiom 1: the people in the relationship are more important than the relationship" (Veaux & Rickert, 2014, p. 400). The emphasis is clear—the focus is on the individual. Being able to design the relationship of one's dreams without feeling guilty about one's wants and desires is beguiling. With the highlighted focus on personal responsibility—it is the individual's duty to do the required work to make the relationship flourish—polyamory appears more other-centered than egocentric. Yet, it is in the latter that polyamory's intra- and interpersonal difficulties often reside. Stated differently, polyamory elevates the individual while blaming the person for not doing polyamory right.

Absence of Jealousy

As a result of the aspirational nature of polyamory, the presence or absence of jealousy and compersion emerge as relational culprits. What is relevant clinically is that these affective states do not arise at random, nor are they purely intrapsychic. Instead, these emotional reactions occur in response to specific people and situations. Their intensity is inevitably exacerbated by past attachment traumas, which may not be consciously recognized. Failing at "a shift in consciousness" may not be a person's fault; yet, it may result in self-blame and lowered self-esteem.

Some people claim to have never experienced jealousy. Secure attachment may account for some of it, but assuming that every person who claims not to be jealous is securely attached would miss the finer points. Polyamorous clients are more likely than monogamous patients to assert that they do not experience jealousy. Yet, the polyamory lifestyle attracts people with all kinds of relational experiences, not merely the securely attached. What possible explanations can be gleaned from the clinical literature on the absence of jealousy?

Clanton (2006) points out how North American, English, and Northern European Protestant cultures often emphasize the repression and denial of negative emotions. This is especially true for males who from early on receive messages to suppress their feelings. Jealousy is perceived as negative and should therefore be repressed. As Clanton writes, "The repression and denial of jealousy are often accompanied by a conscious or unconscious reduction of commitment in a relationship; to avoid being hurt, one may withdraw from a relationship" (p. 423). It is entirely possible that people who do not experience jealousy have learned to repress or deny this feeling; or, subconsciously, they may not value their relationships much and therefore find compersion relatively easy. In contrast, people who struggle with jealousy and lack of compersion may be more attuned to their feelings. They may also value their relationship more.

It is important to explore the nature of nonjealous feelings in therapy, especially when clients report lower levels of relational satisfaction. In my experience (and in line with Clanton's research), men are more likely to assert a lack of jealousy. Men might be better at repressing and denying negative emotions, but it is also feasible that females' socialization makes them more prone to self-doubt. Body-image issues are more prevalent among females than males—girls are more likely to compare themselves to others based on their looks than on their achievements. Compared to males, females receive an overwhelmingly larger amount of attention toward their bodies, whether they ask for it or not. Girls are also taught different interpersonal skills than boys; for females being other-oriented is rewarded and reinforced. From a young age, girls are more aware of other people's feelings, nuances in behaviors, and so on. In contrast, boys' socialization is more self-oriented, with a greater focus on performance, accomplishments, and success. Males are taught to focus more on competition and less on other people's feelings. Indeed, they are encouraged to dismiss their own affects and instead focus on logic and problem solving. For some, this leads to the development of emotional blindness, or *alexithymia*. While alexithymia, which literally means "no words for emotions," is not gender-specific, clinically, the term is more likely to evoke an image of a male and not a female. Given the pressure to repress negative emotions, some males may not be able to recognize jealousy even if they might be feeling it. The latter is in line with Clanton's (1981, 2006) observation that studying jealousy through evaluations and surveys is highly problematic, because jealousy is often denied, repressed, or relabeled. Asking research subjects about how jealous they are is meaningless if they are unclear what jealousy is.

References

Anderlini-D'Onofrio, S. (2009). *Gaia and the new politics of love: Notes for a poly planet*. North Atlantic Books.

Benson, P. J. (2008). *The polyamory handbook: A user's guide*. AuthorHouse.

Clanton, G. (1981). Frontiers of jealousy research. *Journal of Family and Economics Issues, 4*, 259–273. 10.1007/BF01257940

Clanton, G. (2006). Jealousy and envy. In J. E. Stets & J. H. Turner (Eds.), *Handbook of the sociology of emotions* (pp. 410–442). Springer.

Taormino, T. (2008). *Opening up: A guide to creating and sustaining open relationships.* Cleis Press.

Veaux, F., & Rickert, E. (2014). *More than two: A practical guide to ethical polyamory.* Thorntree Press.

Part V
Relational Psychodynamics and Attachment Perspectives

This part of the book reflects theoretical perspectives and psychotherapeutic approaches that I have found to be germane to the understanding and treatment of polyamorous relationships.

15 Tantalizing Objects and Identity Formation: Conscious Choices and Unconscious Motivations

Tantalizing Objects

Ronald Fairbairn introduced the idea of a tantalizing object as represented by a frustratingly desirable person who is simultaneously loving and rejecting—one moment here, the next moment gone. In psychodynamic terms, an object is psychologically meaningful only when it serves some purpose, meets certain needs, or provides some kind of gratification (Mitchell, 2014). In Fairbairn's theory, the tantalizing object was a parent or caregiver who a child had no chance but to attach to, with the hope of making them more predictably available. In polyamory, individuals involved in multiple relationships are like these tantalizing objects, highly coveted and alluring, but frustratingly hard to get hold of.

One of the universally recognizable challenges of polyamory is the allotment of time. There are simply not enough hours in the week for all partners to have their share of affection and love in the amounts they need and crave. Long-term monogamous relationships may suffer from a similar malady when kids are involved; work and children take precedence over sex and intimacy. Work demands do not cease to exist for polyamorous parents; children, when present, require a lot of attention, even if there are more partners to share the task of caretaking. As a result, finding time for romance is an ongoing quest. To make scheduling of dates easier, technology-based solutions such as synched online calendars are often utilized. As efficient and transparent as this practice is, it does not provide reassurance of interest and commitment. Many a patient of mine has sighed with resignation, and at times dejection, that they have to schedule their dates weeks in advance. Seeing the calendar of one's lover filled to the brim can be depressing; it is likely to open old wounds of feeling undesirable and unlovable.

The use of shared calendars to pin down the tantalizing partners is not reserved for people who live apart. It is as frequently used in poly households with three or more individuals living together. This practice does not provide more access to the desirable partners, but it does make their unavailability more predictable. Nonhierarchical polyamory creates another tantalizing object in its attempt to eliminate ranking—it generates an idealized relational vision, one that is challenging to sustain in reality.

In many respects, the entire prospect of polyamory has the characteristics of a tantalizing object. Polyamory as a lifestyle appeals and repels; it rewards and punishes. For many, it is easy to get attached to the idea of polyamory and hoping that, by practicing it right, they will be able to make it more predictable. Aligned with Fairbairn's observations of infants whose ego structures get undermined by the unpredictable and unreliable tantalizing objects, many people get frustrated and disappointed with their polyamorous partners. They try to ameliorate disappointment by looking for someone new to date. The resulting frequent change of partners is not easy to rely on in the long run, but in the meantime, it is an enchanting prospect, filled with possibilities.

Object Relations Reenactments

Object relations theory emphasizes the importance of early attachments in adult romantic relationships. We choose people who can help us re-experience and reintegrate relational wounds inflicted by the family of origin. This theory represents an intrapsychic view of resolving issues from the past; however, partners originally perceived as infallible and gratifying disappoint and hurt soon enough. This disappointment forms the basis of the first projection—you are different from what I thought you were; in other words, you are not who I need you to be. With the passage of time, it gets more difficult to recognize this realization as a projection. Projections are usually met with similar-sounding counterprojections, and painful transference storms start raging within and around wounded partners (Schnarch, 1991).

When an object, that is, another person, is perceived as either good or bad, it may reflect an early stage of development known as the paranoid-schizoid position, in Melanie Klein's terms. This stage is characterized by splitting, which, Klein theorized, allows the good to be separated from the bad. However, splitting as a relational strategy is never effective as it leads to either idealization or devaluation of the other. It makes a person vacillate between the sense of omnipotence and fear of annihilation.

The elements of paranoid-schizoid position can be discerned in poly-amorous patients who move from one relational attempt to the next—the moment a new partner starts making stronger relational requests, she becomes unwanted—she is perceived as too demanding. This is a pattern that a patient, Philip, exhibited. Philip, a warm and solicitous man in his forties, found himself in a vicious cycle of idealizing and dismissing the women he dated. New to nonmonogamy, he searched for the perfect woman, one who would be there for him when he needed her, and who would be content to take care of herself when he was busy with other things. Philip's sense of omnipotence came from his dating success; women found his welcoming smile and friendly manners attractive. His fear of annihilation manifested in the sexual arena; Philip struggled with erectile dysfunction. He assumed that once he found the right woman, his erectile problems would disappear.

The next stage of development, the depressive position, is a maturational milestone that continues throughout the lifespan. The other is no longer perceived as a part-object, but as a whole person, who can be good *and* bad, loving *and* frustrating, reliable *and* ungratifying. To master the tasks of the depressive position, an individual must learn to accept the limitations and incompleteness that accompany any relationship.

As Philip's therapy progressed and his dating involvements provided him with a greater variety of relational experiences, he started seeing women differently. In his telling, they no longer appeared as part-objects; they offered love *and* earning their love required effort. Philip could please them, and he was learning to ask for what he needed without fear of obliteration. Although he still struggled with erectile dysfunction, he started to appreciate how much more was involved in creating conditions for mutually satisfying sex. He came to realize that a woman of his dreams was a fantasy figure. Philip's intelligence and curiosity about his upbringing helped with the transition to the depressive position.

Philip's process illuminates how relational fulfillment and satisfaction are based on one's ability to acknowledge the inevitable losses that come with the choices one makes. Looking at polyamory through the lens of reenactments can reveal which relationships are stuck in the paranoid-schizoid position, as characterized by an omnipotent yearning to have it all, and which are able to accept the inevitable limitations without discarding what is beautiful and functional. When the primitive defense mechanisms characteristic of the early position, such as projection and splitting, are replaced with the more mature emotions of the depressive stance (i.e., grief, guilt, and the desire for repair), relationships are more likely to flourish.

The paranoid-schizoid position can be detected in cases that I came to call *polyfurious*. Those are situations when the partner who argued for opening up is now unable to tolerate his partner's interest in polyamory. He perceives it as a threat that needs to be annihilated rather than worked through. When my patient, Ron, suggested opening up, he did not conceive of the possibility that consensual nonmonogamy may involve more than casual sex. In his perception, the risk of emotional attachment was nonexistent. He imagined that opening up would allow him to enjoy the occasional fun trysts (his wife, too, if she wanted), but when confronted with the reality of his wife developing affection for another man, Ron proverbially lost it. He accused his wife of cheating, arguing that her communication with this other man was not a part of the agreement. In his eyes, the source of her becoming all bad, meaning polyamory, needed to be destroyed. Ron had to split off the bad in order to retain the good, which was his wife. He was unable to conceive that his wife may still love him and at the same time not want to give up on her new friendship. Ron's inability to integrate the good and bad was painful to witness. When his wife pointed out that it was he who suggested opening up, he reacted with fury, shouting back that it was not how he envisioned it. In his eyes, he did not do anything bad; it was she who had acted destructively.

In his fragility, Ron was unable to tolerate therapy either and cut that off, too. In contrast to Philip, Ron was not capable of tolerating the loss and accepting grief as a part of the maturational process.

Managing the depressive position well implies that one has made amends with the shortcomings of polyamory. Contrary to popular imagination, polyamory does not transcend old relational restraints by itself; it comes with its own limitations. Being one of multiple partners comes at the cost of feeling special and uniquely chosen. Giving multiple partners adequate attention is challenging. Forming symmetrical relationships as it is attempted in nonhierarchical polyamory rarely provides all the partners involved with the feeling of equality. These are some of the obvious losses associated with a polyamorous lifestyle, but not the only ones.

Family Systems Theory

Murray Bowen proposed a theory of human behavior that uses systems thinking to delineate multifaceted interactions within the family structure. Bowen's family systems theory describes processes characteristic of most family units: triangles, differentiation of self, nuclear family emotional practices, family projections, emotional cutoffs, multigenerational transmission, and societal-emotional processes. The theory proposes that emotional processing, which is a product of a billion years of evolution, governs human relational systems. People may feel distant from their families, but their origins profoundly affect how they feel, think, and act.

With regard to polyamory, the concept of triangles is worth emphasizing. As relational systems, triangles are thought to be more stable than dyads. A couple in conflict who has a child is less likely to split than a childless couple experiencing relational rifts. At the same time, triangles, which usually have two sides in harmony and one side in conflict, often lead to relational difficulties. Stability is not the same as the lack of struggle. Nonhierarchical polyamory attempts to create greater harmony by eliminating ranking. According to the triangularity theory, polyamorous formations, especially of the nonhierarchical type, should be more stable than dyadic relationships. However, in the cases I have encountered, nonhierarchical polyamory is not any more stable than the hierarchical practice. Partners in a nonhierarchical triangle seldom feel equal. Relational conflicts are not eliminated; on the contrary, they are pushed out of sight but not out of mind.

Bowen's theory depicts systemic processes that influence an individual. One of the core concepts involves differentiation of the self. As outlined by Papero (1990, p. 45), differentiation "addresses how people differ from one another in terms of their sensitivity to one another and their varying abilities to preserve a degree of autonomy in the face of pressure and togetherness." In other words, an individual's reactivity to others varies from person to person, which has relational implications. The degree of differentiation affects the process through which a person manages one's individuality and togetherness in a romantic relationship.

Bowen hypothesized that people fall in love with partners who have similar levels of differentiation, but with opposite defensive styles. These defensive styles complement each other; thus, a man whose primary way of coping with anxiety is suppression of emotions is likely to fall in love with someone who is emotionally highly expressive, even dramatic. This pattern of rational versus emotional complementarity is a familiar challenge in a substantial number of couple's therapy cases.

Identity Formation

We define ourselves relationally—single, married, partnered, divorced, widowed—and in the age of asymmetrical relationships, the phrase "It's complicated" has become another form of self-definition. The phrase captures the relational ambiguity of the heart, or fluidity of boundaries, or both. Relational definitions not only specify who we relate to and how, but they also shape our identity.

Nathan and Emma's case represents one of the most typical poly scenarios that therapists encounter. It also illustrates what can be described as identity confusion or identity reformulation. It starts with two people in a committed relationship deciding to open up. They love each other, but are no longer in love.

Nathan advocated for polyamory and Emma reluctantly agreed, mostly out of fear of losing what she cherished and valued, that is, her relationship with Nathan. Their conflict of preferences became an enactment of attachment wounds, immersed in a question of identity. Erik Erikson's (1950/1993) observation of the stages of development, from childhood to adulthood, provides a valuable perspective on what takes place in poly relationships such as Nathan and Emma's. Two stages are of particular relevance here: Identity vs. Role Confusion and Intimacy vs. Isolation.

Identity vs. Role Confusion typically occurs between the ages of 12 and 18 and is characterized by the search for a sense of self and the development of personal identity. It involves an intense exploration of personal values, beliefs, and goals. For adults opening up to polyamory, this stage comes to the foreground once again—not as a transition from adolescence to adulthood, but as a transition from the hetero- and mononormative type of adulthood to the exploratory and non-normative kind. The parallel between Identity vs. Role Confusion and opening up to polyamory resides in the desire to become more independent and to find a way to fit in in a non-normative way.

Erikson observed that the adolescent mind is essentially a mind in a moratorium, in a psychosocial stage between childhood and adulthood. The mind is in transition between the morality learned as the child and the ethics to be developed as the adult. The notion of a mind in moratorium can be applied to polyamory as well. Transition to polyamory tends to create confusion, even when partners, like Nathan and Emma, claim that they were ready because they had read the recommended books, listened to podcasts, and followed poly blogs.

One of the dominant explorations in the Identity vs. Role Confusion stage involves the sexual search. In polyamory, the search is not so much for who the person is sexually (e.g., heterosexual, gay, lesbian, bi, asexual, pansexual), but what kind of sexual partnership one finds oneself at home with. Nathan and Emma were not in doubt about their heterosexual identities; their goal, at Nathan's request, was to find a way to embrace sexual and romantic liaisons outside of monogamy. Emma was open to occasional sexual encounters with others as long as they were casual and did not threaten their relationship. However, their poly explorations soon started to conflict with Emma's image of herself, and she started questioning her identity. Feeling deprioritized, she was developing a negative sense of self. She agreed to the polyamory terms suggested, or, in her perception, imposed by Nathan. Was she still monogamous? Or should she call herself polyamorous? Emma no longer had a sense of who she was.

Nathan did not merely suggest opening up; upon becoming romantically involved with another woman, he became an advocate for nonhierarchical polyamory. He argued to Emma that this relational format resonated with his long-held beliefs, which, until then, he had been reluctant to reveal. Not sure about her standing in the relationship with Nathan, Emma was becoming depressed.

The next stage in Erikson's model, Intimacy vs. Isolation, typically occurs between the ages of 18 and 40. During this period, the major conflict regards the formation of intimate, loving relationships with other people, figuring out how to share oneself more openly and intimately with those who are not family members. Relationships formed during this stage of development lean toward longer-term romantic explorations and commitments. Successful completion of this stage results in the formation of rewarding and meaningful relationships characterized by a sense of belonging, respect, trust, and care. Mastering of intimacy leads to an appreciation of love. By contrast, when the tasks of this stage are not mastered, they result in avoidance of intimacy, fear of commitment, or engagement in diffuse relationships. If left unresolved, these relational deficits can lead to isolation, loneliness, and avoidance of love and life.

The formation of intimacy, and fear of intimacy, were at the center of Nathan and Emma's polyamorous confusion. They decided to open up two years into their relationship, right at the time when the bliss of a new romance typically ebbs. Nathan and Emma knew each other intimately; there was a certain amount of attachment security present, simply because they had made it so far without breaking up. They also lived together, which was the first time for both. But their sense of safety that comes from familiarity was deceptive. Familiarity makes people relax, but it also breeds boredom; a couple starts longing for more. Nathan met somebody new and experienced NRE. His argument for a nonhierarchical poly arrangement represented a desire for having his cake and eating it too. He genuinely valued his relationship with Emma and the sense of companionship and security it provided. For him, the transition from a monogamous to polyamorous identity was smooth; he did not experience any major conflicts regarding his sense of self, nor did he struggle with the roles he played in his dual intimate relationships. He wanted the two women in his life to get along and, ideally, be more than metamours who relate to each other because they must. Emma began individual therapy in addition to couple's counseling to reconnect with her identity and to explore what she wanted out of her life. Individual treatment helped her to feel reassured that what she wanted relationally—a loving, committed relationship with a man who shares her values—was fine to look for. She desired intimacy that comes with monogamy rather than the loneliness she experienced in her exploration of polyamory.

Polyamory is not just about the successful negotiation of differences; couples of all sexual and relational orientations accomplish this all the time. It is about the uncertainty of belonging, not feeling like you are the chosen one (i.e., Emma) or chosen for who you are (i.e., Nathan). Polyamory is like being on the cusp of adulthood all over again—not sure about the tasks, not sure about the identity one got used to having. Reassessing one's identity while questioning the conventional morality of monogamy is a lot to process.

Nathan and Emma's commitment to each other was solid enough to tolerate the disturbance and distress of polyamory. They realized that the terms proposed and enforced by Nathan needed to be renegotiated if they were to stay together. Emma was willing to make their relationship "monogamish," or at least give it a try. *Monogamish* is a term coined by Dan Savage, and it describes a relationship that is predominantly monogamous, with occasional permission to engage in sexual play with others. Nathan, on the other hand, was able to recognize how forceful and insensitive he had been in his earlier demands. They had more relational work to do and were willing to go down that path.

Like other relational formats, polyamory consists of conscious choices driven by unconscious motivations. The choice of consensual nonmonogamy oftentimes puts one's identity into question, requiring self-examination. The answers one arrives at may be uncomfortable, especially when they are in conflict with what one's partner wants. These struggles regard more than personal identity; they concern relational identity as well. In this respect, Nathan and Emma's case speaks to the relevance of the depressive position in relational development. As partners, they had to figure out how to maintain intimacy without falling into the abyss of isolation. This task of figuring out intimacy forced them to work on accepting losses and limitations without blaming each other for what the other person may not be able to give.

References

Erikson, E. (1950/1993). *Childhood and society*. W. W. Norton.
Mitchell, S. A. (2014). *Relationality: From attachment to intersubjectivity*. Psychology Press.
Papero, D. V. (1990). *Bowen family system theory*. Allyn & Bacon.
Schnarch, D. M. (1991). *Constructing sexual crucible: An integration of sexual and marital therapy*. W. W. Norton.

16 Through a Glass Darkly: Polyamory Through the Lens of Defensive Process

From the psychodynamic point of view, certain defensive processes might be worth a closer examination when working with polyamorous clients. Nancy McWilliams offers thoughtful descriptions of various defensive reactions (2011). One of the defenses in particular, reaction formation, bears an intriguing similarity to the concept of compersion in polyamory. Another defense mechanism worth emphasizing in poly ways of relating is intellectualization, followed by its close cousin, rationalization.

Reaction Formation

Traditionally, reaction formation is the process of converting a negative affect to a positive one. Being able to turn a negative feeling or reaction into its polar opposite is a remarkably human phenomenon, one that becomes evident as early as age three or four. At that age, if a new sibling is born, the older child is usually capable of turning his feelings of jealousy and anger into a conscious affect of love. However, the old emotions of suspicion and resentment of the competitor for his family's attention are not gone. This is often evidenced by an older sibling's actions of "loving the baby to death," showering the newcomer with so much love and affection that they inadvertently hurt the baby.

"It is a basic psychoanalytic premise that no disposition is totally unmixed," writes McWilliams (2011, p. 141). The function of reaction formation is to deny ambivalence. For example, in polyamory, there is a recognition of the complexity of experiencing jealousy and an encouragement that the person feeling jealousy does the work of transforming this emotion (e.g., Anapol, 1997). As described earlier, many polyamory guidebooks provide step-by-step instructions to identify jealousy's inner components and to translate them into workable strategies. It is not an easy process, but people in one's network of relationships, or in the broader community, are usually willing to help. What is not recognized is that the goal to overcome jealousy may serve a further-reaching goal to overcome ambivalence regarding polyamory.

Discerning a genuine lack of jealousy from a wishful desire manifested by reaction formation is clinically relevant, especially when a client's actions do not align with his stated affect. Children jealous of younger siblings are more likely to be told that their conflicted feelings are understandable, whereas adults may struggle with acknowledging emotions they are not "supposed" to be having. Are the clients who insist that they do not feel jealous and would be thrilled if their partners had sex with other people deceiving themselves? Is something else going on? More often than not, these are people who had been married for a number of years, so what role does the longevity of marriage play in such cases? In many situations, that role is significant. Sexual novelty is appealing but hard to find in a long-term relationship. If the spouses of these individuals were to have sex with others, that would be sexually refreshing. It would also affirm that their spouses are attractive to others, hence enhancing one's self-image. Since the threat of jealousy would make it hard to advocate for greater sexual openness, the solution is to eliminate jealousy. The underlying ambivalence usually becomes known when other feelings emerge. It happens when a nonjealous husband encourages his spouse to have sex with another man and then insists, with thinly veiled antagonism, on knowing "all the details" of her interactions with the lover. In this instance, reaction formation may have transformed jealousy into generosity, but without altering the underlying feelings of anger and resentment.

There is a subset of unacknowledged and uncontested rivals present in some poly relationships. These rivals are not other flesh-and-blood partners; rather, video games, board games, and screen-based activities under any other name are frequently the biggest competitors for the limited time resources characteristic of poly reality. By and large, gamers, for whom playing is not merely a leisure preoccupation but a validation of their competence and abilities, prioritize gaming. What often comes up in clinical conversations is that they are more concerned with disappointing the invisible others who rely on their presence to continue the game than they are with upsetting their partners, whose demands are deemed unreasonable. Poly contracts and other negotiations of boundaries fail to mention these all-too-familiar rivals for one's attention—the ones that are impossible to criticize or compare oneself to because they are "real" only in the virtual sense. Yet, they do exist, and they make very real demands on a lover's time.

Reaction formation turns something into its opposite. Rather than being upset with partners who prioritize games, it is easy to convince oneself that, to them, this is an important activity. Similarly, instead of risking conflict by complaining about a partner's extensive use of electronics, it is easier to remind oneself about one's own dependency on technology. The function of reaction formation is to cover up for ambivalence—a person preoccupied with a game has less time to see his other partners in person, and that might be a win.

The power of reaction formation is especially apparent in the desire to convert jealousy into compersion. This is not to deny that some people may genuinely experience compersion, but overall, accepting that one's partner has other partners is easier than delighting in their romantic ecstasy with these other people. In Buddhism, mudita refers to the experience of pure joy at a success and good fortune of others; it is a feeling untainted by self-interest. Yet, even in Buddhism, it is recognized that among the "four sublime attitudes," joy is the most difficult to cultivate. However, since defensive processes are attempts at adaptation, it would make sense that a person who embraces polyamory would try their best to develop compersion.

Intellectualization and Rationalization

Intellectualization as a defense mechanism aims to block confrontations with an unconscious conflict by utilizing thinking instead of feeling. Unpleasant affects are avoided by a call to focus on rational measures and explanations. Thorny relational situations are approached as problems to be solved. What makes this defense mechanism tricky to deal with is that, while intellectualization can be self-serving, it can also help to address polyamorous complexities. What, then, makes intellectualization a destructive defense mechanism that compromises a part of the self, or ruptures a relational bond, rather than one that serves well both the individual and the relationship? As is often the case with defensive strategies, the problem lies in a repetition of a pattern and in avoidance of an underlying conflict. When relational difficulties are repetitively approached as problems to be fixed, the underlying emotions that contain important information about a relationship are suppressed. Only the difficulties evidenced at the surface are addressed, without the need to examine the foundations.

Intellectualization is closely related to the defense mechanism of rationalization. Both use reason, but where intellectualization appraises reality from an emotion-free, logical point of view, rationalization bends the facts to justify one's desires and behaviors. Wanting to add more partners to one's life may signify an ability to love more, but it may also suggest an intellectualized and rationalized wish to bypass the emotional risks associated with monogamous attachments.

Highlighting defense mechanisms that are often at play in polyamory does not imply that polyamory is more pathological than monogamy. By very definition, psychological defense mechanisms start as unconscious adaptations to the realities and vagaries of life. It is possible that polyamory attracts people who are prone to intellectualization, rationalization, and reaction formation as coping strategies. It is also plausible that people who become polyamorous learn to utilize these particular strategies, albeit not under the name of defense mechanisms, since the strategies are valued in poly circles.

References

Anapol, D. M. (1997). *Polyamory: The new love without limits: Secrets of sustainable intimate relationships*. IntiNet Resource Center.

McWilliams, N. (2011). *Psychoanalytic diagnosis: Understanding personality structure in the clinical process*. Guilford.

17 The Ways We Love: Attachment-Based Perspectives

Those who choose polyamory as a lifestyle have the ambition to expand the boundaries of love by embracing concurrent partnerships. It may be argued that this is a quantitative expansion, not necessarily lacking in value, but perhaps less concerned with depth. Wondering about the possibility of loving more *deeply*, I am reminded of Martin Buber's observation regarding love. In his book *I and Thou*, Buber explored what it means to expand the boundaries of the self and perceive the other not merely as *It*, an object that is separate in itself and that can be used or experienced, but as a relational *Thou*. Buber wrote, "Love is *between I* and *Thou* ... Love is responsibility of an *I* for a *Thou*" (Buber, 1996).

It is not only existential philosophy that emphasizes the responsibility of love. Beloved children's books teach that lesson too. This is the message that the fox imprints on the little prince: "'Men have forgotten this truth,' said the fox. 'But you must not forget it. You become responsible, forever, for what you have tamed. You are responsible for your rose ...' 'I am responsible for my rose,' the little prince repeated, so that he would be sure to remember" (Saint-Exupéry, 1943).

For some, this responsibility of love is an obvious assertion, but for others it is an inconvenience that perhaps should not exist. In polyamory, at least on paper, the tendency is to approach relationships more as *I-It*; the concern of the *I* is for its own well-being. One's partners are separate entities responsible for their own well-being. In the *I-It* relationship, the focus is on sensations and experiences. In contrast, in the *I-Thou* relationship, the focus is not on partners as separate objects but on the bond they create. The partners are conjointly responsible for elevating their love's connection to something larger than themselves and, in the process, becoming capable of expanding the boundaries of the self.

This kind of responsibility is diametrically opposite to the axiom in polyamory that it is the individuals in the relationship and not the relationship itself that is most important. However, theorists and advocates of polyamory also claim that by embracing this lifestyle, people will be able to expand the boundaries of the self. Can polyamorous depth come from the dispersed *I-It* rather than the focused *I-Thou*? After all, treating another person as *It* is self-focused. Obviously, there is a range in how poly individuals approach relationships and, at their best, each individual is responsible for their own well-being and concerned with the other's well-being. Working with polyamorous clients, I encourage a development of responsibility in which both individuals in the relationship as well as the relationship itself are the subject and the object, the *Thou*. As the relational perspective teaches us, it is the quality of the bond that people create that cements a relationship.

By connecting existential observations to research on relationships, what insights can be gained from the numerous studies on attachment and the diverse nature of polyamorous partnerships? And how can these insights inform therapy with this population? It could be argued that since the attachment perspective is rooted in hetero- and mononormativity, its ability to explain polyamorous ways of relating might be limited. However, such an argument, should it be made, would place the cart before the horse. The dynamics of attachment influence one's development from the beginning of one's existence, forming and informing an infant's sense of self and others, years before he becomes an adult interested in love and sex. Moreover, as research on attachment behavior indicates, it is the influence of *one* caregiver in particular that has a major impact on the child's sense of self and his later style of relating.

There is no question that1 ancillary attachments with secondary caregivers might be of crucial importance. They may offset the traumatic impact of neglectful or abusive parenting; however, it is the primary attachment that sets the stage. The central tenet of attachment theory is that it is a single individual who becomes the child's primary attachment figure. It is usually the person who is closest to the child: her mother, father, or perhaps another relative who is her main caretaker. Bowlby observed that, even in situations where a child is separated from her primary caregiver (e.g., when hospitalized), she seeks out the comfort of a specific nurse rather than connecting to many aides. This phenomenon is called *monotropy*. Other attachment figures, usually referred to as secondary or subsidiary, are important too and can indeed play a crucial role in the child's development; however, their roles in an individual's life belong to a different sphere of influence. Their presence can have a mitigating effect on attachment wounds caused by the limitations of the primary attachment figure. Being able to relate to more than one person is critical—different relationships satisfy varying needs and assist a child in the development of different aspects of the self.

No two attachment bonds are alike. Parents may claim that they love their kids equally, while secretly knowing that their love and sense of connection varies depending on the child. Pet owners have the same experience. Each person or animal is different, and they evoke different feelings in us. Loving more, as in polyamory, does not imply that one loves with equal strength and commitment. Nowhere else is the power of this selectivity most readily discerned than in the case of NRE. Yet, it is just not so easy to hide the all-consuming NRE, and since honesty and transparency are important values in polyamory, less effort goes into concealing the preoccupation with a new partner.

Attachment-informed therapy for adults originates from Bowlby's (1969, 1973, 1980) recognition of different attachment patterns in children and their impact on future intimate relationships. There has been an abundance of research since Bowlby's original observations, and it has confirmed the presence of an attachment pattern in grownups that does not differ from that of young children. The three types of attachment insecurity presenting in therapy include *anxious-preoccupied, avoidant-dismissive*, and *disorganized* styles of relating. The fourth kind, *secure* attachment, represents the relational model we hope to achieve in adult life. Getting there is not simply a matter of telling oneself, "One day I will be securely attached, and all the pain of the earlier years will go away." It is hard not to be wistful when comparing Bowlby's process of forming a secure attachment to that of falling in love. We want to stay in love and not fall out of it, just as most of us wish to be cradled in the protective embrace of secure attachment—the kind of attachment that allows for safe exploration of the world, without fear of rejection.

Relationships hurt, and relationships heal. Without realizing why, people are unconsciously drawn to partners who represent certain kinds of attachment challenges, fueled by the hope that they will be able to form a healthier, more supportive, and more evolving relationship with the person they love than what they were able to do as children. While I am talking about individual attachment styles that represent early internal adaptations, it is in the romantic, adult attachments that these challenges come into play. The inner workings of one partner quickly fuse in a jigsaw pattern with the internal workings of the other partner, and the attachment dynamic is born. Mature individuals who are supportive of their partner's evolution to the best of their abilities seldom stop and ponder what makes it possible. It is when the attachment patterns are problematic that therapists are called in to help.

Insecure attachments are called insecure for a reason. Anxious-preoccupied attachments are characterized by hypersensitivity to any signs of rejection from others, particularly one's intimate partner. Even when there are none of these signs, the sensitive person easily imagines them. At the core of anxious attachment is perpetual doubt about one's worth. It is usually expressed as an uncertainty that others would be there for her when she needs them most. This fear of abandonment makes the person feel anxious about relationships; therefore, the remedy is to scrutinize all interactions for the slightest signs of danger. This is a pattern of alternating hope and dread; it makes the person hold on to security and fear that it will be taken away. As a consequence, preoccupied individuals often struggle with asserting their independence, because autonomy increases the risk of distance. As Mikulincer and Shaver observe, "This heightens anxious people's ambivalence and causes them to vacillate between an intrusive, controlling posture and a submissive, accommodating stance toward a partner's demands" (2016, p. 273). Pervasive negative self-representations, characteristic of anxious attachment, are not easily quieted by verbal reassurance—this is often perceived as a mere lip service. The craving to merge is a craving for security that words alone fail to provide. Conversely, reassurance provided by acts of care is of limited value when not accompanied by verbal declarations of love and commitment.

Not surprisingly, the shifting ground of poly relating in which new partners can be easily added is challenging for anxious individuals. Already mistrustful of their own value and love from others, they struggle with healthy assertiveness; on the one hand, hoping their partners would show more consideration and, on the other hand, refusing to clearly state their needs. This internal avoidance in anxiously preoccupied attachment translates into circumspect communication, often expressed as, "I shouldn't need to explain what bothers me, he should know it." Alluding to needs while avoiding overt requests makes the person less likely to be heard and understood, which in turn deepens attachment wounds. Fear of rejection, not always consciously recognized, can be overpowering. Anxiously attached individuals may form lasting poly relationships without achieving the attachment security they crave. Relating to multiple partners and their metamours can trigger attachment insecurities, amplifying the existing vulnerabilities instead of alleviating them.

The avoidant-dismissive attachment style is equally pervasive, but the underlying dynamics are different. In this pattern, a person avoids intimacy rather than seeking it, considering too much emotional closeness to be risky and dangerous to one's sense of self. A concerted effort goes into keeping relational intimacy at a safe distance. This pattern creates relational dynamics that can be exasperatingly difficult for the person and his partners to understand and manage. The torment of avoidance lies in a need for intimacy, which is then experienced as threatening. Once an intimate connection is achieved, it becomes the object of mistrust because it triggers the fear of rejection—loneliness and isolation lurk in the shadows. Dismissive people dread appearing dependent and weak. Shaver et al. (2005) describe the difficulty that avoidantly attached individuals experience in decoding the verbal and nonverbal cues, especially those expressed by their intimate partners. This pattern is pronounced when partners' complaints focus on emotional distance. Messages regarding emotional unavailability are often perceived as attacks on one's independence, making dismissive individuals step back even further.

Avoidant people are disinclined to share their thoughts and feelings with others because such acts promote closeness. As a result, their attempts at providing nurturance are more likely to be intellectual rather than emotional. In a poignant example, a female patient described her partner as being very good at listening. He would offer a sensible and thoughtful solution to complicated problems, which she admired but also found intimidating. Her words of praise did not match her anguished facial expression. "What happens when emotions are involved?" I asked. The answer was astonishing. She explained that her partner selects emotions he considers useful and dismisses those he deems less suitable. His approach to feelings made her feel incompetent and inadequate. She was afraid of initiating conversations about her distress, anticipating her partner's scorn. This patient's feeling of inferiority was further exacerbated by what she had gleaned from poly guides, with their tone of pragmatic rationality. The impression that emotions are a matter of choice or, worse, of immaturity, made her struggle in silence, which only increased her sense of relational insecurity. Her partner reinforced the pattern by responding when she presented a complaint in a well-prepared manner and ignoring her when the argument was not well thought through. The nature of their attachment conflicts was glaring. Not surprisingly, this woman's partner refused couple's therapy, considering it a waste of time, since obviously the problem, being emotional, was all hers.

Not all individuals fit into these neat descriptions of attachment behaviors. Sometimes reactions get mixed, as in the case of disorganized attachment, in which a person vacillates between anxious and avoidant tendencies. Their pattern of behavior is incoherent—one moment clinging, the next distancing. The disorganized or mixed attachment style consists of fluctuation between desperate attempts to form intimate connections and frantic efforts to avoid them once they occur. This is a pattern of dramatic pursuit and withdrawal, in which the person is never at rest, trying to manage the challenges of closeness and distance but without having any plan. Disorganized patients lack any strategy of how to relate and how to take care of themselves.

The lack of trust in oneself and others, combined with the difficulty of managing and communicating one's emotions, makes insecure attachments painful to bear. A person may know that rationally what she is sensing or thinking is off, but not be able to calm the distress on her own. Skewed reactions to events in the present are misaligned because they were forged in response to relational dynamics in the past. What once was essential in preserving one's emotional and physical integrity is no longer an adequate response to the current situation.

Strong affect, especially when disproportionate to "the crime at hand," is like a red light, signaling old attachment traumas. Bowlby (1973) made a distinction between what he called the "anger of hope" and the "anger of despair." Anger as a protest against a potential or real relational threat is rooted in the hope of averting the danger. Retaliatory anger, on the other hand, is caused by relational despair, the helpless feeling of not getting the proper attention from one's partner. Other emotions hide underneath anger, notably hurt, fear, sadness, and often grief. Fear might be more directly present in the anger of hope, and sadness and grief in the anger of despair, but in real life, these feelings are intertwined. Because anger is distancing, being able to connect to the underlying feelings is relevant when working toward affective repair. Hurt and sadness are connecting rather than distancing. The fear associated with sadness, rather than expressed as an attack, tends to soften the tension, bringing partners closer together.

In the world of affects, feelings are seldom straightforward. Conflicted feelings are more the norm than the exception; yet, experiencing conflicting emotions is often confusing. When discordant affects are mild to moderate, they appear not so much as contradictory but more as normal reactions to mixed situations. Conflict between work and leisure, career versus relational needs, varying social preferences, and family of origin issues, are all examples of real-life complexities that are likely to evoke contradictory feelings. Disagreements in which it is easy to sympathize with the other person's perception do not strain feelings of empathy. In contrast, when the recognition of the other person's needs is intellectually rather than viscerally felt, it is harder to quiet conflicting emotions. This issue is nowhere as clear as in the realm of sex and love. Intellectually, it is easy to be sympathetic toward a partner who dives into new relationships, perhaps basking in the glow of NRE. Viscerally, it is a very different matter; the conflicting emotions are born.

The interdependence of attachment, caregiving, and sex is crucial to understanding the dynamics of love. Optimally, these three systems function in unison, promoting secure relational bonds. Mutual satisfaction generates a desire to continue the relationship because it is emotionally and erotically rewarding. When the systems' interplay is disrupted, conflicts and distress take over. By undermining stability and trust, the conflicts and distress diminish the overall relational satisfaction. When ignored or poorly addressed, they continue to increase to the point of a relationship breakup. In contrast, when thoughtful attention to the other person's needs is combined with the ability to respond empathically, it fosters the psychological and relational growth of both partners. Feeling loved, valued, and respected generates feelings of gratitude and promotes the desire to invest further in the relationship.

Taken together, this dance of attunement is a picture of attachment security. In a dysfunctional system, the failure to attend empathically to the other person's needs results in emotional distancing. The inability to manage conflict and heal from relational ruptures diminishes the partners' sense of interpersonal efficacy and feelings of self-worth. It makes them feel exceedingly vulnerable and doubtful. The result is increased attachment insecurity.

Attachment-Informed Therapy

History is written into our neurons, and as adults, we are attempting to undo what was once done. We are on an unconscious quest to make relationships safe again, usually without a sense of direction. The goal of attachment-informed therapy is to provide guidance, to make the involuntary and seemingly random more predictable, to make the insecure secure.

In order to achieve greater attachment security, two tasks need to be accomplished, one building upon the other. The first involves creating a safe therapeutic relationship built on openness, trust, and nonjudgmental acceptance—the very picture of secure attachment that is missing from so many patients' lives. Creating a safe alliance is consistent with empirical research pointing to the relationship being the most important therapeutic factor in any form of therapy, from psychoanalysis to behavioral modification. What works in therapy works in life. When and only when this first central step of relationship building is achieved, the second task intrinsic to attachment-informed therapy can take place. This task consists of corrective emotional experiences: "The patient, in order to be helped, must undergo a corrective emotional experience suitable to repair the traumatic influence of previous experiences. It is of secondary importance whether this corrective experience takes place during treatment in the transference relationship, or parallel with the treatment in the daily life of the patient" (Alexander & French, 1980, p. 66).

The centrality of the therapeutic relationship is not unique to attachment-informed therapy. It is emphasized in psychoanalytic relational theory, in Rogers's humanistic psychology, and in most other treatment modalities. Rogers saw a positive relationship as the prerequisite for therapy to work. The client's ability to utilize therapy is dependent on the therapist's capability to create an environment in which it is safe to relate. Relating implies that the therapist maintains unconditional positive regard toward the client. This regard, rooted in deep and genuine caring for the person, and in nonjudgmental acceptance (which is not the same as the lack of discernment), offers the patient an opportunity to be her authentic self rather than who she thinks she should be. To me, the latter is an essential tenet of working with polyamorous clients, in which the clients' tension is so often about being accepted for who they are, with their nonnormative struggles. Their tension is between fitting in and belonging.

Without nonjudgmental acceptance, it is hardly possible to create a therapeutic condition in which an individual or couple can freely explore who they are, rather than who they are trying to be. Because polyamory appears so evenhanded on the surface, some people find it hard to genuinely connect to their underlying desires and conflicts. The deepest form of despair is to try to be someone other than oneself and fail over and over again. The polyamorous lifestyle can easily create despair, not just because the multiple loves it promises are not easy to find and maintain, but because loving you and you and you is hard to achieve without stirring up feelings of insecurity, fear, sadness, and loneliness.

The challenges of dealing with attachment wounds are aptly described by Peter Costello: "Our patients come to us with large areas of silence in their lives about which they have been unable to think clearly and feel coherently. But, in most cases, they do not even know that something is not working right in their lives, that things are not going as they should, that their relationships are not working, or that they are not doing as well in school and career as they should be able to do. Or, they feel anxious or depressed or unreasonably and ineffectively angry. These are the same problems that insecurely attached or disorganized children have in their lives." He continues:

"That which we are unable to communicate because of fear and anxiety gradually becomes obscured and inaccessible, *unknown even to ourselves*" (2013, pp. 193–94, emphasis mine).

Wounds that are unknown to ourselves are not going to be magically healed by access to many lovers. If they were unknown to a person in a monogamous relationship, they will not suddenly become known through polyamory. In individuals whose romantic explorations began with polyamory, attachment wounds may as easily exist as in those who transitioned from monogamy to nonmonogamy. Thus, the proximity of many partners may not increase the opportunity for healing that is sometimes envisioned.

A popular meme says that nobody can meet all the needs and desires a person has. It is an accurate observation, but used as an argument for polyamory, it misses an essential point. It is a romantic dream indeed to find a person who will be one's perfect partner in everything—the best lover, an intellectual equal, someone who is emotionally attuned and supportive, interested in the same things, possessing the same values, and coming from a family one comes to adore. This is Esther Perel's (2007) argument for why those in modern relationships experience so many difficulties. We expect the impossible and, instead of reassessing our expectations, become disappointed with our partners. Perel does not advocate for polyamory; her aim is to explain and soften common relational anxieties. However, the implications are similar. When the choice of monogamy disappoints, because it is marred by unattainable expectations, polyamory may be seen as a relational solution. Some people choose to reach for more rather than reevaluate what they have and, in doing so, hope to stave off the inevitable relational disappointments.

It is not the presence of conflict, but the absence of repair that undermines relationships. If there is such a thing as a therapy mantra, this would be mine. Relationships are not static; relational rifts occur in securely attached couples as they do in anxious, avoidant, and disorganized ones. Affective repair is a key element in the creation of healthy relationships. Secure individuals are better equipped to return to emotional equilibrium, a skill that insecure partners need to develop. The sense of relief and a return to well-being indicate affective repair; the lack of it means the discord has been pushed aside but not resolved. Weathering conflict is a painful process, but when addressed well, it provides partners with a sense of achievement and interpersonal growth.

References

Alexander, F., & French, T. E. (1980). *Psychoanalytic therapy: Principles and applications.* University of Nebraska Press.

Bowlby, J. (1969). *Attachment and loss, Vol. 1: Attachment.* Basic Books.

Bowlby, J. (1973). *Attachment and loss, Vol. 2: Separation: Anxiety and anger.* Basic Books.

Bowlby, J. (1980). *Attachment and loss, Vol. 3: Loss: Sadness and depression.* Basic Books.

Buber, M. (1996). *I and thou.* Touchstone.

Costello, P. (2013). *Attachment-based psychotherapy: Helping patients develop adaptive capacities.* American Psychological Association.

Mikulincer, M., & Shaver, P. R. (2016). *Attachment in adulthood: Structure, dynamics, and change.* Guilford.

Perel, E. (2007). *Mating in captivity: Unlocking erotic intelligence.* Harper.

Shaver, P. R., Schachner, D. A., & Mikulincer, M. (2005). Attachment style, excessive reassurance seeking, relationship processes, and depression. *Personality and Social Psychology Bulletin, 31*(3), 343–359. 10.1177/0146167204271709

Saint-Exupéry, A. (1943). *The little prince.* Harcourt Inc.

18 Fight, Flight, or Freeze: The Neuropsychology of Attachment Psychodynamics

Mona DeKoven Fishbane (2013) remarks, "Throughout life, how we live and how we love shapes our brains and our relationships" (p. xix). Her book bridges findings from years of research and clinical practice on couple's therapy and neurobiology, with a particular focus on neuroplasticity and its power to shape relationships. Our brains are wired for adaptability, and even though we get set in our ways and behaviors with age and experience, we are nonetheless constantly adapting to change. While genes delineate our predispositions, epigenetics influence the expression of genes. It is possible that people who mature within the context of multiple, overlapping love commitments may not only adapt to this lifestyle but also change their expectations of what love is and what it means to be in a relationship.

The key part to this process is how one matures within. Successful relationships, the ones that flourish over time and do not succumb to the numbness of routine and familiarity, are not static. On the contrary, they are dynamic and evolving, integrating at new levels of maturity as the partners successfully master the challenges of life. This is true for monogamous and consensually nonmonogamous relationships.

While some individuals and couples seeking therapy due to the travails of open relationships may represent higher levels of relational maturity, this is not the case for everyone. Relational experience and relational wisdom are not one and the same. Having many partners over time, even if many of them were long term, does not necessarily imply maturity. Similarly, a marriage that has lasted a decade or two, or longer, does not by itself imply relational evolution.

Relationships worth having require ongoing investment. As therapists, we know all too well how many of our clients enter marriages with unrealistic expectations of what commitment means. Most people would readily agree that the Hollywood picture of romance is impractical and naïve; yet, it still seems to shape their views of love. When I first heard a female patient sigh that nobody prepared her for marriage being hard work, I smiled with recognition. When other clients, men and women alike, expressed the same sentiment for the nth time, my smile grew sad. Clichés are easy to dismiss, but they became clichés for a reason; they often express kernels of universal truths. Knowing that successful relationships require a lot of work is a truism; knowing how to do that work is a hard-won skill.

To reiterate an important point, when attempts to address relational hurts repeatedly end in an impasse, it is often due to old attachment injuries. With the partners feeling increasingly more wounded, they default into their predominant survival mechanisms, which renders them even less capable of making repairs. Survival strategies utilized by humans in response to danger are the same as those of other animals—fight, flight, or freeze. Our highly evolved brains do not discriminate between physical and emotional threats; relational perils evoke the same need to protect the self as physical harms do. Survival mechanisms have a defensive and coping purpose, sharing the same aim of escaping real or perceived danger.

Fight, flight, and freeze are, by their very nature, unconscious; we only become aware of them after we have already reacted. Once activated, fight, flight, and freeze responses can be hard to modulate and put a stop to. They feel, and they are, overwhelming. This is what therapists so often witness when working with couples. Seemingly out of nowhere, a calm exchange takes a sudden turn, with one of the partners attacking and the other biting back while simultaneously trying to escape the conflict by leaning as far away from the other person as possible. The argument escalates from arrows to missiles flying back and forth until one of the partners internally collapses. With no enemy to pursue or get away from, the other person's collapse soon follows. A painful silence ensues. Their brains, the conductors and victims of this exchange, have gone from a state of conversational *neutral arousal* to the *hyperarousal* of fight and flight, finally descending to the *hypoarousal* of a freeze. Both hyper- and hypoarousal responses consume large reserves of energy, with one notable difference: fight and flight are action-oriented, easily reenergized by the partner's response. Freeze is a state of ultimate energy depletion; it is physiologically more costly and much harder to recover from (Shore, 2012).

Processing what is going on in order to recover and benefit from this new understanding of attachment dynamics is only attainable when the level of emotional and physiological activation is neither too low nor too high. The state of neutral activation is the realm of therapy; in order to be effective, the psychotherapeutic process has to remain within the edges of the window of emotional tolerance. Once beyond the edges, reflective reasoning is no longer possible as both hyper- and hypoarousal responses interfere with cognitive processing.

The Vulnerability Cycle

While the states of fight, flight, or freeze are distressingly familiar to most couples, very few people are aware of the mechanisms of these responses. More often than not, the three Fs are experienced as out-of-the-blue reactions, their intensity ranging from distressing to frightening, and their course maddeningly difficult to manage. They feel scary, and they leave scars. Like viruses that are first identified by their symptoms, the causes of these intense reactions are not easy to recognize and avoid. Some couples become relatively skillful at diagnosing their triggers, devising more or less adaptive strategies to prevent them from happening, while others resort to more extreme measures of near-complete avoidance of contentious topics. For these couples, communication dwindles down to a few sterile themes, which results in a failure to eliminate the conflict and generate a repair.

Derek and Sandy represent an example of this failure. Unable to make a repair following a conflict, they opted to avoid anything controversial. In therapy, the moment they tried to describe a difficult situation, they erupted in fear and resentment. Derek's explanation of why he was sleeping in the guest bedroom was immediately interrupted by Sandy. She countered his version of events with her account. He fired back, and both, now too preoccupied with making their points, ignored my presence.

Working with couples who swiftly derail is challenging. They do not take the time to listen to each other, never mind the therapist. Their focus is on correcting what the other is saying rather than taking in the message. Michelle Scheinkman and Mona DeKoven Fishbane (2004) developed a model depicting this kind of couple's derailment. They call it the *vulnerability cycle*. The key part of the model is that it depicts cyclical dynamics; one partner's action, verbal or nonverbal, is followed by a reaction, which is followed by a counterreaction, and so on. "The vulnerability cycle highlights the disjuncture between each partner's suffering and the defensive positions they use to cope with that pain. It is these self-protective strategies that keep them in a cycle and lead them to derail. When a couple relates from survival strategy to survival strategy their more vulnerable feelings remain hidden and they become increasingly disconnected" (Scheinkman & Werneck, 2010, p. 493). When hostility is high, it is easy to forget that underneath the anger there are layers of fear and pain. When a couple's survival strategies are blasting, the therapist needs to be active.

It took several weeks for Derek and Sandy to be able to absorb and utilize the details of the vulnerability model. They made an agreement to park difficult topics until our meetings. Their conversations, at least in the office, became calmer. Feeling less urge to correct, they were slowly learning to recognize each other's vulnerabilities.

Psychodynamic and systems theories have long recognized the tenacity of reciprocal patterns of interaction in couples' dynamics. The value of the vulnerability cycle is that it is not concerned with pathology the way traditional analytic theory had been, but instead highlights the ways a couple is *trying to manage* their vulnerabilities. Even if the survival strategies backfire, the emphasis is on the fact that the couple is trying. Partners long to be heard and known, but they do not know how to break out of the problematic cycle. They repeat patterns learned in their own upbringing—the way conflicts were handled in their families of origin. They fight the best way they know how.

Scheinkman and DeKoven Fishbane (2004) use the term *survival positions* to describe beliefs and strategies that individuals adopt to protect and manage their vulnerabilities. The purpose of these positions is to preserve a sense of integrity and control in emotionally undermining situations. Survival positions usually develop before they can be put into words; they are action-centered. Their aim is to protect the self at all costs and are accompanied by little or no reflection. The other person's vulnerability is rarely recognized, and even when it is acknowledged, it is often ignored. What partners need in order to break the cycle is an ability to critically evaluate their strategies. Coaching them to reflect rather than react is the task of therapy.

As therapy continued, Derek and Sandy's levels of reactivity were gradually diminishing. Reluctantly, they were learning to reflect on their survival strategies. They were impatient with the process, but they were making some headway, and that gave them hope. Reflecting critically on the patterns of conflict in their families of origin turned out to be particularly helpful. They were becoming more acutely aware of how these familiar patterns were failing to protect them from feeling vulnerable.

For highly volatile couples, a significant portion of therapy involves learning how to slow down. In the early stages of treatment, my role was that of a traffic cop, giving a motion to go to one person at a time. Their exasperation was obvious; when Sandy stopped talking, Derek would impatiently ask, "Is it my turn now?" and escalate fast. But, when forced to wait for their turn, they were absorbing more of what the other person wanted them to hear. They were evolving in their reflective capacity and developing empathy toward each other. As time went on and neither one of them needed to remain rigid in their survival positions, Derek and Sandy were gradually extricating themselves from their vulnerability cycle.

A day came when Sandy said with a self-conscious smile, "You know, I'm now so much more aware of what I'm doing to make him mad, and I find myself not wanting to do the right thing, but then I remind myself that I have a choice." Derek looked at her in surprise. "You do?" he asked. She nodded. "Yes, I often still feel that it's all your fault, but somewhere deep inside I know it's not the case." Derek reached out for her hand, and they fell into a hug.

They fell into a hug. Behind that hug, there were the years of arguments and lack of repair. Derek and Sandy were one of those couples who believed that opening up would help their marriage. And somehow, in the midst of the arguing, they managed to remain cordial about their polyamorous arrangements. More so, they believed that they would not be together if not for polyamory. Derek and Sandy were a couple against the odds. They got married because, after a few years of cohabitation, it felt like the right thing to do. They were very different as individuals to begin with, and both lacked the relational maturity to manage most conflicts. As their awareness increased, they realized that, while polyamory helped to diffuse some of their relational tension, their marriage was depleted and needed protection.

Feeling less vulnerable in each other's presence, they started to focus on their marriage as a relationship worth guarding.

References

DeKoven Fishbane, M. (2013). *Loving with the brain in mind: Neurobiology & couple therapy*. Norton.

Scheinkman, M. D., & DeKoven Fishbane, M. (2004). The vulnerability cycle: Working with impasses in couples' therapy. *Family Process, 43*(3), 279–299.

Scheinkman, M. D., & Werneck, D. (2010). Disarming jealousy in couples relationships: A multidimensional approach. *Family Process, 49*(4), 486–502.

Shore, A. N. (2012). *The science of the art of psychotherapy*. Norton.

19 Self-Expansion Model: Is Polyamory Expanding the Potential?

It makes intuitive sense that partners include and contain parts of each other. The self-expansion model proposed by Aron and Aron (1986, 2006; Aron et al., 1991) elaborates on this dynamic. This model has two fundamental tenets. The first, called *motivational principle*, is based on the recognition that people seek to expand their potential through exploration, curiosity, or competence. The motivational principle helps them attain their goals. The second, called *inclusion-of-other-in-the-self principle*, observes that humans seek to expand the self through intimate relationships. It is through close relationships that our identities are formed and explored. The other offers resources and perspectives, many of which we incorporate as our own—the other gets included in the self. Even if we are aware of the specific choices we make and conduct in the service of this inclusion, the self-expansion process is not always conscious.

Being involved in a new relationship is frequently connected to a rapid expansion of the self. High levels of energy combined with the positive affect that is usually present in the formation of new relationships support this expansion. This urge to expand is a hallmark of NRE; partners new to each other want more and cannot wait to get there. The obvious contrast to this self-expansion is the precipitous de-expansion of the self. It occurs during a heartbreak, and it accompanies other significant losses that affect one's sense of self.

The model of inclusion-of-other-in-the-self refers to experiencing the world, to some extent, from the partner's point of view. The results of this inclusion are wonderful when the partners' interests are aligned and not so much when they are discordant. Needless to say, expansion of the self does not solely occur when conditions are optimal; we learn through adversity as well. Perhaps this explains why polyamorous communities focus so much on compersion, seeing it as an opportunity to avert de-expansion of the self. If NRE makes jealousy and envy more or less unavoidable, what is better than turning the lemon of jealous feelings into the lemonade of cherishing the expansion of self of one's partner with somebody else?

The self-expansion model parallels the premises of attachment theory. The notion of a secure base allowing for safe exploration has implications for infants and lovers alike. Staying securely connected to the caregiver, the infant's safe haven, while exploring the environment, promotes development and growth—the very model of self-expansion. Secure attachment to the loved one is confidence-building; there is an implicit trust in the support and positive regard of the caregiver. In anxious attachment, the availability of the caregiver is inconsistent—one moment the support is there, the next it is absent. Trying to hold on to the caregiver is the logical solution from an emotional point of view; perhaps they would stay put if one stays close enough to them. Alternatively, other attachment figures may become a relative substitute for the safe base, allowing for tentative expansion. In avoidant attachment, the belief in the loved one being available is long discarded, and the person invests in avoiding the relational risks associated with intimacy.

There is an intriguing correlation between attachment styles and unrequited love. As expected, secure individuals are the least likely to engage in relationships in which love is unreciprocated. Unsurprisingly, anxious individuals are the most likely to hold on to unrequited love, hoping it will morph into a loving relationship if they try hard enough. Avoidant people appear to embrace unreturned love; they experience it less frequently than anxiously attached individuals but more often than securely attached ones. The likely explanation is that unrequited love provides them with the opportunity to be in love, which is culturally valued, but without the risks associated with an intimate relationship (Aron & Aron, 2006).

Over the past 30 years, an extensive body of research has confirmed the initial predictions of the self-expansion model. The rate of expansion skyrockets in a new relationship and slows down when the partner becomes familiar (Xu, Lewandowski, & Aron, 2016). This phenomenon may explain the unconscious drawing power of polyamory; instead of withering within, or resorting to serial monogamy, being involved with multiple partners may provide access to continuing self-expansion. However, this does not mean that long-term relationships, both monogamous and nonmonogamous, are doomed. Research on self-expansion verifies the ongoing need to engage in the kind of motivational activities that promote intra- and interpersonal growth. These are pursuit-type activities, rooted in challenge, novelty, and interest, which, as evidence suggests, not only facilitate sexual desire but also act as a buffer against its decline over time. Engaging in challenging and novel enterprises together increases the possibility of surprise, which in turn promotes a sense of connection and prevents the decline of romantic love.

Self-expansion can be contrasted with what I am tempted to call a not-enough-to-expand model. Spending time together is not enough to promote relational growth; it matters enormously how partners engage with each other. Endless processing not followed by connection-enhancing activities is not enough to expand the relationship. Similarly, scheduling a date night that consists of watching TV (which often feels like a luxury because it occurs so infrequently due to the partners' busy schedules) may feel good, but it is not enough either. *Self-expansion elsewhere* does not enhance *self-expansion together.* When what is left in the relationship is boredom and longing, it is not enough of a foundation to build relational satisfaction upon. Boredom, just like unreciprocated yearning, promotes loneliness; together, they may indicate that the relationship is suffering from too much of not-enough.

References

Aron, A., & Aron, E. N. (1986). *Love and the expansion of self: Understanding attraction and satisfaction.* Hemisphere Publishing Corp./Harper & Row Publishers.

Aron, A., & Aron, E. N. (2006). Romantic relationships from the perspectives of the self-expansion model and attachment theory: Partially overlapping circles. In M. Mikulincer & G. S. Goodman (Eds.), *Dynamics of romantic love: Attachment, caregiving, and sex* (pp. 359–382). The Guilford Press.

Aron, A., Aron, E. N., Tudor, M., & Nelson, G. (1991). Close relationships as including other in the self. *Journal of Personality and Social Psychology, 60*(2), 241–253. https://doi.org/10.1037/0022-3514.60.2.241

Xu, X., Lewandowski, G. W., & Aron, A. (2016). The self-expansion model and optimal relationship development. In C. R. Knee & H. T. Reis (Eds.), *Positive approaches to optimal relationship development* (pp. 79–100). Cambridge University Press.

20 Relationship Escalator Versus Stages of Couple Development

From dating to talk of exclusivity to engagement and marriage (if that is one's preference), followed by a child, then another—these stages of deepening commitment in a monogamous partnership are fairly predictable and more or less taken for granted, so much so that their order is experienced as oppressive by some. Veering off the predictable path, such as when a couple decides not to have children, evokes questions. These internalized dynamics of monogamous life are protected by existing sociocultural norms. The same dynamics can also get destabilized by the disruptive entrance of a third party. The third can come in the shape of a newly discovered affair, overwhelming work demands, serious illness, intrusive in-laws, and so on.

Polyamory and, more broadly, nonmonogamy, may present differently from monogamy, but at the core, they are still intersubjective relational dynamics. In polyamory, the effort to escape the dreaded relationship escalator fails to take into consideration that, akin to individual development, all committed relationships go through developmental stages. Relationships change as partners' intimate knowledge of each other deepens over time. Assessing where the couple is developmentally may provide important information regarding their decision to open up.

The developmental model of couple's therapy proposed by Ellyn Bader and Peter Pearson (1988) has its roots in the work of Margaret Mahler, who delineated stages of early childhood development. The connection between the two is obvious; as children grow up, they reach new levels of maturity. Long-term romantic relationships go through their own stages of development. The first stage, that of the honeymoon, usually receives the most attention, often becoming a benchmark for later comparisons. Who has not heard a struggling couple complain that things are not as they used to be when they were dating? Needless to say, comparing the later stages of a couple's life to this initial phase is not fair; yet, the notion of lost perfection often prevails.

In Bader and Pearson's terminology, the honeymoon period is referred to as the stage of *initial bonding* or *symbiosis*. Falling in love is characterized by the desire for closeness and unrelenting delight in the idealized beloved, who can hardly do anything wrong. New lovers in the throes of passion eagerly focus on their similarities and ignore their differences. Sex is also likely to take center stage, at the cost of other relationships and activities. Tennov (1998) called this period of being intoxicated with love *limerence*, describing it as an involuntary state of intense romantic yearning.

The stage that follows symbiosis is called *differentiation*. This stage carries significant challenges. Sometimes referred to as "make it or break it," it requires a couple to be able to deal with differences and learn ways to resolve conflict. How well partners master this step has far-reaching implications. A couple's overall well-being and a sense of trust depends on successful mastering of this step. Partners who cannot tolerate their differences get stuck in perpetual conflict. In contrast, those who learn that being a couple consists of being two separate individuals choosing to be together are more likely to move on to the next phase.

The *practicing* stage consists of finding the balance between independence and connection, between the demands of the external world and the internal needs of the couple. It is at this point that partners are likely to explore and invest in friendships outside the couple. It is also a time of greater power struggles. Depending on how this balancing act goes, partners' sense of self-worth is likely to soar or suffer. Couples that successfully manage the tasks of comings and goings, who are able to discern between needs and neediness, are likely to move to the phase of reconciliation and reunion, called *rapprochement*.

Couples that reach rapprochement experience a deeper sense of harmony. Aspects of coupledom previously considered ordinary and unremarkable become deeply appreciated. Partners' individual quirks become endearing. In this stage of increased trust and openness, there is much less need to guard against vulnerability, and the couple's sex life often reaches new heights of satisfaction.

The final stage of couples' development is called *synergy*, which is based on the recognition that true partnership makes each individual stronger and more capable than if they were independent. This is the point in a couple's expansion when the deepest kind of intimacy has been reached.

Couples who merely endure, but not thrive, are acutely aware of the torment of their disconnect. In spite of misery and distress, they may not seek therapy until their pain reaches agonizing levels. In the past, when divorce was considered a stigma and the options of changing the marital structure were practically nonexistent, these couples may have resigned themselves to suffering. Divorce no longer carries the stamp of condemnation, but it is not an option that people choose with an easy heart. Many couples endure anguish for a very long time before seeking help; however, when they finally admit that something has to change, their sense of despair becomes acute, demanding immediate relief. Having suffered for so long, many are no longer able to tolerate the pain of working through difficulties. From failing to reach out for help, they now demand a quick resolution of their problems. Many such couples reason that nonmonogamy would solve their dilemma.

The developmental model of couple's therapy emphasizes the importance of the individual as well as the couple's evolution and growth. In other words, they are interdependent. When one of the partners is stuck in an earlier developmental stage, it prevents the couple as a whole from evolving. Alternatively, a couple may come to an impasse upon failing to successfully manage the developmental tasks of a particular stage. When a couple's distress reaches the point of simultaneously seeking therapy and considering nonmonogamy, the couple's developmental level is usually revealed. Sometimes that level is actually quite different from what it initially appeared to be. Considering the phrase used by so many newcomers to therapy, "We're each other's best friend; everything is great (but we have no sex)," it may seem that these couples are in the stage of rapprochement. Oftentimes busy with parenting and careers, they indeed seem to have mastered the developmental tasks of differentiation and practicing, the stages typically imbued with the greatest relational challenges. Many of these couples do present harmoniously, and when describing their relational history, they agree on the details without arguing, together weaving a congruous narrative. It is only when their difficulties with sex and intimacy are explored that their differences emerge.

The discrepancy might be striking at first, but perhaps it is not so strange. The challenges of work and careers can be abundant, but usually there is a lot of understanding and support available along the way. Similarly, being parents can be overwhelming and sometimes lonely, but one is not alone in this endeavor. Access to resources may vary, but there is no lack of validation and assistance when confronting parenting difficulties. Conflicts with families of origin, when present, are usually openly discussed. In contrast, partners in committed, long-term relationships are reluctant to openly admit to their struggles with sex and intimacy. Shame and embarrassment are powerful inhibitors that prevent people from raising the issue behind closed doors, and even more so in front of others. As a result, difficulties accumulate until they finally reach the breaking point.

Furthermore, it is easier to accept differences in leisure-time activities than to tolerate discrepancies in sexual preferences and desires. Even quarreling partners learn to negotiate conflicts regarding spectator sports versus shopping, nature versus city vacations, carnivore versus vegan diet, extrovert versus introvert needs, and so on. Sex, however, is a notable exception. Disagreements regarding physical intimacy are experienced as a threat in long-term relationships. What starts as a seed of dissatisfaction grows into a hedge of conflict. "Why can't you be more like me?" partners ask. Or "You were different in the beginning," which implies "You must be denying me what I need, and I don't understand why." No amount of explaining seems to reduce tensions or increase understanding. The gap grows larger, first getting labeled as a desire discrepancy and finally being categorized as sexual incompatibility. The initial stage of a couple's symbiotic limerence becomes the paradise lost that needs to be rediscovered.

The search for the lost bliss compels some couples to open up, a process full of hurdles. Opening up brings to light what is still vital in the relationship and what is beyond repair. As I described earlier, many couples create a sense of relational safety and security by developing a *fantasy bond* (Firestone, 1987). The fantasy bond, as opposed to a genuine connection, provides an illusion of affinity when love is fractured or gone. This fantasy protects against the vulnerability of loneliness, against emotional deprivation and relational emptiness. The illusory bond preserves the *form* of the relationship while concealing the fact that the *substance* is gone. This emptiness is discernible in communication when the partners communicate with each other as if they are discussing real issues and expressing genuine emotions—their words aim to preserve the illusion that real feelings still exist. However, it is easier to act "as if" in terms of love than it is to fake sexual interest. When the latter becomes intolerable, the state of the first is revealed. The process of opening up may expose the crumbling fantasy bond and lay bare the wreckage of love.

There are no tests or exams that can be taken to grant passage from one developmental stage to the next. But, like a student who excels in some classes and gets by in others, couples may master certain developmental tasks while skimming through other ones. The stages of development are relatively fluid, and the school of life is very busy, with no monitoring of progress available along the way. As a result, certain deficits in a couple's development may not become apparent until revealed by a crisis or some event serving as a catalyst. When a crisis arrives, nobody grades one's performance as harshly as one's partner, usually without comprehending their own contribution to the problem. Many mature relationships seemingly in the rapprochement or synergy stage may be stuck in the differentiation phase in the sexual arena. They may not have developed good-enough skills to manage diverging needs without the entire relationship feeling threatened.

I find it helpful to think about couples' developmental stages from the dynamic maturational perspective developed by Patricia McKinsey Crittenden (McKinsey Crittenden & Landini, 2011). McKinsey Crittenden emphasizes that attachment is not a passive state developed in infancy, but a dynamic, adaptive strategy. Adaptations are context-dependent and, in couples, both partners influence the dynamics of attachment. When three or more partners are closely involved, the combined dynamics of the system influence attachment patterns. As Crittenden observes, security does not require adaptation; everyone survives secure attachment. The trick is to survive danger. It is the other forms of attachment—avoidant-dismissive and anxious-preoccupied—that are actual adaptations to the realities of unsafe contexts. By the nature of its shifts, the relational environment of polyamory is inherently uncertain, and an increase in attachment insecurity can be expected.

Shifting attachment dynamics and mixed developmental stages played out in front of my eyes when I worked with Claire, Larry, and Marilou. The three lived together and came to therapy as a polycule. Their triad was characterized by a strong fantasy bond—"We're a nonhierarchical poly family"—and, as it turned out, rather weak relational bonds. In addition to family sessions, I arranged for a handful of individual meetings to learn what each person was struggling with. The individual appointments illuminated the partners' respective survival strategies; they were a heady mixture of dismissive and preoccupied but never manifested in a disorganized fashion. On the contrary, one person's avoidant tactics co-occurred with another person's preoccupation. It was especially visible in the women's dynamics. Larry reveled in the nonhierarchical polyamory; it satisfied his fantasy of an egalitarian relationship. The women, on the other hand, endured it. Claire and Marilou were "barely there" partners; they found themselves in a living situation that neither of them particularly enjoyed. Secretly, each hoped that Larry would settle with her as the primary partner. In individual sessions, they described the strikingly similar strategies they employed to get Larry's attention. When clear communication of their needs failed, they would resort to avoiding putting almost anything on their shared calendar, with the hope that Larry would notice that something was amiss. At times, the calendar was full of Claire's plans and nearly empty of Marilou's suggestions, and at other times, the picture was reversed. The women did not cease being preoccupied with Larry; it was in the avoidant strategies that they were inversely matched.

According to the dynamic maturational approach, there are three systems of information processing that underlie attachment and development: somatic, affective, and cognitive. As infants, we process information somatically; as the brain develops, emotional processing arises; and finally, as the brain matures, the cognitive organization of information becomes a part of the overall system. These three ways of transforming information into something we can utilize remain relevant throughout our lifespan. Some people favor one type of processing over the others—frequently, it is cognitive over somatic and affective.

Larry was prone to intellectualization; the empty calendar spaces did not tug on his emotions. Valuing cognition to the extreme, he failed to notice his partners' distress, even when it was communicated directly. He was also unaware of most of the physiological signs of discomfort. His de-stressing strategy was to eat and play video games. Larry's avoidant withdrawal was maddening to the women, but because he could eloquently engage in conversations regarding the adaptive advantages of technology (i.e., video games), each woman felt at a loss for words to explain their displeasure. Claire and Marilou were dimly aware of the similarities between their adaptive strategies, but because they were not at ease with each other, they rarely made any comparisons. When I pointed out to the three of them how they were using avoidance as relational adaptations, they were struck. Claire did not feel secure in her attachment to Larry, and neither did Marilou. Larry did not feel safe in a one-to-one attachment, hence his adamant favoring of nonhierarchy. As was his style, he explained his preference for nonhierarchy as ideological; they were equals, so nobody should be prioritized. When he came to realize that, with his introduction of nonhierarchical polyamory, he was achieving the opposite, Larry was flabbergasted. He was protecting himself and, by doing so, had prioritized his comfort over the well-being of his partners.

As a polycule, the three had never experienced initial bonding or symbiosis, although Larry had experienced it with each woman separately—first with Claire, then Marilou. In this respect, aside from sexual openness, his commitment to each woman was not that different from serial monogamy. The triad was stuck somewhere in the stage of differentiation mixed with practicing. The women were committed to being with Larry but not with each other, and as he was savoring the nonhierarchical arrangement, the women's sense of self-worth was rapidly diminishing.

When the capability to recognize emotional and somatic signals is reduced, people lose the ability to use these sources of information to their advantage. Larry processed information cognitively and was cut off from the somatic and affective sources of attachment data. Claire and Marilou were aware of their emotions, but had learned to doubt their validity in the relationship with Larry. If they had been closer to each other, the women might have discovered similarities in their struggles, but because they rarely talked, they could not validate each other's feelings. Recognizing their parallels in therapy helped them to realize the value of affects and somatic reactions as a source of information regarding attachment.

Insight can be hard; what becomes known cannot be un-known. The realization that nonhierarchy was creating inequality, with only one person's needs actually being met, created a predictable fracture in this vulnerable triad. The women could see how their strategies of avoidance were adaptive to the situation, but ultimately not how they wanted to be in a relationship. Our therapy together led to a few behavioral changes, but more importantly, it created a shift in their frame of mind. While still living in the same household for the time being, the women decided to pursue individual therapy to figure out what they wanted.

References

Bader, E., & Pearson, P. T. (1988). *In quest of the mythical mate: A developmental approach to diagnosis and treatment in couples' therapy.* Brunner/Mazel.

Firestone, R. W. (1987). *The fantasy bond: Structure of psychological defenses.* The Glendon Association.

McKinsey Crittenden, P., & Landini, A. (2011). *Assessing adult attachment: A dynamic-maturational approach to discourse analysis.* W. W. Norton.

Tennov, D. (1998). *Love and limerence: The experience of being in love.* Scarborough House.

21 Examining Countertransference: Polyamory in the Heteronormative and Mononormative World

Assumptions About Heteronormativity and Mononormativity

The two most common forms of normativity, *heteronormativity* and *mononormativity*, dominate the theory and practice of psychotherapy. Over the past decades, the concept of heteronormativity was at least partially offset by queer theory, which originated in gay and lesbian studies. Together with feminist perspectives, queer theory has influenced contemporary relational thinking by challenging the perceptions of sexuality and gender norms present in heterosexual narratives. From these perspectives, gender and sexual expressions represent more than biology; they are social constructs. These social influences determine whom one should love, outlining how the relationship of the self to others might be acted out.

If heteronormativity is more willingly questioned, mononormativity—the assumption of monogamy underlying a romantic relationship—is less readily contested. Whether the focus is on heterosexual or same-sex relationships, the common expectation is that the individual or the couple in the therapist's office is monogamous or, at least, tries to be monogamous. This expectation exists in spite of widespread acknowledgment of the challenges of monogamy, especially in long-term commitments. Clinicians, highly aware of the pain associated with transgressions and affairs, are skilled at helping clients to manage the trials of longing for more. Consciously or not, therapists therefore reinforce the binary reality of monogamy: Staying within the bounds of monogamy is healthy; straying from these bounds is problematic. Along those lines, monogamy for life may have been replaced with serial monogamy, but the basic structure of a romantic narrative remains monogamous.

Working with polyamorous clients inevitably pushes clinicians to revisit their assumptions about hetero- and mononormativity. Therapists are advised to avoid concentrating on overt sexual behavior when treating gay, lesbian, or bisexual clients. Instead, they should focus on examining the quality of relationships, as is routinely done in the treatment of heterosexual individuals and couples. This caution applies with equal weight to polyamorous relationships.

The knowledge of whom one is involved with, and presumably has sex with, provides little information regarding the intrapsychic experience of a poly person. As an example, many of my patients talk about their kink or dominance/submission longings. They are usually well-informed about the logistics of these arrangements (i.e., the importance of consent to make the experience feel safe, a clear delineation of boundaries, a discussion of activities that may or may not be involved, and so on). In contrast, these same individuals seldom wonder how they may be impacted by the exploration of these BDSM fantasies. Their experience on the intrapsychic level might be considerably different from what they expect they will feel. After all, a desire for a specific kinky exploration may reflect more than a mere yearning for heightened sexual arousal. In addition, it would be wrong to assume that every person who participates in a kink activity is drawn to this kind of sexual expression. People may agree to play with bondage, dominance/submission, or any other kind of BDSM practice not for their own pleasure but for the sake of their partners. These individuals' inner psychic experience may not align with their overt sexual behavior.

As important as it is to deconstruct traditional categories of gender and sexuality, it is only a part of the clinical work. Being able to help clients own their experience requires transcending the presumptions of what is "natural" and "normal." The assumption of naturalness creates pressures, and polyamorous individuals are already sidelined by mononormative narratives. Simultaneously, polyamory is not any less a social construct than monogamy. Identifying as polyamorous may put a strain on individuals who wish to be poly but struggle with the reality of this relational format. The resulting intrapsychic conflict is often expressed as "not doing polyamory right." The struggle with polyamory is then perceived as an indicator of something being wrong with the person who is not able to demonstrate ease with this lifestyle rather than the possibility that, for that person, polyamory as a social paradigm might be promising more than it can deliver. Working through this intrapsychic conflict is essential for the development of a healthy self-concept—the very opposite of trying to fit in with the label.

The impact of the therapist's self on the therapy process and outcome is well documented (Norcross, 2002; Wachtel, 2008). The task of creating a secure and authentic therapeutic environment in which the process of change can safely unfold is vital regardless of the theoretical orientation of the clinician. The therapist's conscious and unconscious beliefs, emotional reactions, and internal motives are as important to examine as are the beliefs, feelings, and conflicts of the clients. It is relevant in all kinds of therapy, but particularly vital when working with couples, monogamous and nonmonogamous. Most clinicians are trained to provide effective individual treatment, with much less attention given to training in couple's therapy. The risk of unconsciously siding with one partner and alienating the other in a couple's context is very real. This is especially likely when the therapist's beliefs align with mononormativity and one member of the couple is leaning toward monogamy while the other is not. In those instances, retaining the stance of therapeutic neutrality by not revealing one's conscious biases or inclinations may un-consciously reinforce heterosexual and monogamous normativity. To illus-trate, a therapist wearing a wedding band signals her marital status; the ring also evokes assumptions of mononormativity. Avoiding any reference to this therapist's relational status may convey a message that nonmonogamy is not a comfortable topic. In contrast, examining the shared subjective experience between the clinician and her clients in response to the wedding band can promote openness and increase trust.

Therapists inadvertently add to non-normative patients' distress when they fail to recognize the price these individuals may pay for their divergence from normativity. The cost of living in secret can be substantial, but so can be the toll of coming out. Most therapists are aware of the negative impact of heterosexism or internalized homophobia on sexual minority clients. It is not likely that a clinician working with a gay, lesbian, or bisexual individual will question her client's sexual orientation. In contrast, polyamorous clients may be met with doubt regarding their motivation to be romantically involved with more than one person. The risk of a therapeutic injury due to overt or covert skepticism is real. At the same time, the clinical presentation of polyamory can be confounding. Many individuals and couples show up in the therapist's office declaring themselves as poly while struggling with feelings of ambivalence. On the receiving end, a therapist only vaguely familiar with polyamory may feel even more confused than the person or people in front of him.

In pre-polyamory times, if partners in solidly committed relationships hap-pened to experience an extra-dyadic crush, they were likely to feel conflicted about what they wanted, but not confused about who they were. The internal and interpersonal conflict resulting from such a crush could range from mildly to extremely painful, but the options were straightforward—staying with the person one was with, or moving on to explore the new relationship. Both presumed monogamy, so the standard romantic assumption—the social pres-sure to desire a monogamous romantic relationship—remained unchallenged. The key points were romance and monogamy, even if the latter was of the serial kind. Polyamory emerged, representing an alternative view that promotes the possibility of *romantic nonmonogamy.*

Embracing polyamory offers, at least in theory, the graceful resolution of a charged situation when one discovers love and desire for more than one person. Instead of being trapped in an either-or option, many clients con-clude that because they have loving feelings toward two (and sometimes more than two) people, it must mean they are poly. Given the polyamory postulate, it is a reasonable, albeit not necessarily accurate, assumption. Having a new presupposition for the old-fashioned confusion does not dis-solve the conflict. Many individuals and couples seek therapy due to am-bivalent romantic feelings. Some of them may have more exposure to polyamory than the average therapist; however, their exposure does not necessarily make them any sager.

Examined Life: The Power of Countertransference

Emotional and relational confusion combined with intellectual exposure to polyamory are not enough to make a person poly. Identifying as polyamorous is a lived-through, examined experience. Robert Nozick, in his book *The Examined Life*, writes, "To live an examined life is to make a self-portrait. Staring at us from his later self-portraits, Rembrandt is not simply someone who looks like that but one who sees and knows himself *as* that, with the courage this requires. We see him knowing himself" (2006, pp. 12–13). To illustrate the difference between a superficial versus deep *knowing*, Nozick compares a photograph to a painted portrait. A photo is a snapshot. It is superficial in that it freezes a tiny moment of time, only allowing for the surface of a person to show. A snapshot can never have the depth of a painting, which is the result of hours spent scrutinizing every aspect of a subject. The time spent examining accounts for the difference. Reading about polyamory is a snapshot, whereas experimenting with polyamory is like a series of photographs, giving one a sense of who the person in them might be. But in order to know oneself with unflinching honesty, the experience needs to be examined over and over again. The process of learning who one is is not free from confusion and it benefits from therapeutic counsel.

There is a difference between drifting and steering through existence—a life examined tends to be a life worth living. The practice of polyamory presents with a certain paradox in that it encourages people toward examination, while subtly, or not so subtly, limiting that examination to what is deemed socially acceptable in poly circles. An authentic introspection requires openness to all feelings, including the ones that cause distress, such as a desire to be *the one* to one's lover. Because such yearnings fall out of line with polyamorous thinking, these desires are often suppressed or disowned. Being able to differentiate between one's voice and the voices of others promotes the development of a healthy sense of self. Along those lines, my goal for my clients is to make space for examination of their relational choices regardless of the format they may take. Many a time this process involves wavering between monogamy, polyamory, and other forms of consensual nonmonogamy. Indeed, an authentic examination encompasses openness to experience, is benefited by flexibility in thinking, and requires a realistic appraisal of one's environment. When relationships are approached with open-minded curiosity, they reward the seeker with a greater sense of intra- and interpersonal competence. It is a process leading to individual and relational growth.

Authentic introspection in therapy with poly individuals also involves the therapist listening to her countertransference. In order for clinicians to truly "see" a person, we need to perceive their individuality as embedded in the culture and embodied in their relational capacity. Multiple factors, including attachment, social influences, and variations in an embodiment, underlie the formation of the self and the capability to relate. Who the person is and how she is able to relate applies to all kinds of relationships, from traditionally monogamous to polyamorous. This multifaceted perspective allows therapists to better differentiate between the healthy and the pathological. Polyamory juxtaposed with traditions of monogamy may come across as commitment-phobic; however, as a contemporary expression of relatedness in certain sociocultural contexts, it is no longer maladaptive.

What then is healthy and adaptive, and what is unhealthy or maladaptive in polyamorous ways of relating? Psychoanalysis no longer zooms in on sexuality as the core of individual development; sexual emphasis has been replaced with a broader view of a person's overall relational capacities. However, it would be a mistake to overlook the reality that "it is in the sexual arena that core conflicts and personality schisms are played out in a variety of adaptive and maladaptive efforts at resolution" (Celenza, 2014, p. 3).

It is especially in the realm of polyamory that sexual longings and a need for relational safety can erupt into conflict. A therapist working with this population must therefore discern between countertransference as a reaction toward nonmonogamy—a representation of the pathological "other"—and countertransference as a clinically useful response to the underlying pathology *within* the poly context.

The answer to the question of how to deal with countertransference is deceptively simple—therapists need to examine their reactions. They need to notice what belongs where. Are judgments about the person or couple on the couch interfering with their ability to be present? Clinicians often worry about appearing judgmental or, in the case of polyamorous clients, outdatedly conservative. When consulting on poly cases, I advise that it is fine to have reactions and to stand by one's own traditional perceptions, as long as the therapist is able to help the patients decide if what they are choosing is working for them. Helpful inquiries that address the quality of the relationship include: How do the relationships you are in feel to you? Are these relationships of your choice? Is there an internalized aggression manifested by self-blame for not doing polyamory right? Is there an externalized aggression? What other emotions are present when the relationship is described? Envy? Anxiety? Sadness? Anger? Joy?

A clinician's reactions to the material presented contain information relevant for the course of treatment. A case I consulted on comes to my mind. The therapist seeking consultation felt befuddled by a married couple he was working with. They expressed much love for each other and seemed to think highly of their relationship. The couple sought therapy to get help with opening up, to make sure "they did it right." The therapist felt uneasy but tried not to challenge the couple, assuming their decision to be poly was well thought through, given how easily poly terms rolled off their tongues. As I listened to the details, I was struck by the immaturity of this couple. Their perception of polyamory was highly idealized; they imagined that once they worked through the hurdles of opening up, which they assuredly said they were prepared for, each of them would find new partners who would easily fit into their vision of one happy poly family. I asked the therapist what made him feel reluctant to express his doubts about their vision, and learned that he wanted to come across as nonjudgmental. He questioned their eagerness to open up, but knowing little about polyamory, he did not want to appear ignorant or insensitive. As a result, he was at risk for not providing enough of a container for the couple's feelings of hurt and ambivalence. I suggested the therapist revisit the clients' family-of-origin stories in order to better understand what this couple was looking for in polyamory. It turned out that they had not dealt with many life setbacks and had little experience with conflict. They were on a fast track to prematurely open up, with potentially irreversible relational consequences. The open space the therapist strived to provide had counteracted this couple's need to contain what had started to spill out too fast.

As the example above illustrates, when paying attention to countertransference reactions, what might sound like a judgment might actually be clinical acuity. People new to polyamory may not feel concerned with the relational difficulties that open relationships may present, nor be troubled by living on the edge of the normative culture. On the contrary, they may feel energized by what appears to be an elegant solution to a complicated relational situation. Given the increasing popularity of polyamory, they imagine it will be easy to find suitable partners; however, they may not take into account that the process of opening up and forming multiple relationships is likely to be more challenging than they foresee. Online dating, which is the primary way of finding partners for monogamous and nonmonogamous individuals, comes with a lot of promise; what it is able to deliver is a different matter. Finding suitable partners is as unreliable in polyamory as it is in monogamy.

The limited availability of suitable partners notwithstanding, it often strikes me how frequently polyamorous clients hope for so much and end up settling for so little. In polyamory, the term *partner* is applied with equal ease to substantial as well as weak connections. A person one lives with is a partner, but so is a person who lives thousands of miles away and is seen only once or twice a year. In some cases, holding on to such peripheral connections reveals a defensive reaction against loneliness. It is born of comparison of the self to others who appear to be more successful at securing multiple partners. In other instances, a fear of failing at polyamory makes people hold on to flimsy relationships. At times, those secondary connections sound more desperate than fulfilling. A therapist who validates too quickly may inadvertently help solidify something that is not working well for an individual or a couple, thus deepening their sense of personal inadequacy. By contrast, a clinician whose mononormativity-related countertransference makes him take an overly reserved stance may undermine clients' confidence in therapy.

Single individuals whose relational experiences involve polyamory may overtly identify as nonmonogamous while feeling internally conflicted—the limited availability of suitable poly partners being one of the examples of this discord. For some, returning to monogamy is a relief. For others, going back to monogamy is experienced as a personal failure. The latter stems, to a large degree, from how the issue is presented in the poly community. There is a saying in polyamory that "Once you have embarked on this lifestyle there is no return." That saying conveys a sense of the inevitability of polyamory once tasted and experienced. This is embedded in the sentiment expressed by many clients that "polyamory just makes sense," which constitutes yet another example of polyromanticism. The preference for monogamy can be disowned, and when it happens, the consequence is often emotional distress. Anxiety, guilt, shame, and a sense of alienation are often the result of intrapsychic struggles with polyamory. Experiencing oneself as a failure at the relational format that is supposed to be "more natural than monogamy" may increase one's sense of personal inadequacy and tap into hidden reservoirs of self-doubt and other negative self-perceptions. Examining countertransference reactions to such thoughts and feelings can help to facilitate the patient's own exploratory process. If I inquire, "I find it striking that you feel so guilty about leaving polyamory. I wonder why?" my reaction is to the patient's feeling of *guilt* and not to polyamory as such.

When clients present as a couple, their feelings of ambivalence tend to be more in the open. In these cases, it is common to hear diverging stories, one of a spouse who advocates for an open relationship and the other of a partner who unenthusiastically agrees. The advocating spouse often presents a coherent argument that describes how polyamory would fit into their life. The reluctant partner commonly feels that there is no other choice but to agree if their marriage is to survive. As a result, the rationalization of adopting polyamory often sounds more thought through than the less cohesive counterargument of the hesitant spouse. Both arguments are rooted in deep emotions. Each partner fears that unless something changes soon (i.e., they open up, or conversely, they drop the topic of opening up) their relationship will remain in an impasse. Both are right when viewed through the eyes of the rabbi in an old Jewish tale. A couple consults a rabbi regarding a conflict in their marriage. Upon hearing the husband, the rabbi responds, "You are right." Then, it is the wife's turn, and to her, too, the rabbi says, "You are right." After the couple leaves, the rabbi's assistant asks, "But Rabbi, how could they both be right?" And the rabbi answers, "You are right, too." The therapist's task is similar to that of the rabbi—to provide a container for each side so that the multiple angles of a conflict can be contained and explored.

The risk of alienating one of the partners through unexamined countertransference reactions also exists in cases where there is no apparent conflict regarding polyamory. Even if externally there are no signs of ambivalence, doubts about nonmonogamy may persist on a less conscious level. Sometimes the presence of conflict is revealed through an odd clinical presentation, as the following case illustrates. A heterosexual couple in their late twenties sought me out because of a struggle with their sex life. They described themselves as poly and kinky and said this was how they had connected in the first place. To use their language, they were each other's "primaries"; but in telling their story, they made it sound like a fact not worth dwelling on. They provided me with detailed descriptions of who else they were partnered with and how their metamours overlapped. It was a very complicated map with multiple convergences. My attempts to learn more about *their* relationship were futile. The conflict that had brought them to therapy in the first place was glossed over.

I had a sense that we were dealing with something as yet unacknowledged; whether it was related to kink, or polyamory, or both, was unclear. By the time the couple came to a sticking point, they had described seven or eight other people they were in relationships with. One of these individuals, an auxiliary partner at best, had apparently failed to disclose that she had oral herpes. At a party, that woman had kissed the male partner of the couple. That was the extent of their erotic interactions. While trying better to understand the nature of this transgression, I asked the couple about their agreements regarding their sexual involvements with others. Once more, my question was dismissed, but I did learn that the other woman had no cold sores at the time of the party. *What is going on?* I kept wondering.

The term *herpes* has negative connotations, but in reality, the herpes simplex virus is extremely common and does not even need to be sexually transmitted. With this couple, something else was amiss; they were clearly aware of safe-sex practices and, adding to it, the man was a nurse practitioner. Yet, their emotions were as intense as if he had exposed them to HIV. We were nearing the end of the session, and I was still unsure where the problem lay. As we were wrapping up, the woman told me that they were actually shopping for a therapist, so this was a trial session to see if we are a good fit. None of these concerns had come up earlier, and to my knowledge, I was the first person they had contacted. Apparently, I failed. This was one of those sessions that leaves a therapist mystified. I wondered what I had missed, but the couple left, and my puzzlement remained unsolved.

Insight into the dynamics of this session came to me days later when I happened to reflect on the impact of internalized homophobia in gay people. I realized that something parallel might have been present for this couple. Internalized homophobia may retain its hold in spite of one's being out. It can be relentlessly persistent regardless of external acceptance. A number of studies related to internalized homophobia in gays, lesbians, and bisexuals identify common themes, including self-image problems, lack of self-confidence, self-hatred, depression, alcohol and substance abuse, sexual dysfunction, and so on. McCann noted, "An important implication of this for therapy is that individuals and couples may not be open to exploring the meaning of such behaviors and may defend against this by questioning the therapist's own value systems that lead them to pursue certain aspects of behavior in the individual or couple" (2014, p. 83). I was relieved to make this connection; it now made more sense why this couple was dismissive of almost any question I asked. In hindsight, I could see that they were not ready to discuss their relationship, because that would lead to an examination of their polyamorous and kink identities that did not feel solid. Directing attention to a peripheral conflict of minor significance—that of the kiss and the concern about cold sores—provided them with a blanket of false security. For the time being, they could avoid questions that they were not ready to address. Not surprisingly, the couple did not come back, but even if I had had my realization sooner, it probably would not have made any difference. They appeared to have made the appointment in haste; even that one session was, in all likelihood, too much of an exposure. If we had continued, the therapy would likely have agitated their frail relational foundations beyond their ability to tolerate the shiver, and that would have been too much of a risk.

In conclusion, countertransference reaction to polyamory can be conceptualized as a two-layered process. On the broader level, there is the therapist's need to examine how her relational beliefs and experiences affect the work with a person or people in her office. Underlying this straightforward examination, there is a need for a more nuanced discernment of the material presented by patients. It is at this level that the most valuable therapeutic information about a person or a couple is likely to be found.

Transgressions in Polyamory

In spite of the focus on transparency and honesty, polyamorous relationships are not free from transgressions. Betrayals in polyamory are both similar and different from monogamous deceptions, but what they have in common on a human level is that they hurt. Each relational format attempts to prevent transgressions from happening. Monogamous marriages have vows; polyamory is known for its use of contracts. These sometimes fairly detailed agreements delineate what kind of contact is allowed and what is not. Couples new to polyamory often make the mistake of assuming that if they create a contract that addresses all their concerns, they will be able to avoid boundary violations. A couple I worked with described the contract they were drafting. Their contract detailed not only sexual practices but also coordinated care of their son in case one of his parents had a date. My patients' contractual agreement consisted of contingency upon contingency, and while it was too detailed to be helpful, it captured the reality of unavoidable difficulties and accompanying hurts very well.

Transgressions in polyamory can be emotional or sexual in nature but are often a mixture of both. As described earlier, many primary couples establish boundaries regarding fluid bonding (i.e., abstaining from sexual activities with others that involve an exchange of bodily fluids, in particular oral or penetrative sex without the use of condoms). Failure to use a condom with another partner in spite of an existing agreement is one example of betrayal in polyamory. Less obvious forms of betrayal involve emotional slights that unearth longstanding relational disappointments. An example of the latter comes from another poly couple I worked with. It started innocently enough; the husband went to the movies with his girlfriend. When he got home, his wife inquired about the movie they saw. "Nothing special," he said. "Just a silly chick flick." "You did what?!" the wife yelled. She did not try to hide her fury. The husband was startled and clueless. What could he possibly have done wrong? There were no sexual or other kinds of transgressions involved that he could think of. To the wife, this was an act of unfathomable betrayal; she had wanted to see a romantic comedy with her husband for years, but he had always refused. Exploring this affront revealed layers of unhealed rifts. This couple's relationship was harmonious on the surface but underneath rife with distress. They somehow managed to open up without upending the marriage, but the hurts that had accumulated were pushed aside and not dealt with. The seemingly innocuous transgression by the husband became a catalyst for deeper relational work that was long overdue. In their case, it led to a difficult decision to put polyamory on pause and give themselves a chance to focus on their marriage.

References

Celenza, A. (2014). *Erotic revelations: Clinical applications and perverse scenarios*. Routledge.

McCann, D. (2014). Responding to the clinical needs of same-sex couples. In D. E. Scharff & J. S. Scharff (Eds.) & D. Hewison, C. Buss-Twachtmann, J. Wanlass (Collaborators), *Psychoanalytic couple therapy (The library of couple and family psychoanalysis): Foundations of theory and practice* (pp. 81–90). Karnac Books.

Norcross, J. C. (Ed.). (2002). *Psychotherapy relationships that work: Therapist contributions and responsiveness to patient needs*. Oxford University Press.

Nozick, R. (2006). *The examined life: Philosophical meditations*. Simon & Schuster.

Wachtel, P. L. (2008). *Relational theory and the practice of psychotherapy*. The Guilford Press.

22 Clinical Considerations: Ethical Issues and Therapy Tasks

As humans, we seek to make meaning and are prone to duality, at least in the Western world. We seek to explain the world we live in, generating arguments that justify our point of view while attempting to discredit contradictory perspectives. We were either created by a higher power or by evolution (which is a higher power in its own right); it is nature that shapes us unless nurture provides a better explanation. Until recently, gender was binary—we were either male or female, with only fragmentary notions of transgender, genderqueer, omnigender, or gender-fluid realities. Newborn babies with ambiguous genitals were assigned to the category that was most prominent visually. We are taught to separate the rational from emotional, arguing for the superiority of the former while defending the value of the latter, all the while forgetting that both are generated in the very same brains and minds.

The list goes on and encompasses even more elusive phenomena, such as love. Explaining the nature of love in dual terms is not an exception—love is either biological, an argument propagated by Helen Fisher (among others), or it is a social construct, as presented by Robert Sternberg. It should, therefore, not come as a surprise that monogamy is inevitably pitted against polyamory and vice versa, with arguments on both sides about which one is "natural." Somehow there are fewer disagreements about which one is constructed—it is taken for granted that monogamy is, but what about polyamory? Polyamory is declared to be more natural than monogamy by its practitioners, which sounds far sexier than the argument that it is as much a social construct as monogamy.

The reality is that human beings are incredibly complex, capable of adapting to the most unthinkable of circumstances. We are products of nature and nurture, rational thought and emotions; capable of love and commitment and capable of commitment without love. Living in the modern world implies adaptation to more and more complex realities, which includes the rapidly changing essence of relationships. Psychotherapists are called on to assist clients who are single, partnered, married, divorced, widowed, married again, with or without biological children, with or without stepchildren or siblings, and so on. None of these descriptions of relational status conveys the emotional nature of the relationship one is in. There is no way of knowing what makes the person or couple we are seeing happy or miserable based on their romantic and family bonds. I became acutely aware of how true that is when a new patient described her relational status as "dumped." In that single word, she expressed more than ten sentences describing relational complexities could. Not only did I learn that she was in pain, but I also knew the source of her pain. It was a situation with few comparisons; in most therapeutic encounters, we have to ask in order to ascertain what is going on relationally and how it makes people feel. There is no way to know if a person who describes himself as monogamous is content and, if not, why? In the same vein, someone identifying as polyamorous might be distressed by a number of factors that can hardly be explained by their preference for polyamory as a relational format.

Relationships hurt, and relationships heal, and that applies to therapeutic relationships as well. Patients seeking therapy yearn to be *known*—they long to be seen and understood, not dismissed and judged. The greatest insights or skillful behavioral interventions are of limited value when the relationship between the therapist and her clients is tenuous. Adding to it, attitudes toward an effective and beneficial therapeutic stance vary depending on the mode of therapy. Thus, it is important to ask here, what stance may best support therapy with poly clients?

While there is no uniform answer, a compassionate and discerning approach that combines relative neutrality, an open-minded embrace of nontraditional lifestyle choices, and skillful attention to countertransference dynamics is likely to be helpful. While this may sound instinctively right, what does it mean in practical terms?

Compassionate relative neutrality implies neutrality toward an individual or a couple as a whole while acknowledging the relevance of occasionally siding with certain perspectives over others. As an example, myths and misconceptions regarding sexuality, intimacy, and couples' dynamics are very common, and people's perceptions vary enormously, ranging from fairly accurate to grossly misguided. Addressing these issues neutrally may simply not be possible, or worse, it may be detrimental to the couple's process. As an example, siding with the more informed partner (whether they are in the therapy room or not) but taking the step of explaining the reason, can prevent the further accumulation of mistrust and hurt. However, addressing deeply ingrained misconceptions is not always an easy task.

A married couple I worked with comes to mind. This couple firmly believed that something was wrong with them because the woman was not able to achieve vaginal orgasms. No amount of explaining, including references to human anatomy, sufficed; it was obvious that something else was going on. They were suffering in spite of having a remarkably healthy and, by many accounts, enviable sex life. But they were barely able to enjoy what they had. The woman struggled with taking pleasure in her clitoral orgasms because of fear of disappointing her husband. The man believed himself to be inadequate. Ironically, their original narrative that she was the problem served them better than the new narrative that emerged through the therapy process. The new narrative clarified misconceptions regarding female orgasms and made the woman feel empowered. It also happened to further emasculate the husband. Siding with the wife (which was not difficult, being a sex therapist *and* a female) proved to be wholly unhelpful, so the treatment had to take an entirely different turn.

An open-minded stance toward non-normative relationships is not the same as a lack of discernment. Accepting a client's persona and his lifestyle choice is different from the endorsement of potentially hurtful or manipulative behaviors. Striving for objectivity (e.g., avoiding being caught in dysfunctional dynamics) has its drawbacks. To begin with, trying to define objectivity in polyamory can be complicated. More importantly, objectivity makes it hard to utilize countertransference as a valuable therapeutic tool. Referencing the couple above, I assumed that by providing objective information regarding female sexuality and pleasure, I would be helping them. They were hungry for data, asking for book recommendations and other suggestions that could enhance their sex life. What I temporarily put aside was valuable countertransference information regarding his defensiveness. The husband struggled with unresolved traumas from the past; however, he did not see any meaning or reason to explore that ancient history. It made him frustrated and angry. The more we tried to process, the angrier he got toward his wife, and toward me. Therapy was supposed to "fix" the wife, that is, equip her with an ability to experience vaginal orgasms. Any other "talk" was a waste of time. He referenced other women he had had sex with who had appeared to be multi-orgasmic. This man's sense of self, which he had tried to heal through consensual nonmonogamy, was collapsing. Needless to say, the treatment was not going well. We agreed that it might be beneficial if I referred them to a male therapist who would presumably understand better than I could why this man needed to make his wife experience vaginal orgasms.

Polyamory and, more broadly, nonmonogamy may *present* differently from monogamy, but at the core, they still represent intersubjective relational dynamics. They are at the mercy of the same kind of cyclically repeated, contextually based factors as monogamy. These factors originate in and encapsulate early attachments experiences, forming the basis of adult relatedness. Paul Wachtel proposed the term *cyclical psychodynamics* to describe their repetitive nature, later on recognizing the importance of the context in which these repetitions take place. In other words, relational repetitions are context dependent and, consciously and unconsciously, people are drawn to situations that represent the familiar and the longed-for.

Therapists who focus on relationships rather than problems recognize how the early attachment dynamics later evolve into a *way of life*. For therapy to be helpful, it is not enough to appreciate these attachment experiences; it is also necessary to attend to the very real, ongoing consequences of that way of life in the present (Wachtel, 2008). In other words, the past is informing the present in ways that are both real and surreal. The phrase "healing the past" is both accurate and a misnomer. It is in the present that we yearn to be healed, but the secrets to understanding the nature of individual suffering, self- and other-inflicted, lie in the deep past. A therapeutic approach that allows for the exploration of these cyclical, contextual dynamics can be tremendously helpful in facilitating healing. It opens up the chance for a deeper understanding of a person's *particular* ways of responding to specific circumstances, the ways she, for better or for worse, makes choices in life.

Privileged or Oppressed?

One of the confusing aspects of polyamory is that it simultaneously represents a privileged *and* oppressed position. It holds a locus of privilege because of who appears to embody it, which tends to be people who are predominantly white, heterosexual, middle-class, well educated, and with stable careers and incomes. This perception of polyamory demographics may change with more systematic studies (e.g., Balzarini et al., 2019), but the consistency of class privilege appears to be an ongoing factor in consensual nonmonogamy. In their 1972 book *Open Marriage: A New Lifestyle for Couples*, O'Neill and O'Neill reported that 15 percent of people in their sample were in open marriages, and all of them belonged to the upper-middle class. Polyamory's popularity and prominence in the public and academic sphere is rising, which reflects the opposite of oppression or repression. Practitioners of polyamory overtly and covertly consider themselves "more evolved" as individuals, often portraying their lifestyle as ethically superior compared to monogamy, and even other forms of nonmonogamy. With monogamy comes the seemingly inescapable risk of cheating and other transgressions. Being able to openly negotiate extra-dyadic sex, the way it is done in open marriage and swinging, is more ethical than betraying one's partner. It is a step up from monogamy. However, consensual nonmonogamy that is all about extramarital sex is merely an attempt to solve the problem of sexual desire. From polyamory advocates' point of view, love, and not just sex, elevates this lifestyle to a more advanced relational status.

With all of these real and perceived privileges in place, how is polyamory as a principle oppressed? Polyamorous forms of relating are still considered a fringe phenomenon in terms of their nonconformity to established societal norms and practices, and mononormativity in particular, but to a degree heteronormativity, too. Culturally, they are yet to be widely endorsed as valid alternatives to monogamy. Nobody knows what the future of human relationships will look like, but, at present, polyamory evokes more feelings of curiosity and hesitation than of awe and conviction. Early on, the most common complaint among polyamorous clients was that the therapists they contacted did not know what polyamory was and the clients had to explain every term before getting a chance to explain why they pursued treatment.

Needless to say, these conditions did not help to build a therapeutic alliance. Clients felt misunderstood and judged by the clinicians whose help they relied on. This first wave of misgiving might be less of a problem today, but the fear of judgment persists.

Polyamorous people may face discrimination in ways similar to what gays and lesbians experienced when homosexuality was considered a mental health disorder. The price of ostracism can be high; polyamorous individuals and couples might be especially at risk when children are involved. Becoming known as poly can have real-life consequences for the children and their families; schools may become concerned and alert the authorities and so on. There are examples of couples whose application for adoption was refused when it became known that they were poly.

The majority of poly people feel comfortable disclosing their lifestyle to trusted friends and selected family members, but it is less straightforward in work settings; depending on their profession, some people may have reasons to conceal their poly identity to avoid repercussions. Coming out to families can also be difficult; while the immediate family may be more accepting, the extended family may not be as open. Being forced to decide who can attend family events is a challenge that monogamous couples seldom experience.

Ethical Guidance

Ethical guidance for psychotherapy with sexual and gender minorities provides some parallels to clinical work with polyamorous clients. According to the American Psychological Association's (APA) guidelines, "When heterosexual norms for identity, behavior and relationships are applied to lesbian, gay, and bisexual clients, their thoughts, feelings, and behaviors may be misinterpreted as abnormal, deviant, and undesirable" (in Garnets & Kimmel, 2003, p. 759). Polyamory is not currently considered a sexual identity in spite of some arguments for its inclusion in this group. However, the principle of not discriminating in therapy, combined with efforts to ensure competent and effective treatment, applies fittingly to psychotherapy with the poly population.

Seeking supervision, consultation, and training when working with unfamiliar populations represents a standard ethical practice for clinicians. Meanings associated with sexual practices of any kind are inevitably complex, and "[t]he role of psychologists, regarding therapeutic orientation, is not to impose their beliefs on clients but to examine thoughtfully the clients' experiences and motives" (APA in Garnets & Kimmel, 2003, p. 763). Guidelines regarding relationships and families of gay, lesbian, and bisexual people have particular resonance for therapy with poly individuals and couples. There is a significant overlap between LGBTQ+ and poly populations, especially when it comes to reliance on alternative family structures, which, more often than not, are substantially different from the normative makeup of their families of origin.

One client, Olive, identified as bisexual and gender-nonconforming. She would not go so far as to use the pronouns they/them/theirs, but she/her/hers did not feel quite right either. As long as she could remember, Olive had thought of herself as "different." Now, in her mid 30, she wanted to stand by her relational choices without questioning them the way she had in the past. In her early experience, being bisexual was problematic. As she explained, if she were strictly lesbian, her sexual orientation would have been accepted without question. Until polyamory became an option, she tried to fit in by hiding her bi identity. Olive had been previously married, but her husband was not comfortable with her bisexuality, and the marriage eventually fell apart. After the divorce, Olive formed a relationship with a woman whom she loved but who, like her ex-husband, was ill at ease with the thought of her being involved with a man. After that relationship ended as well, Olive decided to pursue polyamory, sensing that this lifestyle would allow her to be who she was without needing to choose between the binary options.

Olive came from a family where everyone, except one cousin, was straight. There were no divorces in her family either. When she first came out as bi, she was surprised to learn that the person she counted on to support her the most, her cousin, was the most critical. In the cousin's eyes, Olive was dishonest with herself, unwilling to admit that she was a lesbian. In therapy, Olive focused on exploring her identity and accepting that polyamory was preferable over monogamy, even if that meant that her family would be even more hostile toward her relational choices. Knowing that she could not reconcile with her family's values, Olive was striving to form a non-normative family of choice in which her bisexuality and gender nonconformity would not be questioned.

Olive's story speaks to the complexity of gender, sexual orientation, and relational dynamics. Ultimately, she was able to find others who, like her, were more comfortable with nonconformity than with mono- and heteronormativity. Olive was lucky to make a home in Cambridge, Massachusetts, which is known to be progressive, and where hiding her identity was not necessary the way it still is in many parts of the U.S. However, the relationship with her family of origin in the rural South continued to be strained. Accepting herself as bisexual, gender-nonconforming, *and* nonmonogamous meant she had to grieve the loss of family connections that could no longer sustain her.

The Concept of Family

For some, polyamory may be reminiscent of something familiar—the intertwined dynamics of a large extended family. For others, it may represent something that is longed for. The very concept of a family has changed enormously in the past several decades, and those choices have implications for understanding the rapid expansion of nonmonogamy. A family is no longer the idealized two plus two plus two, which implied a married, monogamous, heterosexual couple, more often than not of the same race, with two biological children, a boy and a girl, and two pets, a dog and a cat. Rather, a contemporary family can be anything from a single parent with a biological or adopted child; to a blended family consisting of divorced spouses, now single, remarried, or re-coupled, who share the responsibility of raising their mixed-marriage children; to a gay couple who are able to have biological children thanks to egg donors and surrogate mothers; or a poly family into which new children are born or the existing children are absorbed.

A family does not have to include children either. Many people make a conscious choice to not produce offspring. Amy Blackstone's (2019) research on child-free (as opposed to "childless") individuals indicates that our perception of what constitutes a biological clock is primarily sociological. Further, with in-vitro fertilization, egg-donor availability, and birth surrogacy, the lines between who constitutes a parent and who does not have become quite blurry. Oftentimes, the definitions have to be established with the help of lawyers, who draw binding contracts aimed at protecting the rights of everyone involved in bringing into this world a child who is conceived through the tremendously complex process of egg, sperm, and womb donation. Separately, there is a resurgence of interest in polygamy, a practice most commonly associated with Mormonism. Some circumvent the problem of marriage by creating polygamous households without formalizing the ties. As Andrew Solomon, author of the deeply personal and insightful Audible Original series *New Family Values* (Dec 6, 2018), remarks, language aside, the difference between polyamory and polygamy is remarkably small.

All in all, the diversity of existing familial formats, affectionately called "rainbow families," is enormous. If I were to stretch the definition of polyamory beyond its functional limits, I would say that any blended family that manages to form and maintain friendship-based relationships between former and existing partners is in some ways polyamorous. Thus, for people who grew up in families different from the standard narrative, having multiple romantic partners may not be outrageous. On the contrary, it may signify the familiar. For others, it might be a way of life they dreamed about because of what it represents, at least in its romanticized form. The broadening appeal of polyamory is rooted in its principles of honesty and transparency, and for those who experienced parental divorce as a consequence of an affair, such openness might be very appealing. Romantic and sexual connections may shift, but without breaking the family. For therapists working with polyamorous clients, it might be confusing at first. Our society tends to associate commitment with sexual exclusivity. While dating, it is expected that a person will have sex with multiple people in order to determine sexual compatibility, but when the connection becomes more serious, the fledgling couple has a conversation about exclusivity. Not monogamy—exclusivity.

When people decide to open up, their sexual affiliations typically change course. Former primary partners, who often are married, may remain physically affectionate but cease to be directly sexual with each other. For some, it raises the question, why are they still married? Oddly enough, nobody seems to wonder about the same issues when long-term monogamous couples stop having sex. In some respects, it is taken for granted that a long marriage and passionate sex are infrequent bedfellows. Culturally, long-lasting monogamous marriages are not expected to end when the sexual lust fades. The reasons to avoid divorce are multifold and include legal, financial, and, where relevant, parental considerations. These reasons apply as much to polyamorous couples as they do to monogamous ones.

In summary, when taken as a group, nonmonogamous clients tend to be well versed in the language and landscape of polyamory, and they are likely to have more detailed knowledge of this terrain than the majority of therapists. This gap may present a challenge to alliance building and lead to potentially difficult dynamics between clinicians and their patients. Yet, people seek psychotherapy *because* they trust therapists' relational expertise. One example of a potential conflict between the view psychotherapy holds of relationships and that of polyamory involves the relationship escalator. In polyamory, the effort to escape the dreaded relationship escalator fails to take into consideration that, just as in individual development, committed relationships go through developmental stages too. Assessing the couple's developmental level may provide relevant information regarding their process of opening up.

Resolution of Problems Versus Relational Maturity

People seek therapy because they wish for their experience to be validated *and* because they want things to change. Both factors are relevant, but the tension between these two elements is not always easy to reconcile. For treatment to be effective, it needs to promote change; a mere affirmation of experience might provide a desperately needed validation that a person is "not crazy," but it may not be enough to ensure healing and growth. Many schools of therapy have developed an approach to recognizing and naming different parts or ego-states within the self.

The language of parts makes it possible to talk about a conflict *within* a person, usually recounted as a desire to be able to engage differently (e.g., be less reactive), *and* a desire for one's partner to change. The latter usually dominates. The first is real, too, but often more as an aspiration rather than a determination to take the necessary steps toward change. Naming these different modes of experience can help to move the locus of tension from between two (or more) people to within an individual. When the conflict is seen as internal, it creates a shift in the perception of the relational impasse, which can now be seen in a more dynamic and therefore less blaming way.

In many instances, individuals and couples distraught about their relational dynamics enter therapy hoping for a rapid resolution of their problems. As Jeanne Shaw (2012) notes, they seek first-degree change without realizing the complexity of issues that bring them to treatment. They have identified the conflict and are ready to get it solved. For one partner, the idea of opening up may appear outlandishly radical; for the other, it may seem logical. The spouses eventually conclude, although not necessarily with equal conviction, that opening up might be the only way to salvage the marriage. The resolution that promises the end to their suffering seems to be within reach … if only the other person were fully on board.

"The first-degree change occurs when a couple comes with a problem; the therapist suggests resolutions; and the couple complies and resolves the problem," writes Shaw (2012, p. 177). Unfortunately, relational issues are rarely this simple. It is especially the case when sexuality, intimacy, and the complexity of opening up and living a polyamorous life are considered. In first-degree change, "relationship and other issues do not interfere with problem resolution" (p. 177). In therapy with polyamorous clients, relationship and related issues *are* the problem.

When problem-solving strategies fail to address a conflict, an impasse is likely to follow. Couples who praise themselves for being rational get stuck when their solution-oriented skills prove to be insufficient in protecting them from the emotional disasters they worked hard to prevent. It happens when boundaries that have been clearly delineated on paper prove to be inadequate in reality. It also occurs when jealousy is difficult to contain. As a rule, when the hoped-for first-degree change is not attainable, it is because of the complexity of relational matters. As Galit Atlas observes, "We know that people seek sexual experiences for many different emotional reasons: as an attempt to charge their inner objects and self with excitement and realness and aliveness; to express their aggression and hostility; to hide or expose their vulnerability; to bolster the collapsing or fragmenting self; to heal trauma through the repetition of arousal; to achieve recognition and affirmation through the body of the other; and more" (2016, p. 19). Her words capture the multiverse of motivations underlying a person's sexual engagement with other people. Some of these motives are conscious, others not, but they permeate all relationships, whether monogamous or polyamorous. In other words, these motives are at play with a single partner, or with a number of people, in the moment or over a span of time.

With all these complexities at play, are there universal poly themes in particular need of therapeutic support? Absolutely. Negotiating the speed of opening up, establishing or fine-tuning boundaries, working through unexpected conflicts, understanding the impact of NRE, healing from unanticipated betrayals, disarming jealousy, deciding whether to keep polyamory private or come out to family and colleagues, and addressing sexual concerns—these are examples of what is likely to come up in treatment with poly clients.

To Be or Not to Be

Concerns with appearing nonjudgmental may entice therapists to take a cheerleading stance, but being appropriately cautious may serve clients better than being overly supportive. The majority of people who consider opening up contend that it will be difficult but fail to imagine in what way. Here are a handful of questions a therapist may ask to help clients determine whether or not polyamory is the right choice for them:

  –What benefits do you expect from opening up?
  –What kind of short-term and long-term risks do you foresee?
  –Where do you imagine yourself to be in five years? In ten years? What will be important to you then?
  –Are the risks you imagine worth taking?

Naturally, for the partner who advocates for polyamory, it is easier to envision the benefits than the risks; however, the challenges can be substantial. These challenges fall into three categories: personal, relational, and vocational. Having a sense of relational security in the moment is not a guarantee of future security when more people are involved; NRE wreaks havoc; career or family questions may come to the forefront. People without children may want to have them at some point, and they must confront the question of what kind of family they want their kids to grow up in. Where children are already present, the risk of coming out as poly to the wider community might be significant. Having more people to take care of the children is appealing, but having this kind of support depends on the quality of one's relationships.

Negotiations of Boundaries: Contracts and Agreements

Polyamory contracts and agreements may or may not be written down, but no matter how they are constructed, they evolve in a dynamic fashion in response to developments in a couple's life.

Greg and Karina

Greg and Karina were highly detail-oriented and did their best to imagine everything and anything that could go wrong in transitioning from monogamy to polyamory. Armed with friends' advice, they read what they could about contracts and boundary negotiations, discussing the minutiae. The result, they informed me with laughter during our initial session, was a 20-page-long contract. Realizing that such detail only magnified the difficulty, they combed through the contract, removing problematic items, eventually reducing it to nine pages.

   Humor came easily to Greg and Karina, and it was easy to laugh with them about their misadventures. Both were energetic and eager to address their difficulties head on, as their contract enterprise illustrated. But underneath the humor and camaraderie that came from years of knowing and genuinely liking each other, a sense of despair was lurking. Used to being on the same page about most things, they did not anticipate that polyamory could be such a blow to their sense of unity. Greg and Karina had known each other since they were children. Like many couples who married very young, now that they were approaching their 40s, they wondered what sexual opportunities they might have given up on by finding the right person so early in life. They concluded that perhaps it was not too late to find out. They felt confident about their relationship and were each in a good place personally and professionally. In other words, their relationship bore all the signs of a secure attachment, and there were no obvious red flags to alert them to difficulties that polyamory might represent.

The scaled-down contract was an improvement but still too complex to be helpful. In our sessions, we discussed how trust, by its very nature, is implicit rather than explicit, and that there is no contract that would prevent pain and hurt from occurring. Greg and Karina agreed that their convoluted contract was limiting instead of empowering. Not only did it fail to safeguard their relationship, but it also made them feel controlled by the other person. Intended to be a shield, the contract became a weapon. They were angry with each other, and the terms in the contract expressed their agitation.

It would be naïve, however, to blame the contract for the difficulties that Greg and Karina later experienced. It is one thing to imagine what polyamory would be like when contemplating it and an entirely different story when dealing with the not-so-compliant reality of life. While Greg imagined engaging in more or less casual sex with multiple women, Karina was hoping to find one, or at most two, men to form serious secondary relationships with. To their surprise, Karina found herself enjoying casual dating with limited obligations, while Greg struggled to find women willing to sleep with him without further commitment. He settled on looking for one other partner who could be his secondary, but that was not easy to achieve either. In the meantime, Karina was basking in the attention of men who were drawn to her outgoing personality. None of these issues could have been even remotely predicted by the contract they had drawn. Their contract was based on the implicit assumption that theirs was a first-degree problem and that the relationship factors would not interfere.

Managing the Speed of Opening Up

It is seldom the case that both partners in a couple are similarly interested in opening up. For one person, it might be an intriguing thought, like a sexual fantasy best left imagined. For the other, it might be a strong desire that deserves to be put into action. Helping a couple to manage the speed of opening up, so that neither of the partners feels left out, is an important therapeutic task—it is the task of managing accelerators and brakes, to adapt

Emily Nagoski's (2015) metaphor. In sex therapy, it is relevant to help clients recognize their turn-ons (accelerators) and turn-offs (brakes) in order to make the sexual experience as pleasurable as possible. In the case of opening up, where one person wants to accelerate the process and the other to slow down the speed, both of their concerns need to be acknowledged and managed. An example of managing the speed of opening up comes from therapy sessions with Abby and Mike.

Abby and Mike

In couple's therapy, I make clients aware of three interconnected processes: the two individual ones and the couple's process. This applies to individual treatment, too, when a patient is partnered. The partner's process unfolds independently, outside of the therapy room, affecting the joint process. Abby and Mike's processes overlapped in a tense way. Their case was a prototypical mono-poly situation, where one person wants to open up and do it yesterday and the other is highly ambivalent. Mike was impatient to explore the exciting world of polyamorous possibilities; Abby conceded to going to poly events to learn more. Her brakes were on, and she kept her foot firmly down. Mike was revving his accelerator; he had no brakes other than Abby. Each struggled to understand why the other was so eager to stall or rush.

Sometimes people ask how long it should take before they are allowed to take certain steps, and unsurprisingly, there is no quantitative answer to that question. It all depends on the subjective experience of each of the partners. Much of the therapy work here consisted of helping Mike and Abby see where the other person was coming from and learn to empathize with their respective motivations. In their case, his growing understanding of her reluctance increased Abby's confidence in allowing Mike to take measured steps toward greater relational openness. They learned to pay attention to their mutual process—what helped them to move forward and what set them back. As attuned as they became to each other throughout the course of therapy, they never ceased to struggle with the subjective experience of how quickly things should unfold. The way they were different at the core, with their respective preferences for monogamy versus polyamory, did not change much. While much of their focus was on the acute need to figure out the speed of opening up, it was the deeper issue of their core differences that needed to be addressed first.

Exploring Jealousy

Polyamory guides offer plentiful advice on how to manage jealousy. "Managing" something can give the impression that the thing in question is problematic and needs to be fixed—a first-degree change. My approach to jealousy is to give it voice—to separate it from envy, listen to its reasons and grievances, and see how it connects to attachment stories from the past.

Jealousy can be hard to experience and tolerate, but its presence does not need to signify instant dysfunction. People who are jealous may have reasons to feel that way. Their partners might be insensitive or dismissive, pre-occupied with their own desires, and turned away from the pain they are inflicting. Jealousy is a complex relational experience consisting of inter-twined, contradictory feelings. Identifying the emotions that underlie a jealous outburst can help clients to see their reactions in a clearer way. Some of the reactions might be to ghosts from the past; others may reflect unmet relational needs in the present.

Ethan and Audrey

There is no doubt that sometimes jealousy can be intense to the point of being destructive. In these cases, finding a better way to manage the feeling takes precedence. Sometimes people, in my experience men more often than women, are taken by surprise by the intensity of their jealous feelings.

Ethan was taken aback when jealousy hit him; until then, he proudly exclaimed that he was "never jealous." It started when Ethan encouraged his partner, Audrey, to explore erotic liaisons outside of their marriage. However, when Audrey revealed that she had reconnected with a former boyfriend who identified as poly, Ethan became enraged. It became apparent that he had had rules regarding what he called Audrey's "conduct" that he was not aware of until the blow-up. Audrey was scared and remorseful, al-though she was not sure for what. She tried to reassure Ethan the best way she could about her love for him, but he was in too much pain to be able to notice her attempts at repair. For several very intense sessions, the roaring and tears continued, and all I could do was listen and carefully manage the situation to help them both feel safe.

Processing of emotions can occur only after the emotions are heard, and Ethan's affect was the loudest and demanded the most attention. Audrey's affect appeared almost subdued in contrast; it was her body that expressed her anxiety the most. Her hands would shake, and her skin was pale and moist with perspiration. It took a while before Ethan was able to recognize that, like him, she was overcome with emotion and needed reassurance. Ethan and Audrey's respective attachment traumas were in the playing field. Audrey had more therapy experience than Ethan and was able to recognize her triggers more easily. He struggled to understand why I was curious about his past relational experiences. For him, the problem was Audrey in the here and now, not other people in some obscure past.

It would be wrong to attribute the propensity for jealousy solely to early attachment disruptions. As Clanton (2006) points out, experiences of ro-mantic love and loss in adolescence and young adulthood may play a more important role than the developmental wounds of childhood. Adolescents have little relational maturity, and their brains are still developing. Almost everyone remembers their first heartbreak. Young people are only in the beginning of the lifelong process of forming mature attachments, and disruptions of early romantic bonds may leave lasting impressions. Ethan's adolescent love experiences had turned out to be particularly painful and, without realizing it, he was still affected by those early betrayals.

All therapists have experienced treatment situations that make them sweat and wonder about their effectiveness. Therapy with Ethan and Audrey was dominated by his barely controlled rage and her quiet tears. It took months before we were able to stay within a window of emotional tolerance without the risk of their disappearing into fight, flight, or freeze. Managing their affect took a lot of effort, but finally, after a year of treatment, we were able to move on to processing what had brought on their powerful emotional reactions. They realized that not only had Ethan's first love betrayed him with her ex, but she also told him that it was his fault that she had gone back to this other man. Ethan dismissed the significance of his early experience, portraying it as puppy love, not worth dwelling on. On her end, Audrey had grown up with an alcoholic father who was prone to rages. He blamed his wife for his drinking, accusing her of cheating. Until therapy, Ethan and Audrey had had little awareness of how these early dynamics affected their relationship. The introduction of nonmonogamy shook their relational foundation, which they fought to find again.

Exploring Compersion

There are universally recognizable affective states such as anger, sadness, joy, fear, surprise, and disgust. Other feelings are culture-specific and do not easily transcend boundaries. These feelings are taught, categorized, and reinforced by the cultural context in which they exist. Shame, for example, is experienced very differently in the West compared to the East. Adding to this complexity, some visceral emotional states can be difficult to take apart. How, then, do we help clients discern what compersion is? Polyamory guides provide reassurance that it is common to not feel compersion, but that it is possible to achieve this feeling-state if one is willing to learn. Indeed, for most poly patients, compersion is an emotion one is ideally supposed to have. Not surprisingly, exploring compersion in therapy oftentimes implies listening to the pressure to *feel* compersion.

I assure clients that there is nothing inherently abnormal with their inability to feel compersion. Compersion is a social construction that applies to a small group of people; it is a lofty aspiration that is not culturally recognized or influenced outside of polyamory. Aspiring to feel compersion is like aspiring to have religious visions; some will, but most will not, no matter how hard they try. Not experiencing visions does not preclude people from finding comfort in religion or spirituality. Being mindfully aware of one's feelings is likely to be more helpful in the practice of polyamory than worrying about the absence of a feeling that was not likely to be there in the first place.

Some poly people argue that compersion is not substantially different from the feeling of joy a person may have when their partner is recognized for some achievement. One patient, Lizzy, referred to this argument when describing her difficulty with experiencing compersion: "I'm genuinely happy for my partner when he gets promoted, so why can't I feel happy for him when he is sexually excited by somebody else?" she said. "I don't feel insecure; I'm sure he has no plans to leave our relationship, so what's wrong with me?" "Maybe nothing is. Maybe you're wishing that you meant more to him than you do now. Like it was in the beginning?" I responded. "I remember that look in his eyes when he could not get enough of me" Lizzy replied. "I miss it." She got lost in thought. "Perhaps it's enough that I've learned to be okay when he is with his other partners...perhaps that's more than enough."

The Impact of NRE

New relationship energy—some faces light up upon hearing these words; others frown in sorrow. Witnessing NRE in a person you love, but which is directed at someone else other than yourself, is one of the hardest poly experiences to endure. It is difficult for people who are not experiencing it, and it is challenging for those who are in the throes of it. Like a person in love, the individual basking in the erotic vitality of NRE may feel the urge to talk about her object of desire, to display her joy for all to see. Unlike a person in love, a poly partner may try to disguise her experience of NRE in order to protect her partner's feelings. Most people identifying as poly will sigh with resignation: NRE is a beautiful *and* a very hard part of being poly. The impact of NRE is like a magnet that makes two pieces come together while keeping other parts at arm's distance. Even those with extensive poly experience will, at times, find themselves overwrought with intense negative emotion when their partners are in the state of NRE. The earlier discussion of compersion applies here as well. Lacking warm, fuzzy feelings for the partner lost to NRE is the norm rather than exception, but some people will still struggle with expectations to be more at ease.

Trevor (and Anya)

Sometimes, NRE causes more than temporary havoc; its presence and power may restructure the existing poly constellation entirely. One of the patients who sought individual therapy specifically because of NRE, was Trevor. He was married to Anya; they had been together for eight years, four of them as poly, and they were talking about having kids. In the previous six months, however, Anya and her new boyfriend had gotten very serious, and Trevor was not sure how to manage his feelings. He felt left out and was no longer sure if he wanted to have children with Anya, fearing that her interest in him was waning. Trevor expected his negative feelings to go away as time passed; it was reasonable to expect that the command of NRE would lessen after a while. Unfortunately, in this instance, it did not seem to be the case. Anya and her boyfriend were spending more and more time together, and Trevor's struggles intensified. He sought advice from an online poly community, and the responses he got varied from the sympathetic "it's hard," to the dismissive "deal with it, bro; NRE is a part of being poly." Many bloggers were happy to offer practical tools for how to talk to Anya about his feelings.

The advice was somewhat helpful but did not address his concerns regarding kids and family. When I asked him why he chose to come to therapy alone rather than with Anya, I learned that he had suggested counseling to her, but she felt that the problem was his, not theirs. Trevor felt dismissed, just as he felt rejected when Anya's attention was redirected to her new partner. The more I learned about their marriage, the more I got the sense that Anya's NRE was more than just a temporary state. It appeared that she was building a new life with her other boyfriend and was no longer invested in maintaining a vital relationship with Trevor. His biggest fear was confirmed when he finally gathered enough courage to ask her if she still wanted to be with him. Anya replied that while she still loved him, it was no longer romantic. Her feelings for Trevor were like those for a nesting partner with whom she shared a house and the perks of a comfortable partnership. Her new partner made her realize that she could have the relationship she longed for. Trevor felt betrayed and misled; he supposed that Anya followed the poly rules by being open and transparent with him, but how it all evolved did not feel right. It was a point at which the course of therapy switched—rather than managing the impact of NRE on his life, Trevor needed to face the loss of his marriage. It was not an easy task, but he wanted to figure out how to move on without feeling bitter and resentful toward Anya and polyamory.

Coming Out as Poly to a Wider Circle

With polyamory gaining popularity, it may appear that coming out should be relatively stress-free, but that is not always the case. Disclosing one's decision to those who have similar values is easy; the risk of rejection is low. In contrast, other people in one's network of family, friends, neighbors, or colleagues may not be as welcoming. One of the common topics in therapy involves managing the challenges of being out. Family events, such as holidays, weddings, or other parties often raise the question of who may attend and who may not. Couples recognized as such are likely to be invited as usual, but other partners may not be included. Even the families that embrace a person's choice of polyamory may be hesitant to invite her multiple partners to an event because of the difficulty explaining to others who these individuals are. Feelings of this sort are easier to manage in hierarchical polyamory; the secondary partners may not expect to be easily included. In nonhierarchical polyamory, the question of dis-inclusion often becomes a problem. The conflict is not merely external; dis-inclusion may echo an internal struggle of longing but barely belonging. This is true for the non-invited partner, but also for the one who wants to be recognized as non-hierarchically polyamorous. Conflicts like these may bring out old attachment wounds, activating feelings of not being loved, accepted, or respected.

Sometimes families' reluctance to include an indefinite number of poly partners is not solely due to mononormativity. In monogamous dating, people usually wait a while before they introduce a new person as their partner; they want to feel relatively certain about relational commitment before making any wider introductions. Polyamory does not readily evoke associations of serious commitment, especially among parents of young adults. A patient, Dianna, a liberal woman in her early 60s, often comments on how she cannot keep up with her 20-something son's polyamorous adventures. The son perceives her reluctance as judgment, arguing that she should be more forthcoming toward his partners. Dianna's retorts that the women he is supposedly serious with become secondary or start orbiting before she gets to remember their names. Dianna is a former hippie who used to live in a group house. She sees the humor in this situation, remembering her own free-love turbulences.

Another difficulty regarding coming out involves institutions rooted in tradition. People in fields of high visibility and whose authority is ingrained in mononormativity may risk career backlash if their poly lifestyle becomes known. As an example, parents may not want a teacher who is poly to teach their children. Conversely, a conservative school may be alarmed by a home situation of a child whose parents have other live-in partners. Those who have political aspirations may not want their polyamorous preferences to be known. Polyamory is as removed from careless sex as it can be, but some people find it difficult to think of fluid relational and sexual boundaries as safe.

Sexual Boundaries

Compared to the general population, polyamorous individuals are better versed in matters of sexual health. Sexual health is defined by the lack of coercion or exploitation as well as consensual agreements, honesty, shared values, focus on pleasure, and avoidance of risks such as STIs or unwanted pregnancies. Polyamory guides emphasize the importance of negotiating sexual boundaries, and it is one of the first things partners talk about when they open up. Therapists not used to explicit conversations about sex may find it challenging to focus so unambiguously on matters of sexual performance and demeanor. Adding to it, the language of sex in polyamory can be experienced as opaque, clinical, or distancing. While some terms, such as previously mentioned fluid bonding, are widely used in the poly community, other expressions may refer to specific kink practices that not shared by the majority. Sometimes people choose a provocative language to depict their sexual experiences and the terms they use might be rather crude. One example of the latter is barebacking. *Barebacking* is a slang term referring to penetrative sex, predominantly between men, without the use of condoms.

Inquiring about clients' choice of words may reveal difficulties with intimacy or discontent with the existing or proposed agreements. Making love has different connotations than having sex. Barebacking does not convey a sense of emotional closeness or tenderness. Fluid bonding sounds detached and clinical, but beyond these and other phrases, reside emotions that may not come up unless directly inquired about.

Miles and Gaby

Miles and Gaby were polyamorous for a couple of years when they entered therapy. Their relational language was precise, with few adornments and even fewer terms of endearment. When Miles became involved with a new partner, his and Gaby's communication around boundaries at first sounded direct, per their usual. What alerted me to an emotional conflict was Gaby's sharp use of sex-specific terminology. Her tone of voice was flat, but the words felt like needles. "Are you going to do cunnilingus?" she asked. "Does she have femidoms at her place?" and "I hope you are not going to endanger my health by careless fluid exchange." When I asked her how she was feeling, Gaby looked down, averting her eyes. She was good at holding back tears, and she was not going to let them flow now, either. With a halting voice she said that she did not like Miles's new partner; she wished he would not date her, but felt she had no right to demand that he stopped seeing this other woman. Gaby proceeded to describe how another partner of Miles insisted on barebacking, arguing she had a clean bill of health. Miles stepped in to clarify that there was no risk in their exchange of fluids since they both got tested prior to becoming sexual. The language in the session was becoming more and more clinical. I invited Miles to reflect on what he heard Gaby say about her feelings regarding his new partner. Miles became quiet, avoiding looking at her. After several seconds of silence, he acknowledged that he and Gaby had an unresolved conflict regarding sex. Reflecting back on their exchange, I said that it felt like it was not so much the sexual, but the emotional boundaries that got crossed. They both looked at me; my comment hit a nerve. "But how do you define emotional boundaries?" asked Gaby very softly. "I would like to be able to talk about that, but it is so difficult if you want to do polyamory at all." She was right, of course, and they both knew it. As is so often the case, a conversation about the seemingly contained topic of sexual boundaries revealed a field of unresolved emotional rifts.

Cross-Referencing and Cross-Referrals

Therapy with polyamorous relationships, where more than two people are involved, can take many forms. Here are a few examples:

–A poly couple may ask if one of their other partners could join a session or two.

–One of the partners in a couple may realize that what he is dealing with belongs to his other relationship and wonders if it would be possible to change the course of therapy.

–Metamours may ask if they can have a few sessions to help them learn to relate better to one another.

–A new patient happens to be in a relationship with the therapist's current client and was perhaps even referred by this person. Alternatively, she might be in a relationship with the therapist's former patient.

Heather (and Ashley)

Heather's entry into therapy was plain-spoken. She informed me that she was the metamour of a former patient of mine, Ashley, and that it was Ashley who suggested that Heather work with me. Being partnered with the same man, they formed an apprehensive friendship, at some point exploring if they could be more than metamours. Neither one was bisexual, so this exploration quickly ended; however, the attempt got them to know each other better and it was through these conversations that the idea of Heather seeking therapy with me took shape. Both women had had previous therapy experiences and knew that what they were envisioning was unconventional.

Heather's nurturing nature was evident in her wondering if I would be fine with this arrangement. She had given it a lot of thought, she said, and would prefer to work with me rather than with somebody else. "Knowing that you know Ashley, and have a sense of the man I love, will make it easier to explain why I'm here."

It is not only patients who become known through the therapeutic process; clinicians are seen by those they are treating, too. The impressions patients form of their therapists consists not only of what is explicitly expressed, but also of what is implied, sometimes without our knowledge. I wondered what Ashley had perceived when we worked together a few years earlier. I remembered her as a deeply thoughtful woman who did not make rushed decisions. Reflecting on Ashley's introspective nature while forming my impressions of Heather, I detected no red flags. Heather's affect was calm and reflective, and her story was intricately intertwined with that of Ashley. In many ways, they could have been in therapy as a couple, brought to the relationship by chance but doing their best to sustain it. And in many ways, they were doing just that, sequentially in therapy, and out of therapy. Yet, their stories were also independent and both wanted them to be that way. It was enough to be metamours; beyond that association they needed to hold onto their individuality and separateness.

Therapists vary in their perception of what is clinically useful and what is disadvantageous. Some may avoid collaboration with other clinicians when sharing a case (e.g., where one provider sees a couple and the other sees one of the partners in the couple). The rationale is that such collaboration may affect the therapist's objectivity and possibly lead to conflict should she learn about something that has not been revealed to her directly. The opposite view is represented by those who believe that periodic checking in with other treaters may enhance the therapeutic process and thus, benefit the treatment. In my experience, consulting with other therapists involved in a case is more helpful than not, especially in complex presentations. Comparing it to the medical model, it is to the patient's advantage when his doctors are co-ordinating care instead of treating each symptom separately.

Having worked with Ashley before, and now seeing Heather, felt like a strange form of consultation with myself. Through each woman's story, I could see the other individual's struggles and have a deeper sense of their respective longings and challenges. The person whom I knew only through their respective narratives, their partner James, had also become more multidimensional. His influence on the two women in his life was obvious. They tried their best to adopt his cerebral way of approaching relationships. It was evident in their attempts to be pragmatic, problem-solving oriented, and as unemotional as possible. The impression I formed of James was that of a man with dismissive attachment style, who by the virtue of his ten-dency to avoid, came to play dominant role in their polycule. Prone to intellectualization, he formed a polyamorous relationship with two low-demand female partners who learned to take their feelings elsewhere (i.e., to therapy). James seemed to be genuinely kind and caring, but at a loss when it came to affect.

Therapy with Heather was straightforward. She found what she was looking for—a greater sense of comfort with her complicated relational si-tuation. The therapy had ended in an easy, organic way reminiscent of Ashley's end of treatment. After we had finished, I could not help but be in awe for the level of trust these two women had in me and in each other. Partners by association, as all metamours are, they wanted to be as separate from one another as they could be, and yet, they succeeded in forming a distant, but deeply respectful alliance. They had never managed to get close enough to talk about their feelings without restraint, but their emotions were more aligned than they ever knew.

Transparency About Countertransference

There is a reason why I am including countertransference in the list of topics that are likely to come up in therapy with poly clients. Therapists are transitional attachment figures; they play an important role in patients' lives. They are also humans with their own feelings, ethical convictions, and re-lational wounds. Try as we may, we are not always able to hide counter-transference reaction to lifestyles and preferences that are significantly different from ours. Over the years, I have heard many patients describe how they could not work with a therapist they had previously contacted, because they felt judged. Seldom were the judgments expressed directly. More often than not, the clinician's countertransference was communicated through dismissive facial expressions and body language. Many of these patients said they wished that therapists would be more direct in conveying their negative or hesitant reactions.

When an encounter is experienced as insincere, therapy may feel unsafe. Admitting to a lack of familiarity with polyamory while expressing curiosity about the patient's experience is reassuring. Transparency sends a signal of trustworthiness. Clients choose therapists with whom they feel safe and comfortable; these are, after all, the building blocks of secure attachment.

Therapy is never about technique alone, even in treatments that utilize explicit protocols. A thoughtful sharing of countertransference reactions may aid treatment. As an example, some clients use polyamory-specific terms as if their meaning was universally known. During an initial session, when a patient, Rhea, described her situation in a rapid-fire fashion, stating, "I'm a part of a polycule. I entered it as a unicorn, but what I really want is to have an anchor partner. I'm bipoly, but I think I want the anchor to be a man," I could not help but wonder if she felt conflicted about her poly reality or therapy. Since it was our first meeting and we did not have any rapport yet, I made a mental note to come back to this opening if we decided to work together. Some sessions later, I brought it up: "I wonder if you were using all these terms as a shield, perhaps testing how I would respond?" Rhea admitted that she was testing me, although she was not consciously aware of her motivation until I asked. A therapist she had contacted previously told her that what she was engaging in was unhealthy. Later in treatment, we once again came back to this exchange. Rhea realized that, by using poly terminology in this extensive manner, she was trying to erase her doubts about open relationships.

Some patients ask me directly about my thoughts on polyamory. Being asked so directly is a countertransference experience. Inquiring as to why this question is being asked is always relevant, but putting it all back on the client may feel distancing, as many people genuinely wonder about my opinion. There is no simple way to answer this query, but whatever answer I may provide, my response carries weight. Polyamory might be a good choice for some, and not so great for others. Ultimately, our role as therapists is to make space for what Gabor Mate calls "compassionate inquiry," the purpose of which is to dig deeply into the core stories people tell themselves; to get them to see the unconscious aspects of their stories; to see where they came from and learn more about their impact. Once those stories are in the open, the task of compassionate inquiry is to guide people through the possibility of letting go of those narratives, or letting go of the hold those stories have on them.

References

Atlas, G. (2016). *The enigma of desire: Sex, longing, and belonging in psychoanalysis.* Routledge.

Balzarini, R. N., Dharma, C., Kohut, T., Holmes, B. M., Campbell, L., Lehmiller, J. J., & Harman, J. J. (2019). Demographic comparison of American individuals in polyamorous and monogamous relationships. *The Journal of Sex Research*, 56(6), 681–694. https://doi.org/10.1080/00224499.2018.1474333

Blackstone, A. (2019). *Childfree by choice: The movement redefining family and creating a new age of independence.* Dutton.

Clanton, G. (2006). Jealousy and envy. In J. E. Stets & J. H. Turner (Eds.), *Handbook of the sociology of emotions* (pp. 410–442). Springer.

Garnets, L. D., & Kimmel, D. C. (Eds.). (2003). *Psychological perspectives on lesbian, gay, and bisexual experiences.* Columbia University Press.

Nagoski, E. (2015). *Come as you are: The surprising new science that will transform your sex life.* Simon & Schuster.

O'Neill, N., & O'Neill, G. (1972). *Open Marriage: A New Lifestyle for Couples.* M. Evans & Co.

Shaw, J. (2012). Approaching your highest sexual function in relationship: A reward of age and maturity. In P. J. Kleinplatz (Ed.), *New directions in sex therapy: Innovations and alternatives* (pp. 175–194). Routledge.

Solomon, A. (2018). *New family values.* Audible Originals.

Wachtel, P. L. (2008). *Relational theory and the practice of psychotherapy.* The Guilford Press.

Part VI
Love Insists the Loved Loves Back

"Love insists the loved loves back."

—Dante

Dante's personification of love in the quote above resonates with my experience of therapy with polyamorous clients. It captures the deep-seated need for reciprocity in romantic engagements, regardless of the relational format. The following chapters are, in their entirety, devoted to client stories. The narratives presented here give voice to a range of polyamory-related conflicts and difficulties that may unfold in the therapy room.

To ensure privacy and confidentiality, each case is a compilation of multiple patient stories arranged to represent a central theme. Polyamory is not for the faint of heart; this is a warning many hear and just as many ignore. Many therapy clients believe that they took this advice into hard consideration, only to discover the worrisome fragility of their relationship. Intellectual preparedness is very different from the visceral experience of the totally new reality of open relationships. For some people, the difficulties emerge almost at once; for others, the onset is delayed until a catalyst sends a jolt through the system, revealing underlying insecurities. Some triggers are easy to identify and examine; others are harder to name and gauge because the behavior causing distress is incongruous with the expressed level of hurt.

For some individuals, their flirtation with polyamory allows them to rediscover themselves in their relationship, something they were longing for when opening up. Other couples discover that their relationship has been stale rather than solid for a long time and is no longer salvageable. Helping clients to resolve their present conflicts and impasses typically requires an exploration of the past. The unrelenting persistence of hurt in relational dynamics usually points to an old attachment wound that the person is re-enacting.

23 Polycurious: In Search of Greener Grass

Many people find the concept of polyamory appealing. It offers a solution to the loss of sexual and romantic freedom associated with monogamy. This chapter tells the story of a married couple who was intrigued by polyamory and decided to find out what it could offer.

Jack and Sarah

There are different types of polycuriosity—some couples stay at the edge for a long time, slowly exploring what it would be like to open up; others quickly progress into action. Jack and Sarah, a couple in their mid 30s, were of the latter kind; both found polyamory intriguing and, after some deliberation, they decided to give it a try. As they told me, their relationship was good, and they were not prone to jealousy. They felt prepared, having read *The Ethical Slut* and a handful of other books. Podcasts and blogs on nonmonogamy were also part of their daily feed. They figured out which online dating sites attracted people interested in polyamory and set up their profiles.

Soon after he signed up for one such site, Jack started exchanging messages with Lesley. He was open with Sarah about their exchanges, and after a handful of conversations, Sarah approved of him going out on a date. She reasoned that it was going to happen sooner or later, so why not agree to this particular meeting. She did not find Lesley particularly threatening, describing her as a little odd and not overly attractive, and that helped her to be supportive of Jack's new pursuit. On her end, Sarah realized that she needed more time to digest all these recent developments and held off looking for someone suitable until a vaguely defined "later."

Jack and Lesley's first date was comfortable. Not revelatory in any shape or form, but relaxed enough to agree to meet again. Jack did not feel any sparks, but he was interested in continuing. There were no other candidates on the horizon, and he hoped that once he and Lesley got to know each other better, excitement would grow. Their second and third dates involved making out but, per agreement with Sarah, they avoided oral and penetrative sex. For Sarah, Jack and Lesley's progression toward more involved sex felt a little too fast and too soon, but as she reasoned, withholding permission for Jack to proceed further was just an attempt to evade the inevitable. Instead, the pragmatic part of her mind told her to focus on safe-sex practices and protection of marital boundaries. These boundaries included specifications regarding where and when sex could, and could not, occur. The car she and Jack both used was designated as off limits, and so was their bedroom, should the time come for Jack to invite Lesley to their house. Sarah explained that she did not want to have any associations with the couple making out in her car or having sex in their marital bed. They revised the boundaries of sexual practices a few times, finally agreeing that aside from kissing, fluid exchanges were not allowed. Jack and Lesley were to use condoms for oral sex and intercourse.

Agreements to open up that appear synchronous on the surface are not always as harmonious underneath. I learned that Sarah found the idea of polyamory intellectually appealing, but internally, she was not confident about how well it would work in practice. Still, she preferred transparency to cheating. Jack experienced no ambivalence; he was excited about the possibilities. However, he was concerned about their explorations coming to a halt given Sarah's reservations. He hoped for an equal partnership in this polyamorous endeavor—their marriage had mostly been a marriage of equals.

In treatment, Sarah was the more expressive of the two, eagerly engaging in the emotional exploration of her own and Jack's feelings. Jack often referred to her as being emotionally "one-up." There was impatience mixed with admiration in his voice when he talked about Sarah's "command of feelings." He preferred a problem-solving kind of communication, which he knew Sarah to be fully capable of. When emotions got intense, he responded with an affective freeze, erring on the side of saying nothing rather than risking saying "something wrong." He reacted in a similar manner to Lesley, but as Sarah put it, Lesley's odd way of relating matched Jack's dismissive tendencies.

As the intensity of Jack's dates increased, Sarah's yearning for emotional safety was growing—her demand for Jack to show up emotionally was escalating. Jack, unsure how to soothe her distress, sought comfort with Lesley. The couple's relational anguish was rising. A tipping point occurred a few months into polyamory, unearthing an unresolved rift from earlier times. The triggering event was Jack's failure to respect one of the boundary stipulations—to keep any reminders of his sexual connection with Lesley out of Sarah's sight. Driving to work one morning, on the back seat of their car, Sarah found a sex toy that did not belong to her. It was clear that it had been used by the way it was wrapped in a paper towel, "still sticky and gross." Sarah felt violated; she felt that her trust had been betrayed twice. Not only did Jack and Lesley appear to have had sex in the car, but they had failed to use protective barriers. Sarah felt desperately alone vis-à-vis Jack and Lesley's disregard of her boundary requests. Jack's attempts at explaining what had happened did not help much, either. He described how he felt torn between protecting the agreement he and Sarah had made and trying not to reject Lesley. It was Lesley who had surprised him with the sex toy, and Jack had not wanted to hurt her feelings by rebuffing her spontaneity. Responding to Sarah's challenging questions, he reluctantly admitted to being carried away by the heat of the moment. Sarah was livid; she felt betrayed by Lesley as much as by Jack, exclaiming that if she could not trust Jack because "he was just a typical male," at the very least she had hoped that Lesley, as a woman, "would know better."

Virginia Goldner (2014) vividly describes how "[c]ouples in crisis may present in many different ways, content issues and personality styles run the gamut—but whether theatrically voiced or floating in the ether, something is always the same—the shock, the fear of collapse, the profound confusion over what is going on—a situation that incites extreme reactivity, paranoia, [and] hypersensitivity" (p. 403). Sarah and Jack experienced all of these emotions—they were disoriented, unsettled, reactive, and paranoid. In their case, the relational crisis prompted by sexual-boundary crossing sat on top of unresolved family-of-origin issues.

Nobody can hurt one as much as one's beloved. The same person who is a rock, best friend, trusted confidant, supportive cheerleader, and problem solver may, in an instant, become a violator of trust, the source of relational danger and pain. A highly paradoxical attachment situation occurs in which the same person we need is the person we fear. It is far worse than being between a rock and a hard place; when attachment traumas of this kind occur, the brain is not capable of processing the paradox of longing and avoiding. It is only capable of responding to danger and acting fast to escape the threat. The rational mind, the prefrontal cortex that allows us to think and assess, is shut down; the amygdala and the limbic system take the reins. Adding to the problem, it is not just one person's unconscious internal dynamics; it is a two-person system. The triggered partner's state ignites the other partner's unresolved trauma that he is not even aware of. Both partners are dysregulated and in dire need of feeling safe. When it happens in the therapy office, the couple is simultaneously acutely aware of the therapist's person and also actively ignoring her, unable to stop clawing at each other. Those are often the most challenging moments for psychotherapists, novice and seasoned alike. What the clients are experiencing, the clinician is feeling too: the heart palpitations, dry mouth, sweaty hands, the sense of despair, and the need to get to a safer place. Gabbard (1986) aptly described it as physiological countertransference.

My heart beating fast, I was experiencing what Jack and Sarah were feeling. They were like two frightened animals, fighting and fleeing. Jack and Sarah's conflict-resolution styles were more at odds than ever—she was desperate to get his attention; he was frantic to get away. Their dynamics made it difficult to recover, not to mention learn from disagreements, and I needed them to understand their pattern of vulnerability if we were to make any progress. They were aware of my presence at the beginning of the session and toward the end of it, but in between, they were in an open, scary field. For weeks, we could barely make any leeway; all the effort went into containing and stabilizing the shifting ground.

Without any conscious awareness, Jack and Sarah were trying to regulate each other physiologically. For Sarah it was up-regulating. She grew up accustomed to yelling and screaming. In her family, almost anything could set off conflict, whether it was someone passing the salt shaker too slowly or not closing the doors quietly enough. Jack's slow or lack of response was not soothing; on the contrary, it was frightening, making Sarah feel that she was all alone. Jack wanted her to down-regulate. His family avoided conflict; voices were never raised, and emotions were suppressed. As a couple, Jack and Sarah had managed to find a balance by engaging in reciprocally satisfying activities, and it helped that they had a lot in common. For as long as polyamory had felt mutually intriguing, they had been fine but, when the third person, Lesley, had entered the system, the hard-won balance became dangerously tilted.

Multiple losses had occurred in both of their families. On Sarah's side, divorces were rampant. On Jack's side, there were tragic deaths and life-threatening illnesses. Unbeknownst to them, Lesley's presence in their life symbolized these losses. For Sarah, it was the fear of divorce, and for Jack, it was the fear of annihilation. He did not want the relationship with Lesley to die, and he did not want his marriage to Sarah to end on life support. The unconscious parts of Jack's and Sarah's minds were trying to steer them to safety, but what was safe for one person was dangerous for the other.

Jack and Sarah were used to working hard, and they were determined. They wanted their relationship to work, and they wanted to prove (to themselves and others) that polyamory was worth its risks. Their commitment to therapy was strong, but in spite of their efforts, their emotional and physical connection was weakening. As they were becoming more fluent in understanding their dynamics, they were also drifting further apart. In their case, it was not counterintuitive; on the contrary, they had realized how unfit they were to meet each other's emotional needs. Not because they had not tried, but because what they wanted was proving difficult to reconcile. When they eventually decided to part ways, it was with the sadness of acceptance rather than the anger of despair.

Perhaps a year after our therapy ended, a new couple contacted me. They were poly, and they were referred by Sarah. From this new couple, I learned that Jack and Sarah continued to be in touch, but now lived very different lives. Jack continued identifying as poly; he was involved with two women and seemed to manage it well. Sarah was in a monogamous relationship, ready to start a family. For a fleeting moment, I marveled at the fact that it was Sarah who had recommended me to this poly couple.

References

Easton, D., & Hardy, J. (2017). The ethical slut: A practical guide to polyamory, open relationships and other freedoms in sex and love. *Celestial Arts*.

Gabbard, G. O. (1986). The treatment of the "special" patient in a psychoanalytic hospital. *International Review of Psycho-Analysis, 13*(3), 333–347.

Goldner, V. (2014). Romantic bonds, binds, and ruptures: Couples on the brink. *Psychoanalytic Dialogues, 24*(4), 402–418. 10.1080/10481885.2014.932209

24 Frozen Love: Polyamory as a Catalyst

Just like couples in love, couples in frozen relationships are easy to recognize. When they talk, they focus on things that are safe to mention, masterfully dodging risky topics. When such couples start unthawing in therapy, one of the partners may mention polyamory—sometimes revealing longstanding thoughts of opening up flattened by the expectation that it would never be possible. At other times, mentioning polyamory is like a display of nuclear weapons—not intended for use, but meant to indicate the gravity of the situation. For still other couples, it is the emotional flood of unthawing that leads to curiosity about polyamory. This chapter presents two couples whose process of unthawing led to very different results.

Eric and Melissa

Resigned and angry, Eric and Melissa resorted to avoiding each other. They adjusted their circadian rhythms and work schedules, moving through their shared space like ships in the night. Weeks without sex turned into months, then into a year, the avoidance of intimacy readily explained by stress and tiredness.

For Melissa, the contemplation of polyamory began as it sometimes does, with the creation of an online dating profile just to see how it feels, and to explore who is out there. It often is an ego boost to realize that one's profile is being looked at. Melissa tearfully described the pain of her experience: "I thought I was dead and I discovered that I am still alive and apparently still attractive. With sex being gone from our relationship, my sense of self-worth plummeted down. I started to think of myself as ugly and undesirable, becoming really depressed." Melissa was grateful for the encouragement her online activity provided but did not want Eric to think that she was actually intending to find new partners. She was torn—on the one hand, she thought she should take down her profile; on the other hand, she was not ready to do it just yet. The dating site provided the desperately needed affirmation of her aliveness, and she could not bear the thought of going back to the icy state of their marriage. She tried to reassure Eric, and herself, of her love, despite her desire to keep the dating account open. Eric was not convinced; for him, Melissa's unwillingness to close the account was an indicator of her giving up on their relationship. He accused Melissa of being dishonest—she was having her cake and eating it too, and he was left with nothing. Melissa pointed out that since they had stopped having sex, there was barely any cake to eat.

Eric and Melissa were no longer frozen, but they were not any less stuck, still incapable of understanding each other. The previous carefulness and avoidance of anything that tasted of risk had been replaced with loud outcries of despair and torrents of accusations. Compared to the chronic ache of the previous years, they were now acutely in pain. They did what couples may do in situation like theirs—they came to therapy.

Working with couples in distress, I often make a reference to visible and invisible pain, pointing out that the latter is no less disabling than the former. The only difference is that the person in invisible pain has been aware of the relational torment for a longer time than the partner who just got hit by the despair. When Melissa's suffering became intolerable, she moved to action. She had insisted on couple's therapy with greater vehemence than at any time before, and with great reluctance, Eric had agreed to give it a try. He did not like where they were either but did not think they needed help. Eric claimed that he was not ashamed of being in therapy but did not hide the fact that he would prefer they sorted things out on their own. Alternatively, if Melissa insisted on treatment, he thought, she should be doing it individually. His perception of their problems was simple—if only Melissa was less bossy and more willing to show him affection, they would be fine.

For Melissa, the metaphor of invisible and visible pain resonated. She felt validated and relieved, nodding vigorously when I referred to her pain being there all along, even if Eric could not see it. She explained that she had signed up for the dating site in the desperate hope of waking Eric up. Wake him up it did, but not in the way she expected. In my office, he shouted, accusing Melissa of lying and trying to cover her mess up. Eric defended his lashing out—he believed his wife had intended to break up their marriage without even giving it a try. He felt that he was the only one in pain, struggling to understand why she had not said anything sooner. If she were hurting as much as she said she was, and for so long, how could he not have known? The only logical explanation was that she was on a brink of an affair. In his eyes, Melissa had become cold and detached, insistent on playing by her rules.

As Eric's preoccupation with Melissa's duplicity continued to increase, her hope for things to change started deteriorating. Still insisting that she had not looked for anyone else, she explained that she gave in to the temptations of the dating site. It had started with a few careful "likes," the electronic displays of interest. In her profile, Melissa had indicated that she was looking for friends and not for anything serious. It was a gray zone, but there was a truth to it. She was lonely and not on the same page as her friends, who all had young kids. Friends from college who did not have children lived in different states, and getting together with them was not easy. She always got along better with male friends, so it did not seem overly harmful to consider new male friendships. Needless to say, Eric was of a different mindset, feeling threatened by Melissa going out on a "friend's date." He was not kind about it, calling her "stupid" for thinking men would want to stay platonically involved without pushing for sex. While this possibility was not lost on Melissa, she was deeply upset by Eric's condescending tone.

Eric and Melissa were reacting rather than responding; desperate to find each other, they were unable to find a common ground to stand on. Eric was like a fish out of water, one moment thrashing, the next gasping for breath. In an attempt at retaliation, he created his own dating profile and proceeded to go on a date with the first woman who agreed. Melissa was incensed, but also relieved. At least they were on the same page, were they not? Perhaps they could make it work by opening up. From not knowing anything about polyamory, to scoffingly dismissing it as a possibility, Eric and Melissa were now aggressively exploring nonmonogamy while simultaneously destroying the vestigial chances of saving their marriage.

Therapy can hardly save relationships that are rushing toward annihilation, so trying to help such couples can be a particularly challenging task. Witnessing this couple in so much pain that, metaphorically speaking, they were willing to kill each other, was hard. But I could not help but think that, on some unconscious level, perhaps Eric and Melissa knew what they were doing. They were killing off the relationship that had ceased to be viable a long time ago. While still frozen, they had appeared to keep it together. Becoming unfrozen revealed that the process of disintegration was already too advanced to bring life back to their relationship. Their attempt to open up had become the catalyst they needed to finally break apart.

Eric and Melissa's treatment ended the way it started, with a bang. Too hurt and angry with each other, they could not find any reserves of kindness. Once divorce was mentioned, they abruptly terminated therapy and called the lawyers. No longer seeing them, I imagined that they could not tolerate to be in each other's presence and had to put distance between themselves and everything that connected them. Their ability to empathize with the other person's pain was gone—they could only deal with their own hurts.

Cassie and Jared

Not all frozen relationships are dead inside. Every now and then I get a referral for adjunct sex therapy with a couple that has been in treatment for months or years, successfully working through many conflicts in their couple's counseling, but who are unable to move beyond a sexual impasse. Emotional reengagement, which usually involves exploration of various aspects of a couple's intimacy, is often easier than sexual reengagement. For those couples, sex therapy becomes the push they need to finally address their sexual difficulties. In contrast, couples who are acutely aware that their lack of sexual engagement is a major problem in their relationship may engage in sex therapy as a way of avoiding actual physical involvement with each other. Talking about sex becomes the substitute for having sex. In this way, the impasse is maintained while anxiety about the state of the relationship is temporarily assuaged. For those couples, the fear of finding out that there may not be any spark left overpowers the physical longing for sex.

Lack of sexual engagement reopens old wounds and generates new doubts about one's attractiveness, desirability, and ability to satisfy one's partner. With so much at stake, it is not a surprise that many couples prefer avoiding rather than confronting their worst fears. These couples can make considerable progress in therapy, becoming more fluid in their verbal exploration of sexuality, while simultaneously evading any physical contact that could lead to sex. Sex is often the one area in which they remain frozen, waiting for each other to make the move that would convince them that they are lovable and wanted. Their stated wishes and goals are at odds with the need to protect their vulnerable core against the risk of even greater pain. Exploring these dynamics is seldom enough to get out of the sexual freeze, and more often than not, an external push gets things moving faster than therapy could.

Cassie and Jared were in their 30s and hurting. Desperate to escape the icy politeness of their relationship, Cassie turned to perusing online dating sites. "I just want to check what's out there" turned into "I wonder if anyone would respond to my profile, if I had one" then to "It's reassuring to know that there are people out there who are interested in me."

After exchanging a handful of messages behind Jared's back with a man she met online, it became obvious to Cassie that she wanted to meet this new person. She considered not telling Jared but that felt too much like the beginning of an affair, and she did not want to do that. A couple of weeks went by with Cassie making excuses for why she could not meet the new man until she sensed that he would soon lose interest if she continued delaying. Feeling caught between a rock and a hard place, Cassie revealed to Jared that she had created an online profile and had had a handful of exchanges with a man who was interested in meeting her. In the office, Jared's expressions fluctuated between surprise, anger, interest, disdain, curiosity, and fear. Steadying his voice, he exclaimed that he had sensed her distance and had wondered if she was seeing someone else. But, he admitted, he had thought about it too. It was Cassie's turn to show disbelief. "Really?" she asked. Jared explained how he had been reading about polyamory and wondering if it was something that could work for them. A work colleague of his had a husband and a boyfriend, and all three appeared to like and respect one another.

Couples who have been desperately hoping for some shift in their frosty relationship find moments like this invigorating. From anticipating the worst, Cassie and Jared realized how encumbered they were by their situation. Unsure how to change it, both had considered divorce, but neither had actual desire to end the relationship. Now they appeared to be speaking the same language; they felt relieved and reassured by this symmetry. The sessions following this exchange were like a honeymoon, with Cassie and Jared gleefully describing what they were discovering about each other. Going to a poly meeting, they met people who were openly discussing their poly experiences. Their impressions were mixed, but it was refreshing for them to participate in such honest conversations. They went to more poly events, and eventually Jared announced that he was going out on a date with a woman he had met on one of these occasions. Cassie felt conflicted but thought it would be hypocritical to say no. The date went well enough, and the experience gave both of them a sense of reassurance that it was possible to consider dating other people. Cassie was surprised that she was not as distressed as she had feared she would be when Jared went on his date. On his end, Jared was relieved that Cassie did not "freak out."

Cassie and Jared's invigoration led them to conversations they had never had before, and had never believed they could have. Suddenly they were talking about sex and intimacy, about what they liked and what was missing—about their longings for a deeper emotional and sexual connection within their marriage. One night, when they were sharing their sexual fantasies for the first time, their hands started to wander, touching long-disengaged body parts. Before they knew it, they were making love. Sex felt good, although both felt unsure how much the other person enjoyed it. Talking about it in therapy, Cassie and Jared considered the possibility that perhaps they were "a little rusty" and needed to give it more time.

The bliss lasted a few weeks. After three dates, Jared and the woman concluded that there was too little mutual interest to continue. Cassie admitted that she was relieved, realizing that she was not ready for this degree of openness. In those feverish days of emotional rediscovery, they continued having sex but, as they noticed, without feeling really engaged. In therapy, they wondered whether they had become incompatible, or whether they were too preoccupied with all the external explorations to pay full attention to how it actually felt to be together. Once again, Cassie and Jared were overcome with confusion; their "honeymoon" had surely meant something, but it was hard to understand what. Overwhelmed, they were hovering on the edge—not wanting to give up on marriage and therapy and not sure if there was any meaning in continuing with either. Divorce was mentioned again, but to their surprise, this time the feelings were different. They felt deeply sad and not at all relieved at the idea of divorcing. The poly experience had taught them about the value of openness and transparency, and they agreed to continue exploring their relationship while pledging to be honest about their emotions.

Not infrequently, partners who are stuck in their relationship and no longer able to tolerate the discontent, tend to be stuck in other areas of their lives as well: career, work, family relationships, or friendships. With so many sources of discontent, the desire for a change, any change, becomes pressing. And since the relationship usually appears to be the predominant source of dissatisfaction, this is where the need for action first emerges. In contrast, partners who are preoccupied with their work and careers may notice relational distress but have no time or energy to address it.

Compared to Jared, Cassie was less content with her life. She did not particularly care about her job—it paid good money but was not challenging, and she was bored. Cassie's family and friends lived in different states; locally, her network consisted of work colleagues with whom she occasionally went out for drinks. With more time at her disposal than Jared had, she was more acutely aware of her dissatisfaction, accusing her husband of being distant. He defensively agreed that his work was demanding. In a session that focused on the examination of their respective realities, Cassie took an unexpected detour. She told Jared that her coworker and her husband were swingers. Cassie wondered if they should try swinging as it seemed better suited to their relationship. Jared had a vague notion of swingers, not sure how it would look in practice, but he was willing to try.

Although there is some overlap between polyamory and swinging, these communities are based on very different sets of values. In simplified terms, for swingers, sex is recreational; for polyamorists, it is relational. In contrast to polyamorous couples, swingers do not question the basic premise of their relationship; they merely seek mutual sexual enhancement. Interestingly, each community views the other with some amount of derision. While discussing swinging, Jared and Cassie concluded that recreational sex with others sounded more consistent with their values, thus worth exploring. They agreed that they were less interested in finding new romantic partners than they were in having more varied sexual experiences.

Cassie and Jared's initial swinging experience was exhilarating. It took place at a swinger's convention, with hundreds of people in attendance. To their surprise, they were on the younger side of the crowd and highly sought after. Being perceived as attractive was an ego boost. The whole place was teeming with sexual energy; everywhere they looked, people were fully or partially naked and playing. It felt like being kids again, free to run and romp, only with an adult twist.

In the months that followed, Cassie and Jared were discovering that the reality of swinging was not as emotionally contained as it appeared at first. While there was limited risk of either one of them falling in love or experiencing NRE with somebody else, the differences in their sexual experiences became a relational thorn. Cassie was constantly propositioned by other, usually older, men. Jared, on the other hand, had to make the advances. He did not find the women in the group as attractive as the men found Cassie. Luckily, they were able to hear how this reality became tiring to both. Cassie and Jared eventually agreed that the big swinging events were too overwhelming, and they settled on attending occasional private parties with a small group of people who became their friends.

When successful, therapy ends when the patients are no longer in need of support. As a result, clinicians have a freeze-frame picture of the relationship they helped to advance or mend. Sometimes we get a chance to learn how things went when former clients ask for a booster session or decide to return to therapy because of new challenges. Two years after we terminated, Jared and Cassie contacted me, hoping to work through issues related to adoption. I learned that they had settled into their marriage, still allowing for occasional swingers' experiences. It was a balance they could maintain. Through all the turmoil of the previous several years, they had parked the question of children until they felt their relationship could handle such an expansion. Cassie did not want to have biological children, while Jared preferred to have at least one biological child before considering adoption. It was a complex issue, and both felt cornered, struggling to understand the other person's perspective. With their previous therapy experience in mind, they decided that my assistance would be beneficial to help them work through their new conflicted emotions and thoughts.

What made it possible for Cassie and Jared to move from freeze to reconnection, and Eric and Melissa from freeze to disintegration? Needless to say, it was not one thing but many together that accounted for the different outcomes. Couples often complain of not being on the "same page," but Eric and Melissa struggled to be on the "same side." The image I evoke for couples when illustrating the relevance of being on the "same side" rather than the "same page" is that of a river. As long as partners are on the same side of the river with the goal of getting to the other side, it matters more than being in the same boat. Going in the same direction, even if in separate boats, is uniting. Being in the same boat but having opposite directions in mind leads to the boat going in circles; this is what had happened to Eric and Melissa. Both had been paddling hard but they were getting nowhere. After years of struggle, the decision to divorce was the first thing they had managed to agree on. In contrast, Cassie and Jared were worn out at times but energized and hopeful at others. They stayed the course together, while battling the winds, and it was ultimately their most critical accomplishment. They discovered that while polyamory was not for them, they could open their relationship to new, carefully tailored, sexual experiences.

25 Soft Divorce: A Marital Dissolution Through Polyamory

A subset of couples who find polyamory appealing and whose confidence in their marriage is eroding go through a process that can be described as soft divorce. The common denominator of soft divorce is a relative ease of separation—those partners are aware that their relationship has drifted apart.

Garret and Nina

"Isn't what we're doing just a soft divorce?" Garret's question hung in the air. Nina intensely studied the tiniest imperfections of her pale-blue nail polish. Her cheeks were flushed, a telltale sign of her distress. "I don't know," she finally whimpered. "Maybe it is. I didn't think about divorce when I brought up opening up, but perhaps I was fooling myself. What do you think?" With no change in her gaze, it was unclear to whom the question was addressed.

Garret finally broke the silence. "If we end up divorcing, does it mean that we have failed?" he said, looking down.

"Failed at polyamory or failed at marriage?" I asked. Both looked at me, wondering.

"Well, I guess a divorce naturally means that the marriage has failed," replied Garret. "But does it mean we failed at polyamory, or that polyamory failed our marriage?" He looked almost calm, glad for this opportunity to engage in an intellectual pursuit. "This poly thing wasn't my idea, so I don't see myself as failing at something I didn't want do to begin with."

Nina shrank into herself, feebly protesting. "But you said that you'd give it a wholehearted try."

"That I did," agreed Garret. "Not that I had much of a choice. And you can see where it brought us. We have perfunctory sex if we have any, with no passion and no sense of connection. There would be more feeling involved if we were friends with benefits."

Her gaze still cast downward, Nina took a deep breath, straightening her spine. "So, if this is a soft divorce, what do we do now?"

Garret courageously named what many people trapped in open marriages feel but are afraid to confront—the weariness of holding on to a shell of a marriage, functional on the outside and hollow on the inside. For most people, the end of a marriage is associated with a sense of failure, and consciously or not, a soft divorce may be preferable to a hard one; it gives people more time to process. Garret's hopes had dwindled as he felt Nina slipping further and further away from him, and the emptiness of their relationship became hard to endure. Like many couples who embrace polyamory in an attempt to bring vitality back to their marriage, Garret and Nina did so because the thought of divorce was too painful and embarrassing to bear. No blame needs to be assigned when a marriage is failing but, typically, it is. Trying to explain to themselves and others what went wrong, spouses hold each other responsible for the collapse of their relational dwelling—the house they devoted years to building and furnishing until the energy to care for it ran out.

Since relationships do not come with an expiration date that would help justify the decision to discard them, shame, guilt, and fear may weakly hold marriages together. However, these potent emotions make for a flimsy relational glue. Caught between the dreadfulness of a deserted relationship and the terrifying prospect of deserting it altogether, partners turn their energy elsewhere—toward work and career, toward new friends—perhaps with the thrill of secretive transgressions, or toward polyamory. Thus, while the marriage remains moored, the relationship is abandoned, with dubious reassurances that polyamory would strengthen the structure.

Polyamory as the harbinger of soft divorce is common. Over the years, I have seen a lot of polyamorous clients who fall into this category. Although the available data is not necessarily nationally representative, it appears that a large number of people who identify as poly are or have been married at some point. Unmarried couples who open up are more likely to go their own ways, finding less of a need to hold on to a relationship that has run its course.

Nina and Garret's polyamorous exploration followed this pattern. After 12 years of marital trials and disappointments, they felt discontented and were groping for a change. Nina was more restless than Garret, but he too felt stifled and unhappy; the idea of polyamory had started to sound increasingly appealing. As many couples who toy with the idea of therapy but are reluctant to make the call, they simmered in discontent until the crisis of opening up made it impossible to ignore the underlying struggle.

At first, it had appeared that polyamory was the right move. Nina and Garret met new people with whom they got sensually, if not outright sexually, involved. Deep conversations ensued, and excited by the possibilities, they opened up emotionally and sexually toward each other. After years of barely talking, they found themselves conversing about sex and mutual longings into the wee hours, feeling almost giddy with unexpected options: A threesome with a woman Garret connected with? Hmmm…maybe it is worth trying, they said. What about the guy who flirted with Nina at a poly event? Could they go to the cuddle party he told her about? For a period of time, their sex life improved—giving voice to their secret fantasies gave them permission to engage in ways they could not have imagined before. After a few months of this renewed bliss, the old weariness started seeping in. This development coincided with Nina becoming involved with two men who eagerly pursued her, and the relationship with Garret went back to the un-inspiring autopilot of their previous years. In the meantime, a woman Garret was seeing fell in love with someone else and decided to put an end to their casual partnership. Feeling neglected by Nina and with no romantic dis-tractions of his own, Garret became acutely aware of his loneliness and disappointment with their marriage. As he described it in therapy, a small part of him was still hoping their relationship could be saved, or if it did not work, at the very least he would know that he had left no stone unturned.

Ultimately, Garret and Nina's soft divorce led to the legal dissolution of their marriage. It was a relatively amicable process, but not free from con-fusion. Between poly exploration and therapy, they had become better communicators, more attuned to their own needs and less afraid of naming what was hurting them without reverting to blame. Because they were able to communicate with greater ease, they were at times unsure whether giving up on their relationship was the right decision. The final push was almost ac-cidental. Garret half-heartedly applied for a job on the West Coast, not quite believing he would get it. When he was offered the position, he chose to take it, with the hope that starting over in a different state and environment would help him move on and heal.

Nina stayed in therapy for a few months after Garret left. She wanted to work through residual feelings of self-blame for upending the marriage. The phrase I used, "co-creating a relationship worth having," became her motto and inspiration for exploring new relational possibilities.

Alex (and Kendra)

Divorces are costly, both emotionally and financially, and people have rea-sons to delay their finality. For some, a sliver of hope remains that the am-bivalent spouse will "come to their senses and return." These were the words of a heartbroken patient, Alex, after his wife had moved out of the marriage and out of the house. After an intense period of poly explorations that they both had engaged in, Alex's wife, Kendra, met a man with whom she wanted to pursue a relationship. However, this man was not fully available due to his own complicated relational status. "Complicated" is an apt word for many contemporary relationships; a high number of them are characterized by ambiguous boundaries. The man Kendra had fallen in love with was married and monogamous, but not with his own wife. His sexual monogamy was with Kendra, but his emotional status was entangled. Knowing about all of these complications, Alex held on to hope that Kendra would get tired of the ambiguity and reconsider her own marriage.

The main focus of Alex's therapy was on his inability to let go; he was fully aware of being in a holding place with his life. When I asked what made it possible for him to tolerate such an impossible situation, his answer was earnest. He did not want to repeat the pattern of his family of origin in which affairs were widespread. Both of his parents had them, threatening many times to separate and divorce until, after the years of marital disaster, they eventually did. "Which part of the pattern do you not want to repeat?" I asked. Alex looked at me with surprise. I pointed out that he was, in fact, repeating the pattern of tolerating relational comings and goings, but because it was under the auspices of polyamory, it did not look similar to him. Alex sighed. "Yes, but…" the response, "Yes, but," is not a yes, so I followed this clue, asking Alex what he hoped to accomplish by waiting. At first, he did not understand, but eventually he described how, as a child, he had thought that if he was good, he would be able to make his parents stay together and love him the way he needed to be loved. They were too busy having affairs to notice him. Alex's inner child, whose needs were unmet, was engaging in repetition compulsion; he wanted to be noticed and rewarded for his patience. Since he and Kendra never got divorced, he continued hoping that she still loved and cared for him. He was holding on to her the way he could not hold on to his parents.

It was not so much Alex's increased understanding and willingness to break the pattern of repetition compulsion that led to his change of heart. The shift happened on Kendra's front. The wife of the man she was with found out about their relationship and asked for a divorce. It was a hard and quick one. Now free, the man moved in to an apartment, and Kendra moved in with him. Alex finally lost hope that she would come back and filed for a divorce.

26 Poly Repair: The Marriage Saved by Opening Up

For some couples, opening up becomes the grace that saves the marriage. Many of these marriages are held together by a decades-long history that typically includes children. When the relationship is solid, opening up may revitalize their sex life and bring back emotional intimacy. It may also lead to new sexual discoveries.

Danielle and David

It is rare to find a couple in which both partners are equally eager to open up. Usually, one person is the instigator and the other is a reluctant follower. Danielle and David were not any different. Married for 15 years, they had built the life they had long envisioned. A shared dream since their high school days was to have a big, interconnected family with "a soccer team of kids." When the question of polyamory came up, they were dealing with the challenges of parenting three boys and a girl, with the youngest not yet two and the oldest a prepubescent 12-year-old. Their hands were full, literally and figuratively. Between the tasks of parenting and the need to work, it was not a surprise that sex became a thing to wish for (and feel guilty about) but not do. Danielle maintained a small online business selling arts and crafts she was fond of making. It allowed her to work from home and be the primary caretaker for their four kids. David was a well-paid software engineer, and they were financially stable.

It was David who brought up polyamory. Until then, Danielle had never even heard the term, nor had she known what consensual nonmonogamy was about. David's revelation of wanting to open up came as a shock. His idea was bewildering to her and did not match her perception of what their relationship was about. They both had had very limited sexual experience prior to getting married, and their libidos had seemed to match. At least, that was what Danielle had assumed since David had never complained about his sexual needs not being met. On his end, David had felt that it would not be fair to make more demands of Danielle given the time and effort it took to care for their four children.

In therapy, talking about sex was uncomfortable. David and Danielle had figured out what works for them physically but had never learned to communicate about their desires and needs. Both were intelligent and thoughtful, but it was obvious that the topic of sex made them highly self-conscious. Embarrassed by their discomfort, they mused that "it was about time they learned to talk about sex now that their oldest son was on the verge of puberty." If the discovery about their discrepancies in sexual pleasure was an eye-opener, it was no surprise; they were skilled at avoiding unpleasant conversations. Temperamentally, they were similar—slow to react, but having a hard time recovering once upset. Both were more comfortable with logic than emotions, which generally served them well during conflictual situations. In other words, Danielle and David had reason to believe that they were on the same page most of the time. In fact, they believed it so much that, over the years, they had stopped engaging in deep conversations about wishes and longings, assuming they knew where the other person stood.

The question of polyamory opened the gates to explore other untouched topics. Sex was the major one, but there were other issues regarding career, child rearing, and the desire to travel that they had given up on since their kids were born. Realizing how little they knew about each other made them dismayed at first, but as they became more comfortable with difficult but essential conversations, their consternation started to subside. There was a deep sense of relief that they were finally able to engage with each other in this way.

Being able to successfully address less challenging topics made it easier to talk about their needs and desires and inch toward the exploration of polyamory. Danielle explained that, as shocking as it was for her to hear David's thoughts about polyamory, they also made sense. She knew that he was more social than she was, comfortable in groups, and that he enjoyed giving to others. Both had grown up in large families, but while David's was close-knit and eager to hug and kiss on every occasion, Danielle's was formal and aloof. There was very little physical touch among her parents and siblings aside from awkward hugs when absolutely unavoidable. She also acknowledged that sex was never that important to her. She found it enjoyable enough, but not to the point of fantasizing about having other lovers.

A concept sometimes encountered in poly circles is *demisexual*. This term denotes a person with low sex drive who may develop sexual attraction in a stable, emotionally close relationship. Once Danielle and David came across this term, they accepted its meaning without any question. The label seemed to fit their narrative of Danielle's sexuality rather well. However, as it became apparent in our exploration, Danielle *was* interested in sex, but not necessarily the sex she was having. She needed a strong emotional connection, that part did not waver, but she also desired a different kind of touch, softer and gentler, and a slow build-up to get excited. In this respect, she was not different from countless other women, but that was news to her. She assumed that the softer, gentler type of intimate connection was more associated with romance than sex.

Like many men, David had derived his sexual education predominantly from movies and porn. Until that moment in therapy, he had no idea that the way he was approaching Danielle was contributing to her lack of interest. David and Danielle realized that they were facing an unexpected crossroads. On the one hand, they could go home and, with the help of books and videos I recommended, try to build a sexual connection that would be satisfying for both of them. On the other hand, their exploration of polyamory already had some momentum, and it felt wrong to stop it altogether. The fact that neither had much sexual experience with other people was relevant. Naturally, David was more eager to pursue new sexual possibilities, but to his surprise, Danielle was not far behind. "I wonder how it would feel to have sex with a woman..." she said, hesitating. "I cannot believe that I'm saying this out loud. It doesn't sound like me, but maybe it is." She recalled reading an erotic story that involved two women and how it stirred her imagination. "Sex with women seems more intimate, doesn't it?" she asked. Priding themselves for thinking rationally, Danielle and David concluded that learning more about sex by perusing educational materials would no doubt be helpful, but having direct physical experiences with new partners would be even more illuminating.

From not knowing how to talk about sex without blushing, David and Danielle were now discussing bisexual options and weighing in on different forms of nonmonogamy. They agreed that polyamory, which they already had some familiarity with, was still most appealing. Casual sex or swinging were out of the question; it would never work for Danielle, but David did not like the idea, either. It felt too transactional and devoid of intimacy. Polyamory was the only format that allowed for a deeper emotional connection, so they decided to look for people who could become their new partners.

I did not get a chance to witness Danielle and David's process of opening up. The task that brought them to therapy was accomplished; they felt closer together, were able to communicate better, and were more capable of understanding where the other person was coming from. Many of their misconceptions had gotten clarified, and they were hoping to learn more about themselves and each other through new relational explorations. We parted ways with an agreement that they could come back at any time should they encounter new difficulties.

Several months after our final session, Danielle called, wondering about a referral for their oldest son, who was gender nonconforming. I then learned that Danielle had developed a relationship with a married woman who, like herself, was a mother. Their relationship was sexual in the beginning, and this experience confirmed what Danielle had sensed; sex with a woman was more intimate for her. Since then, that relationship had become predominantly emotional. The women were too busy and too tired to make space for sex. Still, having a female partner who "understood" felt really good to Danielle. David, too, had a secondary partner, a polyamorous woman whom he saw infrequently, as she lived some hours away. "Aside from concerns for our son," Danielle remarked with a note of surprise in her voice, as if only now realizing it, "we seem to be doing quite well."

27 Polyfurious: From Dreams to Despair

Patients and therapists alike hope for therapy to be helpful. Unfortunately, that is not always possible. The story below is of a couple who had hoped that by giving voice to their polyamorous dreams they would enrich their relationship. Instead, they discovered that their relational visions were never mutual.

Mark and Eve

When Mark and Eve walked into my office, the air immediately thickened with tension. They looked immensely unhappy. Mark hesitated before sitting down, taking in the décor of my space, as if trying to gauge, by the look of it, whether or not I would be able to help him. Not them, him. Even before they said anything, I had this sense that he was there with a very clear agenda, and that agenda was not shared. Eve, already seated, looked intently at the rug, bracing herself for the blow she knew was coming. It looked like all of her effort went into staying in one piece and not falling apart. She had an agenda too, but hers had to stay suppressed. It took all her energy to withstand the blazing fury of Mark's pain.

Arriving from nowhere conscious, the term *polyfurious* entered my mind. Mark was polyfurious! The intensity of his despair and the palpable agony of their disagreement before any words were exchanged spoke volumes. The story they revealed was a familiar one: they were two people who genuinely loved each other but were riddled with attachment wounds they could not name. Here was a couple who had weathered numerous storms of an unfolding marriage now finding themselves on the brink of dissolution because of their failed attempt at nonmonogamy.

It had all begun several years earlier when Mark first mentioned the possibility of having sex with other women. The remark had led to Eve's tears and confusion; to the processing of what it meant and why he wanted it; to a rift that wanted to be healed, but which was difficult to contain. Time went by. The first uneasy months were filled with the practical challenges of adult life, with its dance of intimacy and tiredness, with exhaustion usually winning. The travails of parenting two children, a boy and a girl, while attending to their professional careers were preoccupying. The kids were young and sweet, but as is the case for any parents who do not have live-in nannies or readily available grandparents, caring for them was demanding. Mark and Eve's respective families of origin lived in different states and struggled with their own conflicts and preoccupations. Work was a source of stress for each but also rewarding as it provided a badly needed validation of their efforts.

The first indicator of an unhealed rift showed up when Mark and Eve had watched a TV show and, without warning, were confronted with references to open relationships. They tried to talk, but it was difficult. Neither could reassure the other that they were on the same page. What Eve could not see was that Mark had quietly resigned himself to lifelong monogamy. He loved her and his two children, and that mattered more than the promise of novel sexual experiences. What Mark did not know was that Eve had continued thinking about open relationships, asking herself why she was so opposed to it and if she could possibly find a way to embrace it. She had started listening to podcasts on nontraditional relationships, and from those stories she learned about this new, bewildering world of transparent sexual openness that could occur without the pain of ending a marriage. A couple of her friends had mentioned ethical nonmonogamy, and what once was unthinkable now appeared plausible. She still did not want to open up, but assuming that Mark's desire to explore sexual relationships with other women would sooner or later reemerge, she was quietly preparing herself for this possibility. It did not take long. Another TV show prompted an abbreviated conversation in which Mark observed that if she were on board, he would be open to polyamory, but since he knew she never would be, he was trying not to think about it. What Eve heard was a verification of her assumption. What Mark heard was a confirmation of his belief that his wife was strictly monogamous and that open marriage was never to be.

Several months went by, with Mark and Eve carefully avoiding the topics of open relationships and polyamory. If they went to the movies, which was not often anyway, they would judiciously pore over the reviews, screening the films for potentially harmful topics. They did not talk about their quiet rating of movies, but the normative PG, PG13, and R, were substituted with their private ranking of "TBA" for "To Be Avoided," "PD" for "Potentially Dangerous," and "OK," for "Safe to Watch." In the midst of this, their sex life was eroding. They did not feel threatened by this erosion, assuming, as some people in long-term marriages do, that it was to be expected. Indeed, their life was very busy; both traveled some for work, which added another demand to their already long list of needs. And sex continued to happen, just not very frequently.

While Mark and Eve's unspoken efforts went into avoiding a relational disaster, without forewarning, a polyamorous reality erupted around them. Mark's colleague revealed that she and her husband were considering either divorcing or opening up. Eve discovered her coworkers were talking about polyamory, too. A male colleague noticed her interest in this conversation and started to pay extra attention, explaining the terms, telling her about the challenges but, more importantly, about the rewards of the poly lifestyle. He and his girlfriend were polyamorous with another couple and found it difficult but, ultimately, highly stimulating. The coworker's attention made Eve realize how deprived of affection she had felt for a long time.

When Eve finally risked telling Mark about her realization, and the context in which it happened, he ignored the part about the lack of affection and zoomed in on the polyamory aspect instead. He wanted to know more about her conversations with friends and colleagues, wanted to know who these people were and what kind of relational lifestyles they were in. Eve felt hurt that Mark had bypassed the affection part, but having his undivided attention felt new and reassuring. She was not surprised by his thinly veiled excitement but was also aware of an undertone of jealousy. Even that felt mostly good; after all, jealousy makes people express things they had been keeping to themselves. Mark's possessiveness felt more comforting than threatening; it eased her emotional deprivation.

Mark took Eve's sudden openness to talk about polyamory as a sign of things changing; his hope of exploring sexual connections with other women was renewed. He did not give polyamory much thought—the distinction between the possibility of having an open marriage, and loving more than one person, was lost on him. Later, when he became aware of the distinction his wife was making, he felt betrayed and misled. In his mind, he had only been talking about casual sex and had never considered the possibility of him or Eve falling in love with somebody else. But at first, Mark was excited. His impression was that finding women ready to sleep with him would be easy given that so many people he knew, or knew about, seemed to be interested in open relationships.

Because of his impressions, Mark was completely unprepared for the blow of rejections. He did not expect to be excluded from the world of people casually sleeping with each other, which seemed to be within such easy reach. Women he approached at conferences and business meetings were, at best, open to flirting, but uninterested in his direct sexual advances. He tried online dating, signing up for a site that he knew attracted more nonmonogamous people than other dating apps. His luck there was limited as well. It surprised him that women he contacted were actually looking for a relationship, even if that relationship was not defined as primary. He never considered sites geared toward married people interested in extramarital flings without their spouses knowing. To him, that was cheating, and it was against his values. Soon enough, Mark became frustrated and angry with his wife for not dropping "the whole poly business," since it was obviously not working. He had had his hopes up for the promise of open relationships and, almost overnight, became disillusioned and hurt. Not knowing what to do with his pain and resentment, he directed his anguish at what he understood to be the source of these feelings—his wife.

Having failed at finding women willing to sleep with him, Mark now poured his energy into securing the marriage. For him, it meant going back to monogamy and doing it fast. To his disbelief, Eve was ambivalent about closing the relationship. Mark was in agony, and his wife did not understand. Eve was perplexed, too; she had not been interested in open marriage or polyamory to begin with and still considered herself to be a monogamous person at heart. She struggled to understand her reluctance; after all, she did not want to add a new relationship to her life, nor did she want to replace Mark with a new man. She knew that Mark would never accept the first, and the latter felt impossible.

This was the point at which Mark and Eve decided to seek therapy. As I soon learned, their understanding of polyamory and other forms of consensual nonmonogamy had never been shared, but that was only a surface problem. Mark and Eve were what I would call an avoidantly volatile couple. There were few confrontations and a handful of encouraging discussions, but overall, their ability to express their emotional needs was restricted. Mark wore his tension as armor; he was quick to overreact to perceived insults and then retract and disappear. Eve's volatility was subdued; she appeared submissive but would not easily yield to Mark's demands.

Since Mark and Eve had never discussed the differences among open relationships, polyamory, casual extramarital sex, and so on, they had developed vastly different perceptions of what nonmonogamy could mean in their case. As a result, they struggled to understand why their attempt at opening up had misfired so badly. Neither one was used to introspection and, as a result, their ability to engage in a therapeutic process that could help them understand the other person was limited. Mark and Eve seemingly agreed on their goal for therapy, which was to restore the marriage. However, their vision of a "good-enough" marriage was as divided as their conceptualization of nonmonogamy. Eve longed for intimacy and connection, which Mark believed he provided. She also desired a more equal partnership. Mark wished their relationship would go back to its mythical origin, that is, a time when Eve had seemed happy in her accommodating position as lover, mother, and homemaker.

More often than not in therapy, Mark and Eve got stuck, with two different conversations happening at once and neither person feeling heard nor understood. Since they were prone to avoid rather than to explore, they continued operating on assumptions, including their expectations of therapy. The treatment reached its final impasse when Mark straight-out demanded that I tell Eve that she should go back to monogamy. "You seem to need my support in telling your wife what you would wish she would do," I reflected back as gently as I could. Mark was not able to take it. He felt betrayed by Eve, dismissive of the fact that it was he who had suggested nonmonogamy in the first place, and he felt deceived by me because I failed to order his wife to obey. He stormed out of the room. Eve and I sat stunned. She finally looked at me with lifeless eyes, asking, "What shall I do?"

That session turned out to be our last. There was no proper termination. In the remaining minutes of that last meeting, I offered Eve a handful of options for how to proceed, but I doubt that Eve heard much of what I said. The following day, she sent me a message saying that, although she wanted to come back, Mark was against it, so she did not think they could continue with therapy.

Reflecting back on the course of treatment with Mark and Eve, I was struck by the bluntness of the term *polyfurious* that had entered my mind in our initial session. Mark's anguish was palpable—he had not come to therapy to explore and understand; he had come to eradicate his pain. He needed me to exorcise the evil that had invaded their relationship. His fury was in response to grief he could not identify, a grief that had existed before any mention of polyamory. Eve had not entered therapy because she trusted it would help; she needed to put Mark at ease. Over the course of treatment, she had discovered that she had needs, but the couple was better off if she did not express them. She was like a dock, rising and falling with the motions of Mark's torment; her seeming lack of agency was an adaptation to the waves of his rage. In hindsight, given the volatility of their situation, which made it hard to establish a good working alliance, there was probably not much I could have done differently to help them. If they had lived in a different time and place, in which there was no notion of polyamory, they would probably have continued weathering their problems as before, without rocking or perhaps even sinking the marital boat. Would they be happier if that had been the case? Neither I, nor they, may ever know.

28 Aspirational Poly: Absence of Jealousy

Among the hopes and aspirations associated with polyamory, the idea of compersion stands out. It goes beyond the vision of harmonious coexistence in multiple romantic relationship; it implies that it is a noble aim to overcome jealousy.

Martin (and Alicia)

Martin claimed not to know or understand jealousy. In fact, he told me, he had experienced compersion a handful of times and was hoping to feel it more often…if only. If only his wife, Alicia, would be more open to exploring sexual connections with other people. Martin and Alicia had a semi-open relationship. They had talked for years about fully opening up, or rather, Martin did. Alicia had begrudgingly gone along with it; she had no interest in polyamory on her own, although Martin had managed to convince her a few times to have a foursome with another married couple. Not surprisingly, he cherished the experience, but for Alicia, it was not something she was eager to repeat. Martin's sexual fantasies involved submission—he longed to be dominated by a strong, assertive woman, a true Amazon. In his description, Alicia's preferences were mostly vanilla, but on a few occasions, she agreed to step into a dominant role during sex. Like with the foursome, she would not have chosen it for her own pleasure, as she, too, preferred to be submissive. But she was willing to play along, knowing how much Martin wanted her to dominate. Martin was even less inclined to play the dominant role than Alicia. Frustrated with the situation, he decided to seek therapy. When I inquired why individual rather than couple's treatment, Martin demurred, saying that it would be "more productive" this way. "How so?" I asked. "You know…," he said, his voice trailing off. "Perhaps it's more about me than about us."

Martin frequently talked about his lack of jealousy, asserting that he would love it if Alicia were with other men, that it would be a big turn-on for him. He emphatically exclaimed that the feeling he experienced when they were sexually engaged with another couple was "nothing but joy for his wife's pleasure—a pure compersion!" Yet, each time Martin described his fantasy of

Alicia having sex with another man, I struggled with a feeling that some-thing was amiss. His words and gestures were almost too grand in their re-assurance, and I found myself wondering about Martin's assertions. It was still early in treatment, and our rapport did not feel strong enough, so I kept my thoughts to myself. I pondered if Martin wanted Alicia to be sexually in-volved with others so he *could* feel jealous of her. When I asked him to describe Alicia, he painted a picture of an attractive woman in her 40s who men found appealing. Martin described her as a fit, petite blonde with a great sense of style. The words were enticing, but there was no energy in Martin's voice, and his description was rather flat. He claimed to be attracted to Alicia, but it felt like he was trying to convince himself about his attraction rather than genuinely feeling drawn to her. Many years into their relation-ship, he appeared to take her for granted. As he told me about the beginning of their relationship, I got the impression that he had chosen a woman with whom he felt safe and who was a great companion, but who did not evoke feelings of pride or admiration in him.

Martin and Alicia had been married for 12 years and had no children. Martin liked his job as a chemist at a pharma company; he felt appreciated and recognized for his skills and abilities. His choice of Alicia as a life partner also provided him with a sense of belonging. He knew he could rely on her, and there was a lot of warmth and trust in their relationship. Yet, his choice of safety had made him see Alicia less as a sex object and more as a sister. He prided himself for not being jealous, and to him, it felt like a significant ac-complishment. Recognizing Alicia's attractiveness, but without actually yearning for her, provided him with a sense of mastery over jealousy. Avoiding jealousy felt more important than subjecting himself to the risk of experiencing it. Martin was dimly aware of his motivation to choose women whom he found pretty but, ultimately, safe—women who were more like sisters than objects of passionate love and desire.

Martin talked about his past and present sexual experiences with ease, giving no impression of ambivalence. Exploring his early sexual history provided clues about his motivation to shun jealousy. Martin had grown up surrounded by all-encompassing female energy; his mother was a stay-at-home mom who took care of him and his three sisters—two older, one younger. He described his mother as a sensual woman, vividly remembering the slinky day dresses she favored, which revealed, rather than concealed, the contours of her body. His mother's unmarried younger sister visited often, and she, too, was very sensual. The women frequently talked about the men the sister was dating, their attributes and their shortcomings.

Growing up with sisters, Martin was accustomed to bras, panties, tampons, makeup, and feminine clothing. Martin was quietly mesmerized by all the mysteries involved in being a woman, but nobody paid any attention to his fascination. In his memory, a lot of activities took place on the second floor of the house, where the children's bedrooms were, with the girls having the command of the floor. It was in his youngest sister's bedroom that he had had his first formative sexual experience. For some reason, his mother and sisters were all on the bed, maybe trying to read, maybe playing, he could not remember. Trying to secure his spot on the bed, he happened to brush against his mother's thigh with his pelvis. She was wearing one of her silky robes, and he instantly got an erection. He was prepubescent, so nobody paid any attention. Preoccupied with their own developing bodies, his sisters mostly ignored the fact that he was a boy. They treated him more like a puppy than a young male.

Martin vividly remembered the exquisite pleasure of that erection, and the terrible dread that he would be found out and ridiculed. He managed to slide down from the bed without his sisters detecting anything unusual, but he thought he saw his mother looking after him. From that moment on, Martin became preoccupied with the intimate connection between his mother and father, listening at night to the sounds coming from their bedroom. It was fascinating and arousing but also hard to endure; he found himself being jealous of his mother. The Oedipal undertone of these memories was not lost on Martin, and he often joked about it in therapy. He had fond memories of both of his parents, but it was his mother who played a central role in his reminiscences. It was during these nightly reveries that his fantasies of being dominated by a stern woman with a hint of a smile on her face were conjured. In this fantasy, the woman bore a resemblance to Wonder Woman; she did not appear overly similar to his mother, although both were dark-haired and tall. The Wonder Woman of his dreams was statuesque and confident, and she subjugated him, commanding him to please her as she wished.

Exploring Martin's choices of romantic partners revealed that Alicia was not an exception. He fell for petite blondes with boyish figures who made him feel strong and protective. He was aware of the differences between the object of his sexual fantasy and the actual women he got involved with, but it was easy to dismiss his fantasy figure as cartoonish. In middle school, Martin had had an enduring crush on an elfin blond girl, so he did not question his later preferences for women. It did not occur to him that the absence of jealousy might have had something to do with his choice of partners—Martin did not need to feel jealous because the women he preferred were safe. He was confident about Alicia's fidelity and commitment to him; their exploration of open relationships had only solidified this impression. She had no interest in sleeping with other men or women on her own, and she only did it on occasion because of Martin's insistence. Thus, it was easy for him to feel compersion when he saw or imagined her having sex with other men.

The motivation to choose petite blondes for romantic partners as a way of preventing jealous feelings was lost on Martin. When I made this observation, he described it as "interesting," but without showing much interest in its meaning. Instead, he assured me that he loved and cherished Alicia and had no intention of leaving her. He could see that other men found her attractive and that pleased him, but without triggering any fear. Between Alicia's clear sexual boundaries and his own lack of possessiveness because she was so reassuringly safe, Martin managed to circumvent jealousy without questioning what made it possible. He cherished the idea of himself as a man capable of compersion, and he was not ready to relinquish that notion.

Unconscious motivations can be powerful, and Martin's story speaks to their influence. Needless to say, not every person who claims to not be jealous is choosing partners who make it easy to avoid this feeling. One of the positive aspects of jealousy is that it makes people examine their relationships and not take one's partner for granted. As Pines (1998) observes, "Most people don't examine their relationships very often, if at all, after they pass the stage of courtship and romance....All this examination takes time and energy most people don't have to spare" (p. 199). Martin was willing to devote time and energy to examining his relationship, as long as it did not challenge the vision of himself as a person incapable of jealousy. That was the boundary he was not willing to cross.

Reference

Pines, A. M. (1998). *Romantic jealousy: Causes, symptoms, cures.* Routledge.

29 Gender and Sex: Bisexual Feelings in Polyamory

There are many forms of bisexuality; when people have simultaneous sex with males and females, it is referred to as concurrent bisexuality. Sequential bisexuality occurs when a person moves from sex with males to females, or vice versa, but without much overlap. In polyamory, experimental bisexuality that involves experiences with same-sex partners, but without altering a person's sense of sexual identity, may also take place.

Alyson and Patrick

Alyson's discovery of her bisexual feelings had come as a surprise. She and Patrick had been married for ten years when the question of opening up arose. At first, she was adamantly against nonmonogamy, feeling deceived and betrayed by Patrick, who, in his matrimonial pledge, promised to love and cherish her and only her. Until Patrick had brought up polyamory, she had never heard the word. The whole concept did not fit with her perception of a sustainable and healthy relationship, in which each partner has an opportunity to evolve and grow in an interdependent fashion. Alyson's parents had a good marriage; after nearly four decades of being together, they were affectionate and loving with each other. Their relationship was a model she wanted to emulate, and polyamory definitely did not fit into this picture.

Patrick had had no such luck. His parents had divorced when he was seven; he and his sister spent their childhood and adolescent years shuffling among three houses, those of their parents and, the most comfortable one, of his maternal grandparents. The grandparents were better role models than the parents, but their relationship was not easy to comprehend. As a matter of fact, their marriage was rather confusing. They were devoted to Patrick and his sister, showering them with affection and kind words. Toward each other they were far less forgiving or caring. Patrick loved being in his grandparents' house but often wondered how they managed to stay together; they bickered constantly. In this respect, Patrick's parents' divorce was easier to understand; they were clearly not suited for each other. In his mind, their decision to escape the suffocation of their marriage was the most sensible step they could have taken. Following the divorce, both of his parents got involved in a string of more or less serious relationships, never finding partners they truly wanted to be with.

Meeting Alyson, with her healthy boundaries and optimistic attitude toward marriage, was a revelation for Patrick; her experiences growing up so deeply contradicted his own. Entering adulthood, Patrick had assumed that he would eventually get established and have kids but did not necessarily expect a relationship to last. With Alyson, he realized, he hoped to grow old together. It was therefore as much a surprise to him as to her when he started fantasizing about polyamory. The more he thought about ethical non-monogamy, the saner it felt. Patrick was apprehensive about Alyson's reaction but reassured himself that, surely, she would see his point. He admitted that he had not anticipated her outright rejection of the idea.

Two months into their discussions about polyamory, Patrick and Alyson's marriage started to deteriorate. She did not want to open up their relationship but also no longer trusted that Patrick would be able to honor their monogamous agreement. It was a double bind—opening up felt like a huge mistake, but not opening up offered little protection against raising mistrust. Reluctantly, Alyson concluded that since their marriage seemed to be on the brink of falling apart, perhaps polyamory could prevent the disintegration. Their sex life had taken a serious hit in the previous few months; it felt like going through the motions when they tried to have sex, both of them robotic and withdrawn.

Seeking couple's therapy was a testament to the fact that hope was not quite gone from the relationship. When I first met with Alyson and Patrick, I was struck by how polite and seemingly at ease they were with each other. However, their demeanor was a mask; their distress was apparent in what they would rather not talk about. They hoped that therapy would be enough of a safe container to help them sail through the experience of opening up. Ultimately, it was not meant to be, but that conclusion came several months later. At first, they went through the predictably unpredictable travails of polyamorous exploration. Alyson was going through the motions of setting up dates with men she met online while struggling to convince herself about polyamory. The dates provided a distraction from the distress she was feeling but did not alleviate her anger and confusion. Patrick hooked up with a woman he had met on a poly speed date. This woman was involved with three other men and hoped to find someone who could be her primary. Patrick found her sexually compatible, but otherwise they did not have much in common.

Through the people they met, Patrick and Alyson were invited to various poly events. One night, at a poly potluck gathering, Alyson found herself engaged in a conversation about bisexuality with a handful of women. As the evening progressed, the casual touching accompanying the conversation became consensually more sensual. To her surprise, Alyson realized that she enjoyed the soft touch of the woman. It was very different from what she knew with men; it piqued her curiosity. The night ended with her making out with another woman, surrounded by the soothing murmur of female voices.

The woman Alyson met at the potluck invited her to other events. Alyson enjoyed their connection; they went to parties, mostly gravitating toward other women. Their public dates eventually became more private. In poly terminology, they were dating, although this term did not accurately capture Alyson's feelings. Discovering new things about her sexuality with another woman was a pleasant experience, but she was not sure she was interested in being in an actual relationship with a female. Patrick, in the meantime, was thrilled. He encouraged Alyson to invest more in this budding relationship, and she liked to see him excited. He talked about compersion and how wonderful it felt to see her engage with another woman. Patrick's unabashed enthusiasm confused Alyson—why was he so happy for her? She was having sex with a woman, but without feeling attracted to women the way she was to men. The matter of her orientation overshadowed the underlying question of her and Patrick's relationship.

The holiday season was approaching. With it, the marital tension came back in full force. Patrick and Alyson were tersely discussing which family events they were going to attend, struggling to find common ground. Both felt hurt and misunderstood—should they keep their poly explorations a secret, or should they come out to their respective families? Patrick voted for coming out; Alyson was against it. The mounting tension became a strain too difficult to bear, and the delicate balance they were striving to maintain tipped. Patrick and Alyson tearfully decided to split. Instead of coming out as poly, they were now forced to figure out whether or not to tell their families that it was polyamory that broke them apart.

In Alyson and Patrick's case, the question of bisexuality was a captivating red herring, allowing them to focus on a topic far less threatening than the reality of their marriage falling apart. When it became obvious that it was no longer possible to salvage their marriage, Alyson's doubts about her sexuality fell aside. She recognized her sexual exploration with women for what it was—an interesting, but ultimately tangential, distraction. She observed, "If it was not for the poly experience, it would probably never have occurred to me to be physical with females."

Samantha (and John)

A very different bisexual story is represented by another client, Samantha. Alyson's bisexual experimentation was circumstantial; she had no real interest in women. Samantha, on the other hand, knew from early on that she was bisexual. Her bisexuality would best be described as sequential; she liked both men and women, but usually not at the same time. Samantha was married, and her husband, John, knew and embraced her bisexuality. They had always had an open marriage, which, according to her, had never evolved into full-blown polyamory. They knew each other's partners, but polyamory did not appeal to them. As Samantha explained, she would go through long periods of preferring either men or women. When she liked men, she would want to be surrounded by male energy only. When she liked women, her interest in men receded to the point of her avoiding sex with her husband. These cold spells had caused occasional friction, which she did not always know how to address. Samantha genuinely loved John and thought he was attractive, but during those times, she found it easier to have sex with him if another woman was present. Fortunately, he liked threesomes, so more often than not, they were able to balance their sexual preferences.

Both Samantha and John had what could be called *flexible sexual scripts.* Their sexual flexibility, coupled with the great degree of trust they had developed in their marriage, allowed them to be involved with others without much conflict. It was in their domestic partnership that they struggled. They wrestled with roles they were willing, or not willing, to play as spouses. Samantha yearned for greater equality, which to her, included a more equal division of labor. John argued that he was contributing as much to the maintenance of the household as Samantha.

The paradox of attraction is that it involves more than physical desirability. In therapy, Samantha described how her bisexual preferences were intertwined with the gender-role undercurrents of her marriage. She wanted to make love to her husband without forcing herself. It was not so much the desire for other women that prevented her from feeling fulfilled during sex with him; it was her frustration with his gendered expectations.

Samantha's initial question in therapy was whether she wanted to move on to a relationship with a woman. She did not want to leave John but wondered if she should give herself a chance to get fully immersed in a lesbian relationship. She was tired of sharing her female partners with her husband to make the marital sex more satisfying. As our therapy progressed, the question of where her bi identity landed faded to the background. Samantha came to accept that she liked both men and women, not necessarily at the same time, but close enough. Therapy helped her recognize that what she wanted to be different was how her marriage was constructed; she wanted to examine and reorganize their gender roles.

Samantha had invited her husband to join in for a session or two, but each time he declined. Eventually, he agreed to attend couple's therapy with a clinician who would not have any preconceived idea about their relationship. Samantha gave me permission to talk to their couple's counselor. The therapist confirmed that what the couple struggled with most was their expectations regarding gender equality. Samantha's husband asserted that he had no problems with her being bi, as long as she was "more caring" when they were together. What caring meant to him was considerably different from Samantha's perception of equality. They were a couple who had figured out nonmonogamy without much conflict, but who struggled to find balance regarding gender expectations.

30 The Tale of the Rings: Renewing Monogamy Vows

Relational outcomes of polyamorous explorations are not easy to predict. Some relationships survive the travails of opening up and flourish while others fall apart; others find their way back to monogamy. The following case is an example of the latter; it is the tale of a couple who came to accept their marriage for what it was, with all of its monogamous limitations and imperfections.

Caroline and Sean

The ring is mighty symbolic. Under most circumstances, it speaks of a commitment to marriage and monogamy. Whether it is a simple band or an ornate adornment designed to one's specifications, the choice of a ring is not random. Just like the person one marries, the anticipation is that the ring will stay where it belongs, on the finger. The ring on Caroline's hand was a family heirloom passed down from her deceased grandmother. Sean's wedding band was inspired by his grandfather's ring. Sean and Caroline did not seek therapy as a result of polyamorous considerations. On the contrary, they had recently married after eight years of dating and hoped to have children in the near future. But sex was a problem. They had never felt sexually compatible and fulfilled, although, as Caroline said, she could not even know what sexual compatibility would feel like—Sean was her first and only partner. What she knew was that sex was painful. Hoping to get pregnant sometime soon, she had embarked on the path of pelvic floor physical therapy.

Pelvic floor therapy can make a huge difference in a woman's life. It can be very helpful for the treatment of vaginal or vulvar pain, but undergoing it is a peculiar experience. More intimate than any form of sex, yet void of any kind of romantic intimacy, the task is accomplished by the physical therapist inserting her fingers into the patient's vagina in order to massage the inner muscles. This manipulation teaches women to release muscle tension on their own with the hope that it will eliminate pain related to sex. This process is followed by the use of dilators of increasingly larger sizes. Unlike a routine gynecological examination, which is typically conducted once a year, pelvic floor therapy requires repeated visits to the office, sometimes for weeks.

Vulnerable at the most intimate level, women who have pelvic floor therapy find it as erotic as the use of tampons.

Caroline bravely endured the dilators, acknowledging the difference the treatment was making. Yet, her desire to have sex of any kind with Sean was nonexistent. He was flabbergasted—after all, why would she go through this bizarre ordeal if she did not want to have sex? Caroline and Sean were miserable and stuck.

Sean's sexual experiences prior to meeting Caroline had been mixed. In high school, he had a girlfriend two years his senior. She was more experienced than he was, but in hindsight he wondered whether she was a victim of sexual abuse. Her behavior was confusing and hard to predict; one moment she appeared confident, the next timid and tearful. As a result, Sean had developed an equally confusing approach to sex, initiating and then abruptly stopping, or waiting for Caroline to give him cues, which she did not know how to do. Throughout Caroline's endurance of pelvic floor therapy, Sean had experienced her as dismissive of his efforts to provide comfort and intimate support. He was eager to progress to penetrative sex, arguing that they needed to do it sooner rather than later if they wanted to have children.

It was hard to tell if sex was the chicken or the egg, but it was apparent that Sean and Caroline's difficulties ran deep. Both were easily provoked, argumentative, hardly able to agree on anything. When attempting to describe the newest conflict, they could barely get past the first sentence before firing missiles at each other. Both felt lost and profoundly misunderstood, desperate for a respite, which seemed as unreachable as a fairy-tale promise of a princess and half of the kingdom. Predictably, therapy was progressing very slowly. The crisis mode prevailed for months as they struggled to find long-lost grounding. Surprisingly, in spite of the vicious fighting, Sean and Caroline never mentioned separation or divorce. Feeling the weight of their unrelenting anger and pain, I finally asked if that was something that had crossed their minds. Without hesitation, they answered that divorce was out of question. They felt committed to each other, hoping to become a family sometime soon. It had been their longstanding dream from the time they had started dating. Both came from large families with many siblings and they wanted to replicate the experience.

Inquiring so directly about the possibility of divorce had a cooling effect on their angry despair. Considering the end of their marriage made them realize their commitment to each other. They continued to disagree on almost everything, but the intensity of their fights started to diminish. It was a welcome relief for the three of us. Finally, it felt like actual therapy rather than emergency room management. However, while their communication skills were improving, their nonverbal signals continued revealing an unresolved conflict: their rings started to talk. Caroline's ring spoke first. It started gliding up and down her finger when she listened, or tried to listen, to Sean's defensive explanations. Sometimes the ring left her finger entirely, like a weary traveler exploring new locations and possibilities. It would slide down on the pinky finger as if measuring its thinness, only to be transferred again. The ring would visit her middle finger, stopping at the impassable boundary of the knuckle and then going up to the tip, touching the nail, before gliding down again. As the ring wandered, Caroline started to express frustration with their lack of sexual experience. She sighed wistfully, saying that she wished she had had more chances to explore her sexuality before meeting Sean. She felt bereft and angry, disheartened with Sean for not being able to touch her the way her body wanted. Two years after the start of pelvic floor treatment, Caroline was fed up with the continuous need to use the dilators. The sterile nature of this endeavor had made her feel even more disconnected from her body, and Sean was not helping her feel sensual and excited.

Sean listened, slumped in his corner of the couch. His head hanging, he seemingly took in what Caroline said. When he finally responded, it was apparent that he experienced Caroline's words as unjust. All he heard was that she blamed him for the difficulties that were not his fault. He was doing what he could, begging her to engage sexually even if it did not involve intercourse, but she would always refuse. As he spoke, Sean got increasingly animated. Defending his position, he started playing with his wedding band. The ring left Sean's finger, quickly migrating to his other hand. Placed between his right thumb and forefinger, the ring would swing back and forth, sometimes playing peekaboo, then disappearing in the palm of his hand. The ring would stay in Sean's right hand for the remainder of the session, only to go back on the left finger as we said our goodbyes.

The rings continued to dance for months. I observed the tale of the rings, many a time wondering if naming the dance would be helpful, each time deciding it was best to wait. My sense was that pointing out the rings' wanderings would upset the fragile balance that Sean and Caroline had struggled to establish. We were only beginning to be able to focus on the process of therapy rather than merely the content of their difficulties. They were still highly vulnerable, and it felt that bringing attention to the rings would be too threatening.

Fascinatingly, the rings never wandered at the same time. It was either one or the other that was actively exploring other territories. When Caroline's ring was moving around, Sean's stayed put on his finger. When his ring started to migrate, hers was immobile. *Are they waiting for the other person to break the spell and talk about their longings, or are they waiting for the other person to come back to their senses, so to speak?* I wondered. One day, when yet another disagreement was aired, the name Lydia came up. They had met her at a party the previous weekend, and Caroline was upset. She accused Sean of spending the entire evening with Lydia and ignoring her presence. Sean denied any wrongdoing; he and Lydia had shared professional interests. Besides, she was a new acquaintance who did not know any other people at the party.

Contrary to her typical response, Caroline did not argue the point. She dropped the topic and focused on something entirely different. Sean did not appear to be relieved by this seemingly fortuitous shift of attention. His face had a passive expression that was hard to read, but his ring did not move. A few sessions later, Caroline mentioned her colleague, Ed, whose work she admired. She had just learned that Ed was polyamorous. It was all new to Caroline and rather incomprehensible. She wondered aloud how people could manage open relationships. I had a feeling that she wanted to talk more about Ed and what he represented, but Sean did not pick up on the subject and commented on something else instead. It was a striking repetition of the exchange from a few weeks earlier, only in reverse. Neither of the rings moved. Soon enough, they were back to the familiar territory of rehashing an earlier fight, arguing who was right and who was wrong, and the rings started wandering again.

Exploration of poly possibilities oftentimes leads to an upsurge of sexual energy in long-term couples. Considering nonmonogamy may work as a catalyst, breaking the icy shield of frozen relationships. Partners start talking about their longings and the state of their relationship in a way they have not done for a very, very long time, or perhaps ever. Breaking the ice releases pent-up energy, making people engage emotionally and sexually in ways they might have thought impossible only days or weeks earlier. Spouses who thought they knew each other to the point of being bored are now wondering, *Who are you?! Do I know you? Why have you been denying me all this before?* Facing the threat of the relationship dissolving, partners dare to show themselves for who they are, or forgot to be, or perhaps long to be, if only the right kind of reassurance were there.

The thrill of this mutual self-and-other discovery can be both amazing and overwhelming. For some couples, contemplating the possibility of engaging sexually with other people leads to an almost manic exploration of their sexuality. Conversations about attraction take place, fantasies are shared, and difficult experiences are discussed without animosity. Bodies become fluid, merging with unprecedented ease. It is like a second honeymoon and NRE combined. Sean and Caroline experienced a variant of such a resurgence, and it came as a surprise.

Sean's half-brother, Danny, with whom they were close, had revealed that his fiancée, Ariel, wanted to open up their relationship. According to Sean, Danny's feelings were divided. On the one hand, it was an unexpected opportunity; on the other hand, it felt like Ariel was ambivalent about their relationship. After all, they had become engaged only recently. *Was it her way of avoiding getting married?* Danny had asked himself. Also, if he went along with it, what would their families say? Danny had admitted to Sean that there was another woman he was attracted to, so his reluctance was muted.

While discussing Danny's situation, Sean and Caroline started talking more openly about their own relational doubts and longings. For the first time, they were able to take in the pain of the other person without shutting it down. Sean explored the impact of his high school relationship in greater depth, and the confusing stop-and-go that it had left him with. He longed for a woman who would confidently show him what he needed to learn so he could become the lover he wished to be. He had had a handful of sexual partners after high school, but these relationships had not lasted long enough to make him realize that his understanding of women's sexuality was limited. Caroline admitted to checking online dating sites to see who was there, wondering if engaging sexually with someone else with whom she did not have the baggage of relational history could help her discover who she was. She recounted how her polyamorous colleague's flirtatious comments made her notice how positively her body was responding. Confused, she described how she did not find this man attractive but was nonetheless attracted to his attention and easygoing manner. She yearned to be with a man who could show her what her body was capable of, and who would made her feel safe and adored. She was tired of being criticized and accused of being cold.

The relief that came with this new openness was confusing. As much as they cherished being more honest and transparent with each other, Sean and Caroline did not know where this path would ultimately lead. Did it mean that they should open up their marriage? As with many couples who contemplate open relationships, Sean and Caroline felt the allure of this possibility. They agreed that it sounded enticing, but could they actually pull it off? Finally, they directly asked for my advice. Their request was understandable; therapists are often asked to tell clients what to do, and there I was, a couple's therapist who specializes in polyamory and open relationships. Knowing their backgrounds, personalities, and relational history, I was far from sure that Caroline and Sean's relationship could survive opening up. Their attachment was fragile, and adding new strings to tug at their unsteady bond felt like too much of a risk. They did not have enough charge in their relational power bank to handle the challenges that accompany non-monogamy. Their history and attachment issues aside, I also had had the benefit of hearing the messages of their wordless story, the story of their rings. The rings that came off only one at the time, but never together, throughout their contentious process. The rings, where one of them always stayed anchored when the other was transgressing.

I did what therapists must do when pressed to give advice. I helped them to arrive at their own answers. As their rings had foretold, ultimately Caroline and Sean decided that they did not want to venture outside of the marriage and look for new partners. Yet, it was this prospect that had helped them to move beyond the painful impasse. They knew that they had more to discover about their sexuality, and much more to work on if they wanted their relationship to thrive. Caroline and Sean's upsurge of erotic energy was reminiscent of the sexual awakening that often follows in the wake of opening up. It was also different in the sense that it helped them realize their commitment to each other and reinforced their preference for monogamy. As much as they fought, viciously and relentlessly at times, Caroline and Sean did not want to risk their relationship. At last they had found the common ground that their rings had known about all along.

31 Veteran Poly: Old Pains, New Tribulations

While the early stages of nonmonogamy present people with more relational unknowns than the later stages of openness, people who have been polyamorous for years may seek therapy, too.
When partners in well-established poly relationships are confronted by new challenges, their sense of trust and commitment to each other might be shaken.

Kurt and Adele

Couples enter therapy with their feelings first—not with a single emotion, although certain affective states dominate, but with many combined. Anxiety is usually high on the list, sometimes mixed with hope, other times with despair. Hurt, anger, resentment, embarrassment, guilt, and shame may all be woven in. Understandably, clinicians pay attention to these first moments of therapy, even before the clients' story unfolds.

Kurt and Adele came in weary. Very weary. The majority of people who enter my office for the first time comment on the many plants that populate the space. This couple did not. They headed straight for the couch, having already determined where each was going to sit. Demurely asking if it was okay to take off their shoes, they curled up in their respective corners, grabbing the white fluffy pillows on the couch, pressing them tightly against their stomachs. A long-ago patient had once compared those pillows to bichons frisés—small, comforting lap dogs. Indeed, the pillows are as often in patients' laps as they are behind their backs. How they are handled sometimes conveys emotions better than words.

Are they looking for protection or comfort? I asked myself. Or both? They feel very wounded, and yet they are marvelously synchronized. Are they even aware of it? Kurt and Adele knew I specialize in polyamory, so there was none of the typical cautiousness exhibited by clients new to open relationships, and none of the concern about the therapist's judgment or lack of understanding of polyamory. They had experience with therapy, and they assumed I would understand.

Kurt and Adele were what I call poly veterans. Both in their late 40s, they had been polyamorous for over ten years. As Adele later revealed, if she had known what lay ahead when they decided to open up, she may not have done it. "I wasn't myself," she said wistfully. "Maybe it was early midlife crisis, maybe something else, but I know that I lost my sense of direction. I wanted to distract myself." Her acknowledgment was not a regret but a recognition of the arduousness of their path.

Polyamory was not in the picture when Kurt and Adele had first met some 15 years earlier, and they had not questioned monogamy as a lifestyle. They proceeded through the steps of the relationship escalator without resistance; dating for a couple of years led to engagement and marriage. They bought a house, changed careers, and moved to a more comfortable house. One deviation from the escalator regarded their decision to have children. Both were ambivalent about kids, leaving it to the other person to decide, and neither felt compelled to insist. Eventually, it became too late to consider biological children, but they had kept the possibility of adoption open.

Like other well-established couples who seek therapy years into polyamory, Kurt and Adele were now presented with a new challenge. A year and a half earlier, Adele had been diagnosed with ovarian cancer, and her body and sense of self were irretrievably altered. The cancer had been caught early, but it required a preventive hysterectomy. Their sex life was put on hold while she was undergoing treatment. Now, struggling with her sense of identity as a woman and having already lost so much, Adele was not ready to give up on what used to be very important—her sex life. She wanted it back, but Kurt was not prepared to take this risk. A part of his concern was whether or not sex would hurt Adele. The other part was his relationship with his other partner, Melanie.

Adele's face fell the moment Melanie's name was mentioned. *So, that's the source of weariness,* I thought to myself. Kurt and Melanie's relationship had started some six months before Adele's diagnosis, and it was a fairly tumultuous experience. Kurt and Adele had lived through the challenges of NRE before but found themselves entirely unprepared for the whirlwind of emotions that had followed the addition of Melanie to Kurt's life. Adele and Melanie's personalities did not mesh well; where Adele was introverted and cerebral, Melanie was extroverted and unpredictable. Melanie was creative and histrionic, and like the collages she was fond of making, her boundaries were ill-defined. For Adele, who shunned ambiguity, this lack of clear boundaries was a challenge. To make matters worse, Kurt tried to downplay how energized he was by Melanie's unrestrained nature. His dismissal only added to Adele's disenchantment. Kurt was deeply loyal to Adele; it was clear that he admired and respected her, but the balance of his two romantic relationships was precarious.

"The presence of Melanie in Kurt's life makes you feel lonely," I ventured, addressing Adele. She slowly nodded. "I have another partner too," she said, "but our relationship is very different. Robert is a friend with both of us." Her relationship with Robert had started almost four years earlier and, to begin with, was not without complications either. Robert was going through a divorce when they had met, and his ex-wife was still in the picture, not always in a peaceful way. Yet, the conflict between Kurt and Adele did not include Robert; over time, the two men became fond of each other. Quiet and reserved, they were compatible personality-wise; they also had similar interests. Being involved with the same woman, whom they cherished and worried about, had brought them closer together.

When it came to poly structure, Kurt and Adele were only marginally concerned with the labels: primary, secondary, hierarchical, or non-hierarchical were merely words, not defining who they were to each other. They simply referred to Melanie and Robert as their other partners. They did not define themselves as a poly family, either, mostly saying, "We're poly, and here is who is involved." There were other partners over time, some of them coming and going, but none of these relationships had challenged the overall balance the way Melanie did.

Listening to Kurt and Adele, each holding on to their furry pillows, I was learning about their conflict regarding sex. They told me that until the cancer diagnosis, they had had semi-regular dates that had involved sexual intimacy. The frequency of their sexual encounters with each other was lower than what they had with their respective partners, but they were comfortable with that arrangement. They described how they managed to maintain a boundary of partial fluid bonding, limiting the practice of unprotected intercourse exclusively to their relationship. With the other partners, they used condoms. As one might expect, advancing through the stages of sexual escalation with others was not always a smooth ride. Both acknowledged that they had learned a lot about themselves and each other through this process.

Adele's diagnosis had altered their patterns of intimacy in more than one way. While she was undergoing treatment, Kurt and Melanie had moved on to having unprotected intercourse. As Kurt remorsefully described, "It happened spontaneously; we didn't have condoms and we were horny." He regretted not having asked for Adele's consent but hoped she would understand. After all, Adele was cautious about penetrative sex. He knew enough about her and Robert's sexual involvement to reassure himself that she would not mind. To his dismay, she did mind. He struggled to understand why Adele described his momentary lapse of judgment as an act of selfishness. She wanted him to know how much it hurt that she could not have sex the way she used to and did not need Kurt to remind her about her limitations.

Already infrequent, Adele and Kurt's sexual interactions dwindled to nothing. They continued hugging and sometimes cuddling, but the sensuality and eroticism were gone. In contrast, the sensual touch and erotic play that characterized Adele and Robert's repertoire felt comforting and reassuring; she felt that not all of her desirability as a woman had been lost.

Love affirms life, but sometimes sex is an even more acute affirmation of one's aliveness. Kurt and Adele had been through a life-threatening experience. Although they were mostly reassured about Adele's good prognosis, they were not quite out of the woods yet. *What made them seek therapy at this particular point and not sooner, when things were far more dramatic, at least on the surface?* I wondered.

The issue of timing is always relevant; I had several questions regarding their case. *Was their marriage at the brink of ending and therapy the last attempt to save it? Were their other partnerships holding the marriage together? What possible traumas from the past lurked underneath this present struggle? Was the conflict about opening up less resolved than it appeared? Were they as deliberate about not having children as they claimed to be? What unresolved issues from the families of origin were possibly activated by Adele's cancer? What about sexual identity?*

I had more questions than answers. Kurt and Adele assured me (and each other) about their love and commitment. What was missing was sex. They did not know how to get it back. Their "pillow language" appeared to confirm their words. No matter what position they took on the couch, sitting or half-lying, they held on to their pillows, but also managed to find a way to touch. Yet, as our therapy progressed, I began wondering whether they indeed questioned the authenticity of their love. Their touch felt like a lifeline to which they clung.

Both had a trauma history; it had taken them several years to learn to trust each other. Given their past experiences, it was truly remarkable that they had managed to survive the tumultuousness of opening up. Under her coolness, Adele was prone to anxiety. Kurt resorted to withdrawal when emotions got heated. Over time, they developed their own version of attachment security; dealing with difficult families of origin showed them how valuable their partnership was—they excelled at being partners in life. They could not imagine being without each other, and the cancer had alarmed them in more ways than they had realized. The cancer and the fear of more losses had triggered old fears, bringing up memories of other wounds. Without any conscious recognition of why it was happening, Kurt and Adele had turned toward their other relationships. In the arms of Melanie and Robert, they sought their way back to each other.

32 Looking for a Family: The Appeal of Multiple Attachments

While the most commonly expressed reason for nonmonogamy is a desire for greater sexual or romantic openness, for some people polyamory represents a vision of an ideal family. Hoping to find love and acceptance in one's connections of choice, and to create a family one did not have growing up, can be a strong motivating factor to explore polyamory.

Veronica

Since her teenage years, Veronica had been drawn to simultaneous relationships. Try as she might, she could not put her feelings into any comprehensible framework for herself or others, she told me in our initial session. Not that the others asked—after all, everyone around her seemed to be equally confused, figuring out the world that was teeming with attractions and rejections. Like many of her peers, she had had intense crushes, but hers had included both boys and girls. It was not until college that she had started wondering why she struggled with being monogamous.

She seemed to be assuring me that being monogamous was something one should aspire to, I thought. I shared my reflection with her, and she replied that there were periods when she was in one relationship at a time, but they did not last longer than a few months. She noticed that others formed lasting exclusive relationships, while she continued to be intensely drawn to two or three people simultaneously.

Veronica had become aware of polyamory when she got her first post-college job at a store that combined a gallery, bookshop, and cafe. The place hosted performances by local artists and attracted artsy people like Veronica. It was easy to meet exciting and unconventional individuals, many of whom identified as polyamorous. Learning about others who did not embrace monogamy was an eye-opener. For the first time, Veronica felt that she had found her tribe and gained language to express her longings.

During our initial appointment, Veronica articulated a desire to figure out her life. Turning 30 in a few months, she felt a need to take stock of her experiences and decide how she wanted her future to look. She identified as polyamorous, but as she said with a sigh, her poly relationships were somewhat messy. Veronica's described her primary partner, Aidan, as reluctantly polyamorous. By that she meant that Aidan was monogamous but tried to engage in poly explorations for her sake. Aware of his disinclination, Veronica felt uneasy pursuing other relationships.

Monogamous men in poly relationships usually find it easier to accept their female partner's involvement with other women. Unenthusiastic about polyamory, they find same-sex partnerships less threatening, often reasoning that it would be unfair to deny their partner's desire to explore their bisexuality. For Aidan, it was difficult to embrace Veronica's intimacy with others regardless of their gender. He tried his best, she knew, and a part of her liked that he was steadfast in his convictions while still willing to "grant her the space to be different." Aidan was her longest relationship to date; they had been together for six years. She loved him, Veronica said, sighing again, but the relationship felt stale.

To say that Veronica came from an emotionally distant family would be an understatement. Her parents had divorced when she was four years old, and although they continued living close to each other, alternating childcare duties, they avoided having any contact beyond the bare minimum. As a result, Veronica spent her childhood years going from one house to the other, oftentimes passing messages between her parents. She had a brother two years younger than herself to whom she did not feel connected. In her experience, he was even more distant than her parents, preferring to be by himself whenever he could. He was "a basement nerd," and she suspected he might be on the spectrum.

With humorous attention to detail, Veronica described the parental houses in which she had dwelled without ever having felt at home. The father's house had a gothic feel—dark in spite of bay windows and high ceilings, and empty of comfort. As she talked, I could almost see the cobwebs in the corners. The mother's house was the opposite, cramped and messy, not quite a hoarder's place, but not far from it. Mice had left gnaw marks on the cardboard boxes that stored "important keepsakes." In Veronica's description, the houses expressed more emotions than her parents or brother had.

With neither of her parents making themselves available, and a younger brother who was not much company, Veronica had sought the comfort of friendships. Growing up, she had two best friends with whom she would spend as much time as she could. The father of one of her friends was a writer, and he genuinely enjoyed interacting with kids. He was a great storyteller, and listening to him provided her with a sense of comfort and love that Veronica missed at home. She was a smart, creative kid who liked to play theater and perform, and her friends' houses and after-school programs were a saving grace from her emotionally distant family.

During an early-winter session, the warm light in my office barely offsetting the gloom of the weather, Veronica observed how she always felt more comfortable knowing that she had more than one person to rely on. Her tone was dispassionate, but her eyes looked sad. "You seem to wonder if you can rely on me alone to guide you through your struggles," I offered. She shook her head, neither a yes or a no. "And you seem sad," I said, trying to mirror her feeling, "and you seem to be uncomfortable with your sadness." Until that moment, Veronica had not thought much about how her family of origin had influenced her preference for polyamory. She became agitated; making this connection made her feel like a victim of the circumstances of her past. What she wanted, above all, was to be an active creator of her life! To forge a life lived with integrity based on conscious choices! She found it hard to sympathize with her own sadness, and she did her best to shake it off.

It was a precarious moment; the seed of doubt about her desire for polyamory had been sown, and that was not what Veronica wanted or expected. She felt disoriented; her view of monogamy as unsustainable and risky was unaltered, but her belief in the suitability of polyamory was shaken. Veronica was concerned that she would never be able to maintain a monogamous relationship for long. She admitted loving the high of NRE, and the thought of giving up on it felt like a loss she did not want to consider.

Despite her conviction, Veronica started questioning the solidity of polyamory. She noticed how her friends in poly relationships were not as happy as they asserted. Making this observation aggravated her, so she did her best to make this consideration irrelevant. "After all," she remarked, "monogamous couples I know are even more miserable." I sympathized with her struggle: "It's hard not to know what's right for you." Veronica nodded; she was discouraged, and she did not know what to do with all her contradictory feelings. She recounted how she had been long-term partners with married men who had claimed to be poly but whose wives, she later realized, were not fully in the know. "Thinking of it, their lack of honesty is inexcusable," she said, wiping a tear from her eye. "It's against the principles of openness and transparency. It feels like a betrayal that I willingly walked into." She fell into silence. "That means that I wasn't honest, either…"

Veronica was connecting the dots; she started seeing how, by rejecting her feelings, she was repeating the family pattern of distancing herself from emotions. She was also learning that, however confusing, emotions could be her guide. That was a lot to take in.

The exploration of Veronica's previous relationships revealed another pattern. The men she was drawn to were usually older, sometimes by a decade or more. The women she got involved with also tended to be a few years older and more experienced and worldly. She preferred creative types, men and women who were highly engaging but who, in their unpredictability, were not always easy to rely upon. Veronica was aware of the pattern of falling in love with people older than her, but less so of how it connected to her past—the search for connection with emotionally unavailable parents, the desire to be cherished and protected, and the fear of being abandoned. "It sounds like such a cliché," she noted more than once, with a smile at first derisive and then sad. "Isn't there more to my preference and confusion about polyamory than the old Mommy and Daddy issue?" she asked.

It was an excellent question, leading Veronica to a deeper exploration of what she wanted out of her life. To begin with, her relationship with Aidan started to take on a different meaning. She was not sure if she wanted it to continue or not, but she could see that the trust and safety it provided were essential for her emotional stability and well-being. At the beginning of therapy, Veronica had thought that if only Aidan were more on board with polyamory and willing to pursue his own partners, it would solidify their partnership. Now she could see the value of his reluctance. Aidan remained dubious about polyamory, not because he was an advocate of monogamy, but because he had witnessed enough bad poly relationships to not be excited about this prospect.

As Veronica's perception of Aidan started to shift, his approach began to feel measured rather than dismissive. It was an important realization that clarified some of her relational needs. She became more aware of wanting a stable primary relationship, whether it was with Aidan or another man. Veronica realized that her earlier discomfort with this need had been based on the idealization of nonhierarchical polyamory. She saw how strongly she was influenced by discussions with people in her poly circles who saw more pros than cons of nonhierarchy, so being able to stand by her own relational preference was momentous.

These insights were the beginning of Veronica's process of differentiation from the ideology of polyamory, whose impact she had only vaguely recognized. As we explored the difference between influence and preference, a clearer vision of her relational needs started to emerge. The essential part of this exploration was not so much the realization of what she needed, which was a solid primary relationship to build upon, but that she did not feel guilty about her need. It was a melancholy relief for Veronica to see how her unconscious efforts to protect herself from potential abandonment had made her disregard what she sensed underneath—her deep-seated longing to belong and be safe, whether it was with one partner or more.

Final Thoughts

"No single event can awaken within us a stranger totally unknown to us. To live is to be slowly born. It would be a bit too easy if we could go about borrowing ready-made souls."

– Antoine de Saint-Exupéry

The time has come to return to the original question that shaped this book: *Jak to się je?* (How do you eat it?). I hope that I was able to show that there are many ways to "eat" or conceptualize polyamory—how it came into being, what makes it appealing, and whether or not it is going to continue evolving or will remain but one of many forms of the human bonding experience.

This book has provided an overview of polyamory from the clinical perspective, which, with all of its focus on relational quality, is intersubjectively and inevitably mine. I am more equipped than many to speak about polyamory, and as humble as anyone who embarks on this path. I have learned a lot; my clients were my teachers, and the very process of writing this book has made me examine my own observations and thoughts. I am not advocating for either polyamory or monogamy. Instead, I remain deferentially in awe of the preciousness and difficulties of our immensely complex relational lives. Hopefully, this book provokes questions and provides insights. To live is to be slowly born.

Glossary

Polyamory-related terms are proliferating, but in this glossary, I am including only the terms that I have used in this book.

ANCHOR/NESTING PARTNER: A partner with whom one creates a nest and/or who anchors the relationship.

ASEXUAL: A person with no sexual feelings or desires.

BAREBACKING: Penetrative sex without the use of condoms.

BIPOLY: A person who identifies as bisexual and polyamorous.

COMPERSION: The opposite of jealousy; a happy feeling of seeing one's partner experience sexual and romantic bliss with another person.

CONSENSUAL NONMONOGAMY (CNM): An umbrella term that includes polyamory, swinging, and other forms of sexually non-exclusive relationships.

DEMISEXUAL: A person who does not experience sexual desire unless there is a strong emotional connection.

FLUID BONDING: An agreement not to use barrier protection during sex/permission to exchange bodily fluids with one's partner.

HIERARCHICAL POLYAMORY: A ranking system among partnerships in polyamory.

METAMOUR: One's partner's other partner, with whom one does not have any sexual or romantic ties.

MONO-POLY: A relationship between a person who identifies as monogamous and a person who identifies as polyamorous.

NEW RELATIONSHIP AGONY: A response to witnessing one's partner experience NRE with somebody else.

NEW RELATIONSHIP ENERGY (NRE): Heightened emotional and sexual preoccupation characteristic of a new relationship.

NONHIERARCHICAL POLYAMORY: An agreement to not impose hierarchy onto the existing relationships.

OPEN RELATIONSHIP/OPEN MARRIAGE: A permission for one or both partners in a committed relationship to be sexually involved with other people.

PANSEXUAL: Sexual attraction toward others regardless of their gender and sexual identity.

POLYCULE: A romantic network of closely connected partners.

POLYCURIOUS: Curiosity about polyamory, with or without an intention to open up.

POLYFAMILY: A set of people who live together and identify as polyamorous.

POLYFIDELITY: An agreement to be romantically and sexually exclusive within the existing partnerships.

POLYFURIOUS: A strong negative reaction to polyamory.

POLYROMANTICISM: A perception of superiority of polyamory over other relational formats.

PRIMARY, SECONDARY, TERTIARY: Relational designations describing the degree of involvement among partners.

RELATIONSHIP ESCALATOR: An expectation regarding intimate relationships to proceed through predictable stages of deepening the commitment, from dating to engagement to marriage and family.

QUAD: A polyamorous relationship involving four people.

SATTELITE/ORBIT: A nonprimary, occasional partner.

SWINGING: A form of CNM involving recreational sex outside of a marriage or committed relationship.

TRIAD: A polyamorous relationship involving three partners.

UNICORN: A hypothetical woman who is willing to be equally involved with both partners of an existing heterosexual couple and not with anyone else.

VEE: A relationship among three people in which one person is sexually and romantically involved with two other partners who themselves are not sexually or romantically connected.

Index